Jobs That Matter

Find a Stable, Fulfilling Career in Public Service

Heather Krasna

With a foreword from Max Stier,
CEO and president of Partnership for Public Service

jist Works
America's Career Publisher®

Jobs That Matter

Published by JIST Works, an imprint of JIST Publishing
7321 Shadeland Station, Suite 200
Indianapolis, IN 46256-3923

Phone: 800-648-JIST Fax: 877-454-7839 E-mail: info@jist.com

Visit our Web site at **www.jist.com** for information on JIST, tables of contents, sample pages, and ordering instructions for our many products!

Trade Product Manager: Lori Cates Hand
Development Editor: Heather Stith
Interior Designer and Page Layout: Aleata Halbig
Cover Designer: Honeymoon Image & Design Inc.
Proofreaders: Chuck Hutchison, Jeanne Clark
Indexer: Joy Dean Lee

Printed in the United States of America

15 14 13 12 11 10 9 8 7 6 5 4 3 2

Library of Congress Cataloging-in-Publication Data

Krasna, Heather, 1973-
Jobs that matter : find a stable, fulfilling career in public service / Heather Krasna.
p. cm.
Includes bibliographical references and index.
ISBN 978-1-59357-787-2 (alk. paper)
1. Civil service positions--United States. 2. Nonprofit organizations--United States--Employees. 3. Vocational guidance--United States. I. Title.
JK716.K686 2010
351.73023--dc22
2010012800

ISBN 978-1-59357-787-2

Foreword

"Everybody can be great... because everybody can serve."
—Martin Luther King, Jr.

Our country is at a crossroads. We are facing numerous complex challenges, from climate change to health care to terrorism, not to mention the effects of the economic recession and all that has come with it—soaring unemployment, families losing their homes, and a society in need of services as our nation works to get back on its collective feet. More visibly than ever, our government and nonprofit public service organizations are playing a critical role in the lives of Americans, addressing issues of poverty, education, preservation of the environment, safety and security for all our citizens, and more.

Our public servants, who face these challenges each day on our behalf, are the unsung heroes of our country—often denigrated as "bureaucrats" or "paper pushers" when nothing could be farther from the truth. Joining the public service—in whatever capacity you choose—is one of the most rewarding challenges of our time, and opportunities abound.

Good government starts with good people, and America depends on those who serve to be many things: bright, motivated, dedicated, creative, talented, and willing to take on even the toughest of challenges on our collective behalf. Let me be frank: It takes a certain kind of person to be successful in government and other public service jobs, one who is committed to change, who is mission-focused, and who will be dedicated to facing and overcoming obstacles along the road to success.

That said, our country needs you, and reading this book is a smart step on the journey to both finding a fulfilling job and serving the nation. Author Heather Krasna has put her considerable experience as a career counselor to great use to share the secrets of public service with you. She explains why government work is extremely important; provides insights into a wide array of exciting career opportunities; shares real stories of public servants; offers advice on finding the right job; and lays out details on how to apply, interview, and negotiate for a position.

I hope you'll make good use of this informative guide, join the talented cadre of public servants, and bring your unique gifts to our country and to the American people. After all, this is *our* country and *our* government. You'll never do anything more rewarding.

Max Stier
CEO and President, Partnership for Public Service
www.ourpublicservice.org

Dedication

To Elizabeth Maybelle: Raising you is the job that matters most.

Acknowledgments

First and foremost, I thank all of the people who volunteered their time to write profiles of themselves or be interviewed for this book, including Vanessa Casavant, Jill Lane, Craig Newmark, Richard Hendra, Johari Rashad, Ed Barocas, Hillary Tabor, Amy Whipple, Ngozi Oleru, Loreen Loonie, Tom Melancon, Hugh Ho, Kristen Taddonio, Fred Henson, Steve Scofield, Giovannina Souers, Cathleen Berrick, Jack Bienko, Vicki Aken, Matthew Perkins, Jeff Abramson, Ron Neubauer, John Burns, Carol Dunn, Jon Dean, Hope Johnson, Kitty Wooley, Jimmy Lee, Brian Hill, Laura McGrew, Maggie Jarry, Steve Damiano, Monica Rich, Christopher Mayberry, Rob Schwartz, and Anna De Santis. Their inspiring stories and words of advice were very motivational as I continued writing this book. I especially thank Lori Cates Hand and Heather Stith, who are wonderful editors and guides.

This book would not have been possible without the guidance of my good friend and writing mentor, Carol Pinchefsky, an excellent author. Several other people were very helpful in orienting me to the book-writing and publishing world, especially Jessica Trupin, Kathryn Troutman, Wendy Enelow, and Jason Alba. The wonderful Rebecca Blakewood volunteered to review the first four chapters, and I would like to thank the others who reviewed sections of the book, including Kay Sterner, Emily Orling, Jill Lane, Carol Pinchefsky, Loreen Loonie, Kitty Wooley, Anneclaire De Roos, Fred Henson, Hugh Ho, Jack Bienko, Vicki Aken, Ron Neubauer, Jonathan Dean, and Dan Koifman.

I also thank all of my wonderful colleagues, students, alumni, and employers at the Evans School of Public Affairs, from whom I've learned a great deal about the world of public service. Some of the profiled individuals are alumni of this great program. I thank Barry Wall for his visual representations of the job search. I also sincerely thank my former colleagues from Baruch College for their friendship and wisdom over the years and my former students for all they taught me. The teachers and guides from my graduate program at Milano The New School for Management and

Urban Policy and my former mentors at Support Center for Nonprofit Management helped me start on my current path. In addition, the Partnership for Public Service taught me much about the federal hiring process.

A number of people helped me find the fascinating people whose profiles appear in these pages, especially Carol R. Anderson from Milano The New School for Management and Urban Policy; Elyse Mendel of Baruch College's School of Public Affairs; Steve Ressler, founder of GovLoop.com; Takako Nagumo of the United Nations; Amiko Matsumoto, Sarah Howe, and Samantha Donaldson of the Partnership for Public Service; and Jessica Trupin, Mei Hua, and my friends and connections on Facebook, Twitter, and GovLoop. I also thank the many people who provided recruiting advice, including Michaela Favre of the Washington State Department of Transportation, Elizabeth Streett (former HR in the U.S. Army), and Andrea Lowe of the City of Seattle.

Last but never least, I must thank my family. In retrospect, it seems inevitable that the child of a renowned and brilliant professor of political science (my father, Paul Abramson) and a wonderful and creative professor of English (my mother, Janet Abramson) would wind up writing a book on public service careers. If it weren't for my parents proofreading some of my high school essays, I'm sure I wouldn't be the writer I am today. I especially thank my mother for proofreading this whole book—twice! I thank my brother, Lee, for being the most inspiring person I know. Above all, I thank my wonderful husband, Stuart, who gave me the greatest gift in the world.

Contents

Introduction

"How wonderful it is that nobody need wait a single moment before starting to improve the world." —Anne Frank

Do you want to make a difference in your community, your country, or the world? Are you inspired to make the world a better place? Do you believe strongly that people who are vulnerable should be cared for and empowered, the natural environment should be protected, the nation should be shielded from terrorism, people in developing countries should have a better life, everyone should have access to a good education and health care, or that your town should have clean water and less sprawl? Then you have heard the "call to serve."

Whether you are exploring your first career after college or graduate school, have worked for years and now want a job that aligns more directly with your personal values, or are returning to the workplace after time away, this book is for you. It provides you with the tools you need to help you focus your job search, prioritize your interests and values, find opportunities, and make yourself a great candidate for jobs that make a difference.

What Is a Public Service Career?

Public service used to mean, and to some extent still means, careers in government. But over the last few years, the definition of public service has broadened to include work within nonprofit organizations, universities, nongovernmental organizations, and some parts of the private sector and any other work that contributes to the public good. In this book, I define public service careers as those that make a significant contribution to solving problems in society or the world.

What am I leaving out? Mainly, careers in which the key function is to make a profit for a corporation or private individual rather than to benefit society as a whole and organizations that primarily benefit their members rather than the public. I also omit some jobs that, though clearly a part of public service, are beyond the scope of this book. These include many of the skilled trades and hands-on jobs such as paving roads, setting up electrical cables, or delivering mail.

This is not to say that the jobs I am leaving out do not matter. To a large extent, any job can become meaningful depending on your attitude toward it. Being happy at work has much to do with enjoying your job function, getting along with coworkers, feeling competent at what you do, and having a good working environment. Yet working for an organization that also has a mission that you care about and believe in can make a world of difference.

Why Is a Public Service Job for You?

There are many reasons that you might consider a career in public service. For most people, the three biggest are mission, job function, and work values.

Many people are drawn to public service because they are passionate about an organization's mission. Perhaps you are reading this book because you care about saving the environment, making government more accountable, protecting your country or your neighborhood, or raising public awareness of the challenges faced by refugees. Chapters 3 through 9 explore careers categorized by mission in more detail.

Some people are interested in certain job functions or job titles that exist mainly in public service, like social worker, forester, or foreign service officer. A job title or function might intrigue you, but it is hard to tell what a job with a particular title actually entails. Reading a job description might be a great place to start, but this book provides profiles of people with careers in public service so you can get a sense of what kinds of careers are available in these fields. There are also resources for exploring different careers and information on the most common types of positions within different types of organizations.

Lastly, perhaps you are drawn to this book because you have heard that government jobs are more secure and provide better benefits or that nonprofit organizations have a more relaxed work culture. Perhaps you are drawn to a career in international development because you like world travel. Throughout this book, the benefits and work-related values of public service careers will be highlighted.

First-Time Job Seekers

Perhaps you are just finishing school and have not figured out how your studies translate into a job. Maybe you have been a serial volunteer. Maybe you founded a student organization to help raise money for a homeless shelter or a school in Bolivia. Maybe you completed an AmeriCorps program or a stint in the Peace Corps, but now you need a job with a paycheck and benefits. This book can help you explore your interests, skills, and abilities and will provide an overview of the many ways in which you can make a difference. Not only that, it will provide a toolkit for identifying the right kinds of jobs and careers for you, finding people who can help you on your path, and successfully obtaining a "job that matters."

Career Changers

Perhaps you have had an established career, but something is telling you it is time for a change. It could be any number of things: a sense that you are not sure how your job contributes to the greater good; a feeling that your work has become monotonous and you have nothing more to learn; stress and burnout from long hours, a difficult boss, or a toxic workplace; fear of layoffs. Perhaps you have been in denial for a long time that you might have to make a change, but now it is staring you in the face. Or maybe you have retired, and now want a rewarding second career.

Do not worry—career change is not unusual. In fact, it is a fairly normal part of the career process. Although most people assume they will find a job, move up the career ladder, and work happily ever after (and yes, there are people who do follow that path), in reality most people change careers (careers, not just jobs) several times during their working years. Career re-invention has become a fact of life ever since companies began downsizing, right-sizing, re-engineering, and reducing headcount (don't you love those euphemisms for layoffs!).

Change may be coming your way, but it is important to look before you leap. This book will come in handy as a self-assessment tool to help you determine whether you need to switch careers entirely, whether you might want to switch industries and fields, whether it is worth pursuing further education, or whether you just need a few weeks of vacation. If you decide it is time for a change, this book will equip you to take your next big step.

How Is This Book Organized?

This book is designed to be flexible—you can skip sections and still find it useful. If you are unsure of which direction to go in, or what career or job might be a good fit for you, Chapter 1 provides a series of self-evaluations and career exploration exercises. Chapter 2 explains the three sectors of the economy—public, private, and nonprofit—and outlines some of the careers that could fit into any issue area, such as program management, executive positions, fundraising, human resources, advocacy, and elected office.

Chapters 3 through 9 identify some of the major organizations in each field, highlighting the main job types involved and listing additional resources for each area:

- Chapter 3, "Helping People Through Human Services and Health" discusses the fields of human services (helping children, the elderly, people with disabilities, and so on) and health.
- Chapter 4, "Educating People and Defending Their Rights," covers education, worker protections, and civil rights.
- Chapter 5, "Protecting the Environment and Managing Infrastructure," describes the fields of natural resource management, parks and recreation, protection of wildlife and animals, pollution prevention, and infrastructure-related fields that are sometimes linked to the environment, such as energy, transportation, utilities, and urban planning.

- Chapter 6, "Managing and Developing Financial Resources," discusses those careers that keep the economy running, build communities through economic development, support nonprofit organizations through philanthropy, regulate trade, and ensure tax dollars are well spent.
- Chapter 7, "Helping the World: International Development, Relief, Relations, and Trade," discusses international careers.
- Chapter 8, "Keeping People Safe," focuses on law enforcement, the legal system, international security, and defense.
- Chapter 9, "Working with Arts, Culture, and Religion," covers these areas.

Once you have gone through the career exploration exercises in Chapter 1 and explored the different career areas highlighted in Chapters 2 through 9, you will be equipped to start your search for the perfect career. Chapter 10 provides time-tested advice on preparing for the job search, including advice on writing resumes. Chapter 11 offers the secrets of job searching in organizations that have a special hiring process, with tips for getting hired in the federal, state, and local government, information on civil service tests, and suggestions on the transition into nonprofit organizations. After you have found an opportunity and navigated the application process, Chapter 12 guides you through a successful interview and salary negotiation and even offers suggestions for getting promoted and building a satisfying new career. Throughout the book, links and resources are provided. To get these and many other links online, and to get updates for this book, visit http://heatherkrasna.com and sign up for the mailing list.

The job search is a journey, and every journey begins with a single step. So let us get started!

CHAPTER 1

Exploring Public Service Careers

"If one advances confidently in the direction of his dreams, and endeavors to live the life which he has imagined, he will meet with a success unexpected in common hours." —Henry David Thoreau

You're inspired to change the world—now what?

Have you said any of the following? "I know I want to help change the world, but I don't know how." "I want to do something for the environment, but I don't know where my skills fit in." Or, "I know what I don't want, but not what I want."

On any journey, finding your way is easier if you have a goal in mind. I am not saying that careers should take a direct path—in fact, contrary to popular opinion, they rarely do. However, before jumping in to the job search process, you have some important work to do: figuring out who you are, identifying what is important to you in a job or career, assessing what your skills are, and then determining which opportunities fit with what you have discovered about yourself. This chapter will help you define what you want to do and what matters to you. Even if you are fairly clear on what you want to do, completing the exercises in this chapter can help you when you have to make a decision about whether to accept a job offer.

A Career Exercises Caveat

It is easy to get caught up in what a career assessment exercise tells you and assume it will give you the "right" answer. Yet there are few absolutely right answers in career decisions. For every person, there are multiple possible career choices that could be satisfying.

By doing the exercises in this chapter and conducting career research, you may discover that you are only a few small life changes away from career happiness. Or you may find that changing to your ideal position is a long-term goal that requires you to meet several short-term goals along the way. Perhaps you are ready to take the leap into a brand-new career. You may also find that you need a transitional phase of exploration before deciding your next step.

Career Exploration Exercises

Keeping the preceding caveat in mind, try some of the following exercises to see if they help clarify your career goals. Set aside some quiet, uninterrupted time to focus on these exercises to see where they lead; and then consider finding a friend, fellow job seeker, trusted mentor, or career counselor to discuss the exercises with and to get some impartial feedback. After each exercise, consider writing a list of questions or concerns that have occurred to you, and make a plan of action about what you need to research next.

Dreams and Fantasies

Do you have any recollections of what you wanted to be when you grew up? What daydreams did you have, and what games did you play? What did you do for fun, and what hobbies were you passionate about? What were some of your favorite classes in school? Often, unedited childhood or teenage career fantasies can give some hints about what you would like to do.

In this exercise, you will examine some of your past career dreams and fantasies. This exercise requires a small leap of faith. Although you may feel the need to start critiquing yourself or telling yourself why something is not possible, try to simply do the exercise without any mental criticism about what you come up with—and don't feel silly about what you write.

Dreams and Fantasies Exercise

Complete the following statements:

When I was a child, I wanted to be

____

When I was a teenager, I wanted to be

____

When I was a young adult, I wanted to be

____

What about those dreams appealed to you?

____

____

What career questions arise from this exercise?

____

____

Look at the dreams you listed and compare them with some of the career ideas you have been considering lately. Are there any careers that relate to your earlier dreams? List them here:

____

____

What information about these careers do you need to obtain?

____

____

Missions

Some people are especially motivated by the mission of the organization they want to work for (Chapters 3–9 detail different kinds of missions). By doing this exercise, you will start to unearth the real reasons why you are passionate about a certain mission or issue. You may discover that you really do not know why an issue is important to you or what the history of the issue is. This important insight indicates that you need to do further research before you decide to pursue a certain career. The next few chapters of this book will point you in the right direction for further exploration of each of these issue areas.

MISSIONS EXERCISE

Review this list of possible missions that benefit the public and put a check mark next to the ones that you find the most exciting:

- ❑ Advocacy
- ❑ Animals and wildlife
- ❑ Art, music, drama, culture
- ❑ Building community

(continued)

(continued)

- ❑ Children and youth
- ❑ Civil rights or empowerment of underrepresented peoples
- ❑ Communication
- ❑ Disaster relief, management, and recovery
- ❑ Early childhood education
- ❑ Economics and economic development; improving business, commerce, and trade
- ❑ Education: higher education
- ❑ Education: K–12
- ❑ Elderly people and seniors
- ❑ Energy policy or energy efficiency
- ❑ Ensuring government accountability
- ❑ The environment: preserving natural areas; preventing pollution
- ❑ Financing public work and budgeting
- ❑ Health care
- ❑ Health research or finding cures for disease
- ❑ Helping local neighborhoods
- ❑ Housing and homelessness
- ❑ Immigration
- ❑ Influencing policy, creating new legislation, or serving in elected office
- ❑ Information sharing and libraries
- ❑ International relations and understanding
- ❑ International relief and development
- ❑ International trade
- ❑ Maintaining safety, security, or law and order
- ❑ Philanthropy
- ❑ Preventing and alleviating poverty
- ❑ Regulating trade and commerce
- ❑ Religion/spirituality
- ❑ Rural development or agricultural issues
- ❑ Technology
- ❑ Transportation
- ❑ Urban planning and issues of cities
- ❑ Volunteerism

On a separate page, make a list of the missions you have checked and put them in order of their importance to you. Write the top three to five missions on your list in the space provided. Next to each, write a reason why that mission appeals to you.

Mission	Reason
1.	
2.	
3.	
4.	
5.	

Pick your top mission area and have a friend ask you—sincerely—the following questions, pausing between each:

1. Why is this issue important to you? Why should anyone care about this issue?____

2. Have you had a personal experience that inspired you to pursue this issue?

Job Functions/Interests

While some people are most motivated by a career that serves a specific purpose or mission, others are more motivated by doing a particular task or having a particular job function. (Of course, because you are reading this book, you are probably also motivated to work for an organization that helps the world and creates public value.) You may be the type of person who does not mind what organization you work for as long as it does not conflict with your values and allows you to do specific things you enjoy, such as help people reach their goals or fix broken systems.

Dr. John L. Holland, a psychologist formerly at Johns Hopkins University, created a well-regarded career theory that helps organize jobs and careers into six broad career categories: realistic, investigative, artistic, social, enterprising, and conventional (sometimes abbreviated RIASEC). By looking through descriptions of these categories, you may be able to identify which job functions are of the greatest interest to you. The following descriptions of each of the six career categories include most of the public service jobs described in this book so you can see where they fit in. (Note that most individuals and most jobs don't neatly fit into one of these six categories, but usually have two or three top categories.)

Realistic careers are hands-on and practical, careers in which people work with physical objects, tools, machinery, or plants and animals. If you enjoy fixing things, doing things with your hands, or being outdoors, you may have some realistic career interests. Specific realistic jobs discussed in this book include

- Foresters, fish and game wardens, civil engineers, scientists, park rangers, and recreation specialists/park naturalists (Chapter 5)
- Uniformed police officers, firefighters, corrections officers, and military (Chapter 8)
- Museum technicians and set designers (Chapter 9)

Investigative careers often involve working with ideas, thinking through problems, or understanding science or medicine. They also often require advanced education. If you enjoy academic work, analyzing issues, coming up with innovative ideas, understanding and testing theories, conducting research, diagnosing problems, or finding new ways to understand the world, you may be looking for an investigative job. Specific investigative jobs described in this book include

- Policy researchers and legislative analysts (Chapter 2)
- Doctors, scientists, epidemiologists, and, to a lesser extent, nurses and counselors (Chapter 3)
- College/university professors, to a lesser extent (Chapter 4)
- Urban planners, environmental scientists, foresters, fish and game wardens, and civil engineers (Chapter 5)
- Detectives, lawyers, and security analysts (Chapter 8)

Artistic people have an aesthetic appreciation or creative talent that informs their worldview. Artistic careers involve self-expression and do not require following clear rules. Many, though not all, of the careers in the arts are freelance or entrepreneurial in nature, and some artistic individuals make much of their income from sources other than art, but there are many people who make a good income from artistic work, including photography, design, writing, editing, and musical performance. Communications and public affairs positions that require writing and public speaking are artistic as well. If you are particularly sensitive to art, music, theatre, or books or enjoy writing, drawing, making music, or acting, you may be inspired to find an artistic career path. Artistic jobs described in this book include

- Communications/public relations managers and specialists, and training and development managers and specialists (Chapter 2)
- Teachers, preschool teachers, and student life program managers (Chapter 4)
- To a lesser extent, urban planners and park rangers (Chapter 5)
- Musicians, music directors, set designers, museum technicians, and clergy (Chapter 9)

Social careers focus on helping others through listening, caregiving, teaching, or counseling. If people typically come to you with their problems, comment on your sensitivity to others, see you as a genuine and caring person, or open up to you about their feelings easily, you may be a social person. Social careers discussed in this book include

- Training and development managers and specialists, human resources managers and assistants, and, to an extent, elected officials/legislators (Chapter 2)
- Social workers, counselors, and, to a lesser extent, human services aides, doctors, and nurses (Chapter 3)
- Teachers, guidance counselors, preschool teachers, college/university professors, student life program managers, vocational education teachers, and, to a lesser extent, librarians and school administrators (Chapter 4)
- Park rangers, recreation specialists/park naturalists (Chapter 5)
- Emergency planners and parole officers (Chapter 8)
- Clergy (Chapter 9)

Enterprising jobs involve influencing people through persuasion, sales, or leadership or starting and managing projects. If you started a lemonade stand as a kid, often have ideas for new businesses or initiatives, find it easy to convince people of your ideas, easily win over people and make new friends, don't mind taking risks sometimes, and enjoy leading others, you may be enterprising. Enterprising jobs in this book include

- Managers, executives, communications/public relations managers and specialists, human resources managers and assistants, fundraisers, contract administrators, information technology specialists, advocates, elected officials/legislators, accountants and financial managers, campaign staff, and community organizers (Chapter 2)
- Social workers, to some extent (Chapter 3)
- School administrators, college administrators, and student services staff (Chapter 4)
- Urban planners (Chapter 5)
- Community loan officers, asset managers, real estate managers, compliance officers, inspectors, and tax collectors (Chapter 6)
- Foreign service officers (Chapter 7)
- Detectives, lawyers, and, to a lesser extent, uniformed police officers, corrections officers, emergency planners, and parole officers (Chapter 8)
- Musicians, music directors, and clergy (Chapter 9)

Conventional careers are a perfect fit for people who enjoy maintaining order and following systems. Conventional people are good at correctly following and enforcing procedures, keeping track of data or finances, and keeping details organized in an understandable structure. If you enjoy extracurricular activities that involve following set patterns (such as cooking or sewing), or enjoy balancing your checkbook and seeing the numbers add up, or organize your personal papers alphabetically in a filing cabinet when no one is looking, a conventional career path may be perfect for you. Examples of conventional jobs include

- Accountants and financial managers, administrators, and, to a lesser extent, managers, executives, contract administrators, and information technology managers and specialists (Chapter 2)
- Human services aides (Chapter 3)
- Librarians and some higher education administrators (Chapter 4)
- Community loan officers, asset managers, real estate managers, compliance officers, inspectors, and tax collectors (Chapter 6)

Job Functions/Interests Exercise

Which of the six Holland categories—realistic, investigative, artistic, social, enterprising, and conventional—speaks to you the most? Write the top three categories, in order of how relevant you think they are for you, here:

1. ______________________________
2. ______________________________
3. ______________________________

What career questions arise from this exercise?

____

____

The exercise and information presented here is just a brief overview of this approach to career choice. To get a more in-depth view, consider taking a career assessment to help narrow down your career interests. A career advisor can help you take the Strong Interest Inventory or you can try the Self-Directed Search (available online for about $10, see reference list at the end of the chapter) to find out what Holland code combination fits you best and what careers match that Holland code.

Work Values

In addition to job functions and mission areas, there are a lot of other variables about jobs that are important to consider: location, salary, stability, work-life balance, benefits, and so on. These variables are known as *work values.* Many people are strongly motivated by certain values more than they are by a particular mission or even job function. Values also can change as a person's life circumstances change. For instance, you may not be worried about work-life balance until you have a child. You may also find that some values are non-negotiable for you. For example, you may be unable to move to a new location for a job due to family commitments and a mortgage on a house. Or you may be unable to accept any job offer less than a certain salary. As you begin a job search, it's important to have a list of your non-negotiable items, followed by your "nice to have but not as essential" items.

Work Values Exercise

Look through the following list of values and circle those that are most important to you.

Job Functions/Qualities

Role/tasks involved with job

Types of clients served

Skills needed to perform the job

Autonomy—ability to work independently

Volume/speed of work (fast- or slow-paced environment)

Variety of work

Advancement opportunities

Prestige/respect of job

Level of responsibility

Stress level of work

Level of risk involved with work

Other: ______________________________

Culture of the Organization

Work-life balance (hours of work, etc.)

Travel

(continued)

(continued)

Structure of the organization (hierarchical or not)

Friendliness of coworkers

Personality of supervisor

Stability/security of the job or organization

Size of organization

Location/commute

Dress code

Reputation of organization

Environment of work (outdoors/indoors)

Other: ______________________________

Compensation

Salary

Bonuses and opportunity for promotion

Training offered

Insurance and retirement benefits (health insurance; dental, vision, life, and disability; retirement fund, 401(k), pension)

Tuition reimbursement benefits

Vacation/sick time/flextime benefits

Onsite day care or other child-care benefits

Relocation benefits

Other perks: ______________________________

Look at the values you circled and determine which are the most important to you. What are the top five to seven values you seek in a job? Write them here, and circle any that are non-negotiable:

1. ______________________________
2. ______________________________
3. ______________________________
4. ______________________________

5. ____
6. ____
7. ____

What career questions arise from this exercise? How will this exercise help you if you receive a job offer and need to decide whether to accept it?

____

____

____

Skills

Besides knowing what is important to you in a career or job, you also need to know what you actually can do. By thinking about some of your favorite accomplishments, you may be able to identify some of your top skills, abilities, and knowledge areas. Most importantly, you can start to determine not just what you are good at, but also which skills you enjoy using.

Start by writing at least six stories of times when you accomplished something you were proud of. These stories can come from jobs, volunteer activities, internships, coursework, or hobbies and recreational activities. These accomplishments don't have to illustrate that you did something totally earth-shattering, solved a crisis, or won an award—though those kinds of stories often make great examples. What is important is that you enjoyed doing these activities and felt a sense of accomplishment from your end result.

When you write your stories, use the Problem-Action-Result (PAR) method. (This method also will come in handy later when you get ready for job interviews.) This method has three major components:

- **Problem:** Think of problems that you have solved—employers love problem solvers! Describe the situation. What were the circumstances? What task needed to be done? What challenge did you face, and why was it important? What was at stake—what would happen if you failed? Use concrete nouns or numbers to illustrate why it was a problem and why an employer should care.
- **Action:** How did you analyze the situation? What actions did you take? Go step-by-step and think about exactly what you did—how many phone calls did you make? How did you write your report? What research did you have to do? Describe your role. Although many accomplishments are achieved through a group effort, you can still claim a personal accomplishment by focusing on what your role was in a group achievement.

- **Result:** Describe the result. Quantify your accomplishments whenever possible even if you have to make an estimate. (How much money was saved? How many kids went on the trip you organized? How can you prove you accomplished something? Why was it important, and how did it solve the original problem?) Don't choose stories with a negative result.

Here's one of my accomplishment stories that demonstrates the PAR method:

> *The nonprofit organization where I was interning, which provided training and support to 600 other nonprofit organizations, had to separate from its parent organization and had no cash reserves. This was a major problem because every year the organization had slow times with little revenue and had to borrow, then pay back, up to $70,000 from the parent organization. Without a cash reserve, the organization might be unable to continue functioning (Problem).*
>
> *I researched 50 potential donors using the Foundation Center's foundation database as well as the organization's past donor history, cowrote a 10-page grant proposal to ask for operating support, and submitted the tailored proposal to 15 of our best prospective donors (Action).*
>
> *The grant successfully raised $70,000, doubling the cash reserves of the organization and ensuring its ability to continue providing services to the 600 nonprofit organizations it served (Result).*

This is another one:

> *In my last job, I helped maintain filing and accounting systems. I discovered that many of the files were out of order and needed to be reorganized. This was a problem because it took me and the rest of my unit much longer to retrieve important client information and historical data than it should have. We sometimes received urgent data requests from the director, and without quick access to information, the unit could not fulfill them in time, which affected our reputation with the director (Problem).*
>
> *To fix this problem, I first ordered some filing supplies, including a filing cabinet and folders. I then made alphabetical files for each client and took some time to organize any loose papers and alphabetize them. I took the initiative to start scanning some of the files so they could be digitally accessed, and also made an index of what information could be found in each file (Action).*
>
> *By reorganizing the files and coming up with a more logical and organized system, I was able to reduce the turnaround time on retrieving data for the director's requests by 50 percent and reduce the amount of staff time spent on managing data by more than a half day per week (Result).*

Skills Exercise

Write your own Problem-Action-Result statements below. (Note that even though there's only room for three, you should write at least six of these if you can.)

1. Problem:____

   Action:____

   Result:____

2. Problem:____

   Action:____

   Result:____

3. Problem:____

   Action:____

   Result:____

Once you have written your PARs, use the following checklist to check when you have used these skills. Look for repeated use of particular skills.

Interpersonal/Leadership Skills

Skill	PAR 1	PAR 2	PAR 3
Listening	❑	❑	❑
Serving clients	❑	❑	❑
Persuading, motivating, or selling	❑	❑	❑
Supervising, delegating to, and evaluating people	❑	❑	❑
Working in teams/groups collegially	❑	❑	❑
Coaching, mentoring, or counseling	❑	❑	❑
Teaching or training	❑	❑	❑
Facilitating meetings or discussions	❑	❑	❑
Negotiating or resolving conflicts	❑	❑	❑
Representing others	❑	❑	❑
Interviewing others	❑	❑	❑
Making judgments or assessments of others	❑	❑	❑
Critical thinking	❑	❑	❑
Being aware of others' feelings	❑	❑	❑

(continued)

(continued)

Communication Skills			
Skill	**PAR 1**	**PAR 2**	**PAR 3**
Public speaking	❑	❑	❑
Speaking clearly and concisely	❑	❑	❑
Writing and editing	❑	❑	❑
Fundraising/grant writing	❑	❑	❑

Information/Research/Idea Skills			
Skill	**PAR 1**	**PAR 2**	**PAR 3**
Conducting qualitative research	❑	❑	❑
Doing quantitative and/or statistical research	❑	❑	❑
Interviewing for research	❑	❑	❑
Developing new programs	❑	❑	❑
Developing evaluation strategies	❑	❑	❑
Analyzing problems and identifying solutions	❑	❑	❑
Imagining or creating new ideas	❑	❑	❑
Starting up or establishing new organizations	❑	❑	❑
Forecasting, predicting	❑	❑	❑
Memorizing	❑	❑	❑

Organizational/Managerial Skills			
Skill	**PAR 1**	**PAR 2**	**PAR 3**
Organizing information and data	❑	❑	❑
Taking instructions	❑	❑	❑
Handling details	❑	❑	❑
Managing finances and budgeting	❑	❑	❑
Planning events	❑	❑	❑
Managing or running an organization	❑	❑	❑
Coordinating tasks	❑	❑	❑
Enforcing policies	❑	❑	❑
Identifying resources (including personnel, financial)	❑	❑	❑
Managing time, being punctual, meeting deadlines	❑	❑	❑
Planning, setting, and meeting goals	❑	❑	❑
Managing material/physical resources	❑	❑	❑

Physical Skills			
Skill	**PAR 1**	**PAR 2**	**PAR 3**
Working with machinery, tools, or instruments	❑	❑	❑
Maintaining, installing, or repairing equipment	❑	❑	❑
Manipulating materials (crafting, sculpting)	❑	❑	❑
Constructing or building	❑	❑	❑
Gardening or outdoors skills	❑	❑	❑
Choosing equipment	❑	❑	❑
Other physical skills: ____________________	❑	❑	❑

Knowledge/Content/Technical Skills			
Skill	**PAR 1**	**PAR 2**	**PAR 3**
Having specific "industry" knowledge/exposure	❑	❑	❑
Relating to specific groups of people (such as wealthy donors, homeless teens, elected officials)	❑	❑	❑
Speaking foreign languages	❑	❑	❑
Using specialized computer skills	❑	❑	❑
Designing, drawing, or other art-related skills	❑	❑	❑
Using skills in science, mathematics, engineering, or statistics	❑	❑	❑
Other technical skills: ____________________	❑	❑	❑

List your top skills here—the ones that showed up in most of your PARs, or that you enjoyed using the most:

____

____

____

Of this list, what are the three to five skills you enjoy using the most and are most interested in using in a job?

1. ____
2. ____
3. ____
4. ____
5. ____

(continued)

(continued)

What career questions arise from this exercise?

____

____

Which skills do you want to develop, but have not had a chance to use very much yet?

____

____

How might you start working on building those skills?

____

____

Specific Organizations

Perhaps you've watched glamorous movies about the FBI or CIA; or you have always been intrigued by the workings of the U.S. Congress; or you really want to work for the Red Cross. There might be some specific organizations you had in mind when you bought this book. Make a list of them—but don't stop there. Make sure to do some additional research. Visit their websites, especially any career pages they have, and reach out to people who work in these organizations to learn more about what they do. (For tips on learning more about organizations through their people, check Chapter 11).

Organizations Exercise

List the organizations that interest you and basic information about them.

Organization name:______________________

Website:______________________

Contacts:______________________

Organization name:______________________

Website:______________________

Contacts:______________________

Organization name:____________________

Website:____________________

Contacts:____________________

The Total Picture

Now that you've identified the various qualities you are seeking in a job or career, it is time to prioritize them. Go back through all of the career exercises and look at the complete list of qualities you came up with, focusing on those that you can't live without. Perhaps you will find that some career qualities are less relevant than others, while the lack of other qualities is driving you to consider a career change. You might even find that there is one burning problem with your current situation that you can solve with a change of perspective, change of boss, or change of job, rather than a change of career.

Total Picture Exercise

Write a list of your 5 to 10 most important career qualities here, in order of how important they are to you. This list will help you identify which jobs or careers are most closely related to your career interests.

1. ____________________
2. ____________________
3. ____________________
4. ____________________
5. ____________________
6. ____________________
7. ____________________
8. ____________________
9. ____________________
10. ____________________

For some people, working in a certain mission area (environment, social services, etc.) is of paramount importance and other factors (such as job function) are less important. Others seek a certain job function or certain values (family-friendly policies, job security). Your job search will be different depending on what is most important to you.

In most ways, a "mission-oriented" job search is the most straightforward to pursue, because you can target your search to a particular set of organizations. Most of the middle chapters of this book, which each focus on a different mission area, help guide individuals who are mission-driven. If you are focused on a job function, such as running a program or doing research, rather than a certain mission area, read Chapter 2 to learn about jobs that fit all mission areas and Chapters 3 to 9 for examples of different job types. In addition, you can learn more about different job types from reading the profiles of the various people in the book.

The most challenging job search, in terms of finding the right job or organization, is one that is mostly motivated by certain values. In particular, it is sometimes difficult to find out whether an organization or a certain job has a good work-life balance until you start working in the job. You can find some hints about what certain careers are like by reading the profiles of people in the book, which illustrate the lifestyle involved in certain careers. In addition, you can find more about the work-life balance–related policies of different organizations by visiting their websites or speaking to their employees in informational interviews.

None of These Exercises Work for Me!

If you've read through and tried doing these exercises, but you end up with more unanswered questions than answers, don't panic! There are many perfectly good reasons why these exercises might not work for you.

First, you might not have enough variety of life experience to know what you like or don't like. Maybe you need to start branching out of your current situation and trying new things. Here are some suggestions:

- Read job descriptions in the fields you are interested in.
- Start doing ongoing research in your field—consider keeping a career journal and keeping track of blogs or articles in the field.
- Conduct informational interviews (see Chapter 11).
- Take a class or workshop in the field you are interested in.
- Research professional organizations in the career fields you are considering (these are listed in the following chapters).
- Volunteer a few hours per week in an organization whose mission you appreciate.
- Ask people if you can "job shadow" them—go with them to work for a day or two and sit next to them and observe what they do on a day-to-day basis.
- Intern in the field you are interested in.
- Take a part-time job in the field you are interested in.

Perhaps you are just having trouble making decisions in general and need someone else to talk things over with. Consider finding a qualified career counselor through an organization such as the National Career Development Association or National Board for Certified Counselors. Or, if available, try contacting your college's career services office or a friend who can help you talk through your career ideas. Sometimes a neutral, trusted third party can help you discover what careers fit you.

Above all, before you panic that you don't have "the answer," know that finding a career path takes time and experience. In the process of searching for a job, you also might find "the answer," or you might take a job without even realizing that it will be a step in the right direction on your career path.

Lastly, not everyone defines himself or herself through a job. Some people work mainly to earn an income and define themselves through other parts of their identities, such as their hobbies, activities, family, or religion. Therefore, take some of the pressure off yourself to find the absolute answer and just try to enjoy the self-exploration process.

Researching Careers

Now that you have looked within to examine your skills, interests, and values, the next step is to look outside yourself for more information in order to see where your interests and skills match with possible careers.

Reading this book is a great start to your research. The next few chapters will give an overview of some of the specific career opportunities available in the government or nonprofit sectors, as well as profiles of people in the field. Each chapter also points you to resources for additional information, such as websites, professional organizations, books, and magazines.

Other places to research careers in general include the Department of Labor's *Occupational Outlook Handbook* and the O*NET. Much of the information about specific careers in this book, including salary and job growth data, comes from these sources. The *Occupational Outlook Handbook* is available online at www.bls.gov/oco/. This site is maintained by the U.S. Department of Labor Statistics and includes job profiles, education and experience requirements, average salaries, and the future job outlook for numerous positions.

O*NET Online is available at http://online.onetcenter.org/. This comprehensive database of job descriptions and worker attributes even includes an Interests section in each listing that lists the top Holland codes (discussed in the earlier "Job Functions/Interests" section) for that career.

Also, be sure to research careers by talking with people in the field. Many people have generously agreed to be profiled throughout this book, but it's also a good idea to speak with people in person about their careers.

Matching Your Skills and Interests with Careers

Once you have done your research (and read the rest of this book), you will know more about what employers look for in the field you want to enter. The next step is to match up your skills, interests, values, and goals with the careers you have learned about.

You may want to create a worksheet in which you list your top interests, skills, values, and so on in one column and then list a job or career pathway in another column. Look at both columns to see whether your knowledge, skills, and abilities match with what employers are seeking, and whether the career you are interested in matches your values. The following example shows a comparison between what a person might want and what his or her prospective employer is seeking and can offer.

I Want and Can Offer	ABC Youth Services Wants/Offers
Mission: Human services	**Mission:** Human services
Value: Work-life balance	Some positions have long hours
Value: Integrity of the workplace	Good reputation in community
Job Function: Research (investigative) and/or helping people (social)	Few research positions, but many hands-on helping roles
Skills: Interpersonal and research skills	Seeking interpersonal skills, as well as social work license for many positions

This person might have a gap or two—for example, she or he may need to pursue a social work license for this particular agency. The person may also want to look at other agencies that offer more research-oriented jobs or shorter hours.

After doing this comparison, you might have a picture like this (image developed by Barry Wall):

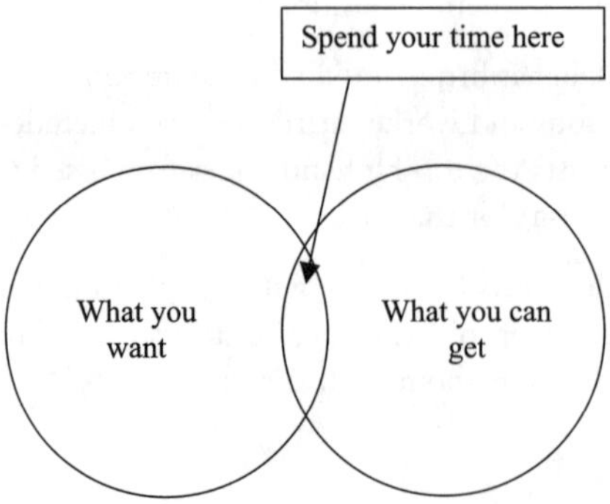

Or perhaps your picture will look like this:

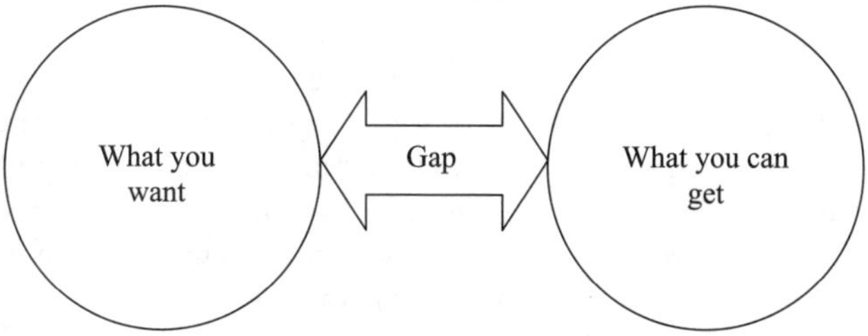

After doing your research, make a list of any gaps you discover between the job you want and the job you can get. The next section explains how to bridge this distance.

Handling Gaps

There are three types of gaps that prevent people from entering a career field they are interested in: skills or experience, values, or education. If you discover a gap, do not despair. There are solutions. Knowing how to solve a gap will help you decide if you want to jump right into a new career or whether a career change might be a longer-term goal for you.

Skills or Experience Gaps

In your research about jobs, you may find that specific skills or experience is required for a new position. Or you may keep seeing job listings that require five or more years of experience—and you have only two. Finding the jobs that will give you the relevant experience that will lead you in the direction of your ideal job takes patience and creativity, but you can certainly do it.

Also, is this a perceived or a real gap? Perhaps you really do have the skills and experience needed for a new career, but you don't realize it. Look again at your problem-action-result statements to identify the skills you may be able to transfer to a new career. Talk to some friends and reach out to people in your chosen field to find out whether you might be able to bridge a perceived gap.

To fill a skills gap, consider taking on a part-time internship or apprenticeship or see if there is some aspect of your current position you can restructure so that you can obtain experience that is more relevant to your future career goals. Consider looking for jobs that are at a more entry level than your current role, but give an opportunity to build essential skills. In addition, the importance of volunteering in the public service world cannot be overestimated. Take a few hours per week to do some volunteer work in your field of interest.

Values Gaps

The second type of gap is a values gap. Through research, you may discover that the job you want requires you to do something you don't want to do, such as take certain risks, live in locations you don't like, work long hours, or be physically uncomfortable. Perhaps you've discovered that your dream job pays less than you think you need. Or maybe it requires a perfectly clean criminal record or credit history, and unfortunately you don't have one. Therefore, you may have to reassess whether this career is for you. Or you may need to try to expand your definition of what you want in order to bring it a bit closer to what you can more easily get.

Are your job requirements non-negotiable? Can you compromise on something? For instance, can you decide to work very long hours for two or three years so that you can get a less stressful job later? Take a long look at what you really need and what is really important to you, and talk it over with friends, family, or a career counselor.

Education or Training Gaps

The third type of gap is education, training, or specific skills. Some jobs require a bachelor's or master's degree, a license or a certification, or a particular language or computer skill. There are few substitutions for this type of requirement (Chapters 3 to 9 list the education requirements for various jobs).

Think carefully before you decide whether you need to invest in additional education or training. Education is valuable for its own sake, but it can cost a significant amount of time and money. Unless you have lots of both to spare, you should be clear on why you need a new degree. Remember, too, that just having a certain degree will not guarantee you a job in that field.

If you decide additional education is necessary, research the programs available through professional associations or accrediting agencies or the websites of the various schools you are considering. Ask for additional materials about each school, try to visit if possible, sit in on classes, and speak to faculty, admissions staff, career services staff, or alumni whenever you can. You can also refer to more general resources such as the *U.S. News & World Report,* though keep in mind its rankings can be somewhat subjective.

In addition, some graduate programs have certain entrance requirements (test scores such as the GRE or GMAT, professional experience, undergraduate grades) that are important to consider to determine whether you will fit into their programs. Check with an admissions counselor to see which programs are a good fit for your background, and consider whether you are ready to pursue further education.

When looking at investing in additional education or training, you should consider these factors:

- Curriculum and focus of studies; academic course offerings and specializations
- Research areas of faculty
- Admissions requirements (GRE scores, grades, work experience)
- Cost of tuition; availability of financial aid
- Job or internship placement resources; employment outcomes of recent graduates
- College rankings (check what they are based on)
- Geographic location
- Awards and recognition
- Size of the school
- Student-to-faculty ratio
- Alumni network and employer partnerships
- Culture and atmosphere of the school
- Teaching methodologies used (applied/hands-on versus theoretical, individual studies versus team projects)
- Demographics of the students
- Internship or practicum requirements
- Availability of evening courses (if, for example, you are going to school while working a full-time job)

Financial Aid

Don't let the sticker shock of continuing study deter you from furthering your education without first determining how you might be able to fund your education. Be creative! Consider applying for any scholarships or fellowship programs you can find. Some employers (especially the federal government) offer college loan repayment or may pay for your continuing studies.

Also, note that because of the College Cost Reduction and Access Act of 2007, individuals working in public service may be able to pay back some of their federal student loans on an income-based sliding scale. For individuals who work for 10 years in public service (a very generally defined term), the remainder of their student loan debt may be waived.

Graduate Programs

Although there are many graduate degree programs that offer skills for specific public service careers, such as Master of Public Health, Master of Urban Planning, Master of Social Work, and so on (many of which will be discussed in future chapters), one in particular is broadly useful for a range of careers in government, nonprofits, or public-service-related private sector jobs. This degree is the Master of Public Administration and its cousin, the Master of Public Policy.

Master of Public Administration (MPA) degrees focus on preparing professionals for managing, organizing, running, or leading government or nonprofit organizations. Courses in this degree typically include policy analysis and formulation, political science, organization management, ethics, economics, statistics, and budgeting. Master of Public Policy (MPP) programs focus more heavily on policy analysis, using research methods including quantitative and qualitative analysis to better understand policy decisions. Coursework tends to focus on statistics and analysis of data, economics, finance, and program evaluation and less on policy implementation and management. There are more than 260 MPA or MPP programs in the United States.

There are also other, similar programs available, such as Master of Science in Nonprofit Management, Master of Urban Policy, Master of Arts in Policy Studies, Master of Arts in International Environmental Policy, Master of Science in Community Leadership, Master of Government Administration, and so on.

References and Resources

For more information on the topics presented in this chapter, refer to the following sources.

Career Exploration Exercises

Farr, Michael, and Shatkin, Laurence; *50 Best Jobs for Your Personality,* Second Edition (JIST Publishing, 2009)
National Board for Certified Counselors, www.nbcc.org
National Career Development Association, www.ncda.org
Self-Directed Search, www.self-directed-search.com

Researching Careers

Occupational Outlook Handbook, www.bls.gov/oco/
O*NET Online, http://online.onetcenter.org/

Handling Gaps

American Society for Public Administration, www.aspanet.org
Go Public Service, degree information, http://gopublicservice.org/degree.aspx
National Association of Schools of Public Affairs and Administration (NASPAA), http://naspaa.org
Project on Student Debt, income-based repayment information, www.ibrinfo.org

CHAPTER 2

Understanding Public Service Jobs in Every Sector and for Every Mission

"Change will not come if we wait for some other person or some other time. We are the ones we've been waiting for. We are the change that we seek." —Barack Obama

The U.S. economy has several different sectors that serve different functions and operate in different ways. In order to provide some perspective about what public service opportunities are available in the United States, the first part of this chapter defines the scope of these different parts of the economy and what each does to benefit the public good.

In addition, while other chapters of this book focus on jobs that are specific to particular issue areas, certain types of public service jobs are found in nearly all non-profit and government agencies. The second half of this chapter covers these jobs in more detail.

Where Are the Public Service Jobs?

Public service jobs are available in multiple parts of the U.S. economy: the public sector, the nonprofit sector, and even the private sector. The following sections describe each of these sectors and explain the benefits and drawbacks of working in them.

The Public Sector

The public sector is another term for government—city, county, municipal, state, federal, and even international government. Public sector organizations are generally funded by taxes, which only the government has the power to levy.

These organizations and agencies provide more jobs than you might think—about 16 percent of jobs in the United States, or a total of about 22 million people in 2006. The federal government employed about 2.7 million civilian employees as of 2007 and is the nation's largest single employer. (Note that this number doesn't include the millions of jobs in the private sector that are dependent on federal government contracts.) Local government employees numbered more than 14 million, and state governments employed more than 5 million people in 2006.

Governments provide many benefits that people take for granted. Things such as public education, parks, clean water, insured bank deposits, transportation and transit, libraries, electrical utilities, public safety, national security, international diplomacy, the legal system, and protections for public resources such as clean air or water are provided either solely or mainly by government. Table 2.1 provides a snapshot of overall government employment (federal, state, and local combined) in the United States.

Table 2.1: Total Government Employment by Function

Function	Percent of Total Government Employment	Number of Jobs
Education and research	53%	11,800,000
Security, defense, law enforcement, and judicial system	12%	2,800,000
Health	8%	1,780,000
Infrastructure, utilities, and transportation	7%	1,400,000
Other	6%	1,200,000

Function	Percent of Total Government Employment	Number of Jobs
Environment and parks	4%	800,000
Postal service	4%	770,000
Human services	3%	696,000
Community/economic development, trade, finance, and government finance	3%	687,000

Source: U.S. Census Bureau, 2006 data.

There are three points to consider about government jobs:

- Government exists at the federal (national), state, and local/municipal levels.
- Government is divided into three branches: executive (for example, the President, a state governor, a mayor, and the many agencies reporting to them), legislative (the U.S. Senate and House of Representatives, a state legislature, or the city or county council), and judicial (the Supreme Court and other courts and judges).
- Some government positions are elected or appointed, and others are considered *civil service* positions.

The next several sections provide an overview of the levels and branches of government so that you can get a sense of which does what—and how you can be a part of it.

The Federal Government

The federal government is nationwide and covers a vast array of agencies and career opportunities. Employees at federal agencies serve as diplomats to other countries, protect food safety through the Food and Drug Administration (FDA), provide assistance for low-income individuals through programs such as the Supplemental Nutrition Assistance Program, produce important information for the public through agencies such as the National Weather Service, and research diseases through the Centers for Disease Control (CDC) and National Institutes of Health (NIH). They also manage records for the National Archives and provide burials for military veterans through the National Cemetery Administration. Although one out of nine federal government employees works in Washington, DC (according to the Bureau of Labor Statistics), the majority work in all of the 50 states and internationally.

Most federal employees work in the executive branch cabinet departments:

Agriculture	Energy	Labor
Commerce	Interior	State
Defense	Justice	Treasury
Education	Homeland Security	Transportation
Health and Human Services	Housing and Urban Development	Veterans Affairs

The executive branch also includes various independent agencies such as the CIA, Amtrak, Environmental Protection Agency, Federal Reserve, NASA, the Peace Corps, the Securities and Exchange Commission, and the Social Security Administration.

On the elected executive level, the President has a staff of about 1,730, according to the Office of Personnel Management. The legislative branch employs 30,000 people, many of whom work directly for an elected official as staff, advisors, researchers, or constituent liaisons. Others work for agencies that report to Congress, such as the Congressional Research Service or the Congressional Budget Office. On the judicial level, about 34,000 employees work for the Supreme Court and other federal courts.

To get an idea of what missions most civilian federal employees serve, take a look at Table 2.2. This table provides an overview of federal employment according to the mission (or *function,* as it is called in the table) of federal agencies. Table 2.3 provides a snapshot of federal government priorities by listing the federal financial outlays by function.

Table 2.2: Federal Civilian Government Employment by Function

Function	Percent of All Civilian Federal Employees
Postal service	28%
National defense	26%
Hospitals and health	11%
Police, correction, and judicial/legal	7%
Natural resources and parks	8%
Other	6%
Government administration	7%

Function	Percent of All Civilian Federal Employees
Social insurance, public welfare	3%
Transportation	2%
Space research and technology	1%
Housing and community development	1%
Elementary and secondary education, libraries	1%

Source: U.S. Census Bureau, 2007 data.

Table 2.3: Federal Outlays by Function

Function	Amount of Money (in Billions)
Social Security	$586.2
National defense	$552.6
Debt interest	$430.0
Medicare	$375.4
Income security (retirement, housing and food assistance, unemployment compensation)	$366.0
Health	$266.4
Education, training, employment, social services	$91.7
Transportation	$72.9
Veterans' benefits	$72.8
Administration of justice	$41.2
Natural resources	$31.8
Community development	$29.6
International affairs	$28.5
Science, technology	$25.6
Agriculture	$17.7
General government	$17.5
Commerce, housing credit	$0.5

Source: U.S. Census Bureau, 2007 data.

State Government

State government handles welfare, unemployment benefits, Medicaid, state laws and regulations, school issues, and state prisons and state highways, among other things. State agencies vary in their names and functions between different states and in the ways in which they relate to federal and local government agencies. For example, the state government of Washington includes the following departments:

Employment Security	Agriculture	Corrections
Transportation	Revenue	Personnel
State Senate	State Patrol	Health Authority
Natural Resources	Ecology	Fish and Wildlife
Liquor Control Board	The Governor's Office	State House of Representatives
Parks, Recreation, and Conservation	Archeology and Historic Preservation	

Table 2.4 lists the percentage of state employees that serve in each general function. Elected officials at the state level include a governor; independently elected superintendents, commissioners, or officials; and the state legislature.

Table 2.4: State Government Employment by Function

Function	Percent of State Employees
Higher education	46%
Police and fire, judicial, legal, and corrections	15%
Hospitals and health	12%
Government administration	5%
Public welfare and social insurance	6%
Transportation, transit, and infrastructure	6%
Parks, recreation, and natural resources	4%
Other	4%
Elementary, secondary, and other education	3%

Source: U.S. Census Bureau, 2007 data.

Local/Municipal Government

Local/municipal government encompasses cities, towns, and counties and includes police and fire departments, schools, solid waste departments, local roads, and more. According to the U.S. Census Bureau (2002 data), there are about 87,500 different local governments, including 3,000 county governments, 19,400 municipal governments, 16,500 townships, 13,500 school districts, and 35,100 special districts. Together these governments employ more than 14 million people.

Cities, counties, and towns vary in the services they provide and the offices they have. Some typical departments of a city include city administration and policy, boards and commissions, animal shelters, fleets and facilities, environmental protection, code compliance, a city-run television station, arts and cultural affairs, libraries, parks and recreation, aquariums and zoos, human services (such as prevention of child abuse and homelessness), housing, public health, economic development, planning, public utilities (such as provision of clean drinking water, sewage and wastewater treatment, and solid waste management), electricity, transportation, civil rights offices, and public safety departments (police, fire, jails). Most localities also have an independent school board that oversees public education.

On the elected level, larger cities may be run by a mayor-council (or mayor-commission) form of government: A mayor is elected to serve as the executive branch of the city government and a city council is elected as a (unicameral) legislative branch. Many small to mid-size cities use a council-manager (or commission) form of government, in which a city council makes policies and legislation and appoints a city or town manager, which is a high-level civil service position.

On the judicial level, cities have municipal courts, and judges handle violations of local ordinances, including parking violations, landlord-tenant problems, building code enforcement, and public nuisances. Table 2.5 lists the percentage of local government employees that serve in each general function.

Table 2.5: Local Government Employment by Function

Function	Percent of Local Employees
Elementary and secondary education	55%
Police and fire, judicial, legal, and corrections	13%
Hospitals	4%
Transportation and transit	4%
Higher education	4%

(continued)

(continued)

Table 2.5: Local Government Employment by Function

Function	Percent of Local Employees
Government administration	4%
Water, sewer, and utilities	4%
Parks, recreation, and natural resources	3%
Other	2%
Public welfare	2%
Health	2%
Libraries	1%
Housing and community development	1%

Source: U.S. Census Bureau, 2007 data.

Reasons to Work in the Public Sector

People choose to work for the government for many different reasons. The following sections describe the top four.

Making a Difference

You can have a national or regional impact by working for state or federal government, or you can work in local government and make changes that you can see in your own neighborhood. Most of the government employees I have met care deeply about delivering real value on each taxpayer dollar, and they see, on a daily basis, the way their agency helps average citizens with things that are essential to their lives. Government agencies can make policy or legislative recommendations or start or improve programs that have a positive impact in society. In addition, some of the biggest changes in society are created through policies and laws made by elected officials.

Job Security

No job is ever 100 percent secure, but many government jobs are much more secure than those in the private sector. For example, the Bureau of Labor Statistics reports that in January 2009—in the midst of the economic downturn—the layoff rate for the private sector was 2.1 percent, but for government it was only 0.6 percent. In fact, while the layoff rate from January 2008 to January 2009 rose for nearly every industry (including for state and local government, though the rate was still lower than it was for the private sector), the layoff rate actually fell for the federal government.

During economic downturns, layoffs (sometimes called *reductions in force*) do happen, as do *furloughs* (required unpaid leave). However, the government generally has a very strong preference for retaining current employees, reassigning them to new positions, or re-employing them after layoffs. For example, federal agencies often have an interagency career transition assistance program, which is designed to re-employ individuals who have recently been laid off in other agencies and give them priority for jobs.

In addition, many agencies give a strong preference for hiring current or past government employees. For example, a large number of positions in the federal government are open only to current federal employees. These positions are also available for individuals who recently left federal employment, who worked at a federal job for several years in the past (and achieved *career tenure*), or who served in the military.

Lastly, a large percentage of government employees are protected by unions, which allow for a grievance process with management as well as additional protections from firing.

Benefits and Salary

Jobs in government often pay a comparable salary to jobs in the private sector, though in some fields they pay less. In general, though, government jobs provide a good income and offer a number of benefits, often including better health and retirement benefits (sometimes including defined benefit pensions) than are offered in the private sector. For example, the federal government provides a pension based on a percentage of the average of an employee's highest three years' salary combined with number of years of service, as well as a thrift savings plan. New employees receive 13 paid vacation days per year, increasing to up to 26 days after 15 years of service. Other benefits can include telework, numerous paid holidays, funding for ongoing professional training or education, and student loan repayment.

Career Opportunities

From park rangers to policy analysts, government provides a vast array of career opportunities. In addition, according to the U.S. Office of Personnel Management, more than 33 percent of current federal employees are eligible to retire (and federal workers aren't getting any younger—their average age is nearly 47), and this trend also exists in many state and local governments. This means that the government is likely to be hiring more people for a long time to come. Also, because so many higher-level managers are retiring soon, new employees may be promoted faster than they might be in other sectors.

Reasons Not to Work in the Public Sector

Some people choose not to work in the public sector for several reasons. First, numerous regulations often impede employees from making quick changes in government, which can be frustrating.

Relocation is also an issue to consider. Although there are 14.2 million positions in local government, these jobs are spread out across 87,500 different organizations, which gives an average of only 162 positions per local government (obviously, New York City has many more positions than Topeka). As a result, opportunities for advancement in small cities can be limited. To advance in state government, you might have to move to your state's capital city. To advance in federal government, you may have to be willing to move to another state or Washington, DC.

Also, the heads of agencies are typically appointed by the executive in power (the President, a governor, or a mayor), which means the agency's priorities might change with a new administration. Depending on how high-level your job is, each new election can create some turmoil. Working under an administration you disagree with can sometimes be hard (though some people relish the chance to defend the work of their agency under different administrations).

Lastly, the government hiring process can be lengthy, and the background checks can be elaborate. Most federal positions are only open to U.S. citizens. Yet, whether you must apply by U.S. mail or fax as some agencies request, or whether you must take an extensive written or oral exam as the Foreign Service might require, Chapter 11 of this book will give you tips about the application process for government employment.

The Nonprofit Sector

The nonprofit sector employs about 8.7 million people or 5.9 percent of the workers in the United States and represents $1.4 trillion in total revenues (and $1.3 trillion in expenses, according to the National Center for Charitable Statistics) and about 5 percent of the gross domestic product. In addition, this sector is especially important in the United States, where there is a historical resistance to government providing certain services that are often provided by government in other countries.

Yet the organizations in the nonprofit sector are often defined by what they are not. They are not part of the government, meaning nonprofits do not have the power to impose a tax to obtain funding. They are not operating in order to earn a profit; their goal, typically, is to serve the greater good.

However, these definitions can be misleading. Some nonprofit organizations, even though they are technically nongovernmental, work hand-in-hand with government and receive much of their funding from government agencies. Other nonprofits are entirely independent and receive their funding from donations or other sources.

Also, nonprofit organizations can generate revenue and even surplus funds (see Table 2.6), as long as the surplus funds are used to advance their mission. And even though nonprofits don't earn money for investors, people who work for nonprofits can certainly make a good living.

The 1.6 million different nonprofits in the U.S nonprofit sector represent a vast array of organizations, including hospitals, private schools and universities, opera companies and symphonies, art museums, religious institutions, international non-governmental organizations, and policy institutes and think tanks. Groups ranging from small, all-volunteer organizations to membership-based organizations and even political parties can be classified as nonprofit organizations.

However, when people talk about nonprofits, they are mainly referring to organizations that fall under the IRS's 501(c)(3) tax exemption. To get a sense of the number of these nonprofits in different areas, see Table 2.6. Note that organizations that lobby for specific laws are not tax-exempt in the 501(c)(3) status. (They might be referred to as *advocacy organizations* and will be described in this book as well even though they fall under a different tax status.) Some nonprofits (especially religious organizations or those with incomes less than $25,000) may not be required to file tax returns.

Table 2.6: 501(c)(3) Organizations by Area

Purpose	Number of Organizations	Revenue (in Billions)
Education	61,987	$260.8
Health care, mental health, and medical	42,918	$788.6
Human services	42,539	$110.2
Arts, culture, and humanities	37,851	$32.5
Recreation and sports	28,027	$11.2
Religion-related	21,470	$12.5
Housing and shelter	17,046	$19.5
Community improvement and capacity building	16,288	$15.7
Philanthropy, voluntarism, and grant-making foundations	16,103	$37.9
Youth development	8,148	$7.0
Environment	7,781	$7.9

(continued)

(continued)

Table 2.6: 501(c)(3) Organizations by Area

Purpose	Number of Organizations	Revenue (in Billions)
Animal-related	6,753	$5.6
International, foreign affairs, and national security	6,408	$28.4
Public safety, disaster preparedness, and relief	6,114	$2.0
Crime and legal-related	5,962	$6.7
Other: public benefit, food/agriculture, science, civil rights	17,775	$52.8

Source: National Center for Charitable Statistics, based on 2009 annual filers.

NOTE

A large percentage of existing nonprofits are either entirely volunteer-run or might have one paid staff person. They might be wonderful places to volunteer or have an internship but are unlikely to offer longer-term, paid job opportunities.

Reasons to Work in the Nonprofit Sector

There are many positive aspects to working for a nonprofit. The following sections describe the major ones.

Passion for a Mission

Most people who are drawn to the nonprofit sector share a passion for a particular mission, which means you are likely to work with people who believe as strongly as you do in the mission of the organization. Because many nonprofits provide direct services to the community, a job in a nonprofit organization can allow you to see clearly the positive impact of your work, which is very satisfying.

Culture, Flexibility, and Independence

Nonprofit organizations often provide services that greatly benefit the public but are not provided by government and would not be profitable for a corporation to provide. Nonprofits are often able to be more creative, entrepreneurial, or experimental in their mission and provision of services than government because they are independently run and not subject to the will of the voters or the many rules and regulations that affect government agencies. Similarly, nonprofit organizations have more freedom to experiment than corporations because, though nonprofits must break even to keep functioning, there is not usually any pressure to earn surplus income.

Some nonprofit organizations also have a less formal or traditional work culture. Many work to empower the powerless, so they are less hierarchical and are interested in hearing the opinions of people at all levels of the organization.

Unique Opportunities

Nonprofit organizations also offer opportunities that don't exist in the other sectors. For instance, nearly all religious institutions are nonprofits; many organizations that provide arts and culture that appeal to particular audiences are nonprofits; and organizations conducting advocacy work tend to be nonprofits. If working to advocate for social change from outside the established system appeals to you, you may prefer working for a nonprofit organization. Benefits in nonprofit organizations are often very generous as well.

Reasons Not to Work in the Nonprofit Sector

Nonprofits do not fit everyone. They typically pay less than the private sector (and often the public sector), though it is quite possible to make a reasonable salary in a nonprofit. In addition, sometimes nonprofits are short-staffed; this situation, combined with a strong passion for a mission, can mean long hours, which can lead to burnout.

According to the Bureau of Labor Statistics, most jobs in the nonprofit sector are in organizations that employ fewer than 50 employees. Some of these smaller nonprofits also have limited career mobility, especially when the organization's founder is still in charge (though transferring between organizations is common).

Job security in the nonprofit sector is also a more difficult matter than in government. During an economic downturn, nonprofit organizations tend to receive fewer donations. Those with endowment funds also may suffer because endowments are typically invested in the stock market, which means their value falls in most recessions.

At the same time, some organizations, such as those that serve homeless people and others in need, may see an increase in donations as donors recognize an increased demand for their services during recessions. During the recession of 2009, for example, the federal government stepped in by infusing some cash into certain nonprofits through the American Recovery and Reinvestment Act (ARRA).

Many nonprofits are resilient and have the flexibility and creativity to adapt during a downturn, perhaps taking on an influx of volunteers (including some who have been affected by layoffs elsewhere!). When the economy recovers, those organizations that stick to their missions are often in a stronger situation than they were in before.

The Private Sector

Encompassing the great majority of the U.S. economy and about 115.4 million workers (according to U.S. Census figures for 2007), the private sector includes corporations and organizations whose main goal is to make a profit. It includes organizations ranging from small sole proprietorships to huge, international, publicly traded corporations.

Although the main focus of these organizations is their bottom line, many of them also strive to be good corporate citizens through philanthropy and social responsibility. Some corporations, such as consulting organizations, often have large government or nonprofit contracts and play a major role in implementing projects for the public good. Although this book focuses on the public and nonprofit sectors, it also touches on some of the ways you can add to the public good while working in the private sector.

Reasons to Work in the Private Sector

Salaries in the private sector are usually higher than those for the public or nonprofit sector. Because a great deal of the work of government agencies is done by private sector contractors and consultants, there is a broad variety of available career opportunities. Consultants in the private sector also can have much variety within their jobs, because they move from one project to another or manage multiple projects at once. Also, the hiring process for contractors is usually much faster than it is for government. Often, the speed and volume of work completed also are faster in the private sector. Lastly, the private sector's size and scope mean that it has the potential to have a broad positive impact on society.

Reasons Not to Work in the Private Sector

Private sector consulting firms must continually solicit new contracts from their clients, so a certain amount of salesmanship is involved in many private sector jobs, which is not for everyone. Because private sector organizations must make a profit, some people feel they do not have the same "purity" of mission as nonprofit or government organizations. Private sector jobs also may be more fast-paced than some government and nonprofit jobs, which isn't a good fit for everyone. Lastly, job security is typically less in the private sector.

Jobs That Fit Every Mission

The next few chapters discuss various career fields grouped by mission or issue area. However, certain public service jobs exist in any or all mission areas. These jobs consist of two main groups: management and support jobs (which support the service delivery or *line* positions discussed in the next few chapters) and policy or political jobs. The rest of the chapter explores these groups of jobs.

When you read through these job descriptions, consider how each of the following job types might fit in with the issue area you are interested in. For example, if you like managing programs and care about the environment, consider a program management career in an environmental organization. Then read Chapter 5, "Protecting the Environment and Managing Infrastructure," for more information specific to your area of interest.

Management and Support Positions

In order for any organization to function, certain roles must exist: management of people and programs, communications and public relations, human resources, accounting, and more. Certain roles, such as fundraising, exist primarily in the nonprofit sector; others exist mainly in government. In a tiny organization, all of these roles might be rolled into one position. In large organizations, these roles become quite specialized. The following sections describe the jobs that keep public service organizations running.

Executive Positions

> *"Inventories can be managed, but people must be led."*
> *—H. Ross Perot*

Every organization needs a leader. In the nonprofit sector, leaders tend to be called executive directors and typically report to a volunteer board of directors. In a small nonprofit, the executive director (or E.D.) might perform all administrative and managerial functions, including fundraising, program management, events planning, budgeting, and community outreach. In a larger organization, an executive director will be the spokesperson for the organization; be involved with building community partnerships; manage, hire, and fire staff; build relationships with donors, volunteers, and community partners; handle long-term strategic planning; and create and oversee budgets.

In government, titles for leaders vary. For example, the top administrator at a city government for a city with a council-management form of government is called a city manager or city administrator and typically is not an elected official, but reports to the city council. City managers handle a variety of duties, such as overseeing the activities of city departments, managing the budget for the city, responding to requests for information from the city council, attending city council meetings, and representing the city in external affairs and events.

For a state agency, a division manager may be the top person at an agency. The division manager provides strategic oversight of an agency, leads staff, manages a budget, creates policy recommendations and legislative proposals, and monitors program performance. The typical trajectory for such a career usually starts at an entry level, includes positions that involve technical expertise in the division's mission area, and progresses over a long time at one agency.

Top executives of federal agencies are often appointed directly by the President, though other top positions may include regional directors for field offices and others in the Senior Executive Service, which is the top level of federal civil service. Top managers in local government earned a median of $74,950 in 2006; members of the Senior Executive Service can earn from $117,787 to $177,000. According to the Professionals for Nonprofits Salary Survey (2005), nonprofit executive directors range in salary from the mid-$40,000s for a very small nonprofit up to $350,000+ for a huge one.

Program and Project Managers

Program managers are at the heart of many services, initiatives, projects, and activities that are provided by nonprofit and government agencies—they are the people who make things happen. In the nonprofit world, they tend to be called program or project managers. In government, they may be called management and program analysts, project managers, program analysts, or program specialists. Their tasks typically include

- Developing programs to fit with the organization's mission.
- Coordinating and collaborating with other units within the organization as well as with external organizations. At a nonprofit, these groups may include community partners and funders. In government, these groups include partner government agencies, contractors, and nonprofits.
- Managing and implementing projects. This task often includes writing reports, handling the program budget, and, in government work especially, ensuring milestones or goals are completed within a specific timeline.
- Evaluating the success and effectiveness of a program.

Being well organized and efficient and communicating well are essential to a career in program management, as is having prior experience in the field or a background in project administration. An entry point into the field may include starting as a program assistant or a more technical worker in the field. For example, a social worker may transition from providing direct case management for homeless individuals to managing a broad-based program to help the same population. A variety of educational backgrounds can fit well with a career in program management, though most organizations seek at least a bachelor's degree and some hands-on experience in the field.

Management and program analysts in the federal government earned a median of $79,830 in 2008 (according to the Department of Labor's *Occupational Outlook Handbook*), while those in state government earned about $55,590. Social and community services managers in nonprofit organizations earned an average of $25.07 per hour.

Communications and Outreach

"The sources of information are the springs from which democracy drinks." —Adlai Stevenson

Communications, public relations, and public affairs are careers that exist in nearly every government and nonprofit agency. (In government, communications staff members are typically called public affairs, as opposed to public relations, professionals.) People in such roles make sure that the organization interfaces effectively with the public. They also may answer questions from the public; serve as press contacts; write newsletters, web content, and blog posts; and perform outreach activities to ensure the public is aware of the organization's services.

People in these roles have strong writing and editing abilities and should also be comfortable in public speaking, graphic design, and web design. Increasingly, organizations are looking for individuals who can bring the organization to the Web 2.0 era of increased transparency and web-based interactivity or social media, because many people have become accustomed to having direct communication and access to people through the Internet and now require their government and the nonprofits they care about to be responsive to them in a new way. Some organizations choose to outsource their communications efforts to consulting firms that produce marketing materials and perform outreach in the community.

In general, public relations is a field which is expected to grow faster than average, though at the same time, competition will be fierce because many people are interested in these careers. Median salaries of public relations specialists in local government were about $51,340 in 2008.

PROFILE: VANESSA CASAVANT

Content Strategist/Writer for Electronic Media, The Collaboration to AdoptUsKids

How did you get involved in journalism and public affairs?

I was a really disengaged citizen living in New York City at the age of 21 and pursuing an acting career. I had a temp position in downtown Manhattan across the street from the World Trade Center. I had only been there a month when 9/11 happened. I was in my office on the fourteenth floor when the second plane hit, which shook our building. We evacuated just in time. After two years

(continued)

(continued)

of working through the post-traumatic stress, I asked myself why I didn't know who Osama Bin Laden was or how our government worked. I started reading the newspaper every day and took classes on politics, government, and media during my studies at Hunter College. I became more active and became a reporter for my college's online paper, which led to an internship in Albany covering state politics for *The Legislative Gazette.*

When I graduated, I got an internship with *The Seattle Times,* which led to a job as a reporter with the *Peninsula Daily News* in Port Angeles, Washington. I later got a job with the Quileute tribe in La Push, Washington, a reservation of about 300 people from a tribe of about 700 members. (I'm from a tribe in North Dakota, the Turtle Mountain Band of the Chippewa.) I was originally hired to start a monthly newsletter for them called *The Talking Raven.*

One thing I really worked on as a communications director and as a journalist was to bring awareness that tribal governments have their own courts, laws, policies, constitutions, roads they build, and so on. However, continued funding for my position at the tribe was uncertain, which led to me pursuing my job as the Communications Writer at the Evans School of Public Affairs at the University of Washington and eventually to my current position.

What do you think is the future of a career in public relations for government or nonprofits?

Even though the economy is slowing down, it seems there's still job growth in the area for people working as digital media strategists. With print journalism dying, there are fewer journalists trying to cover the same amount of news and fewer and fewer outlets for organizations and agencies to get their messages out. So viral marketing through media like social networks is becoming essential. Today it's essential for those who want to work on campaigns or in the public sector to know how to use social networking in a way that clearly gets your message across. In a few years, it won't sound odd to have a job as a digital communications strategist for a government agency.

Human Resources (HR) and Volunteer Coordination

Human resources is a field that exists in nearly all organizations: corporate, government, and nonprofit. The field encompasses a broad spectrum of career opportunities, ranging from benefits administration to labor relations and from recruiting to training and development.

Opportunities in the federal government exist in the federal Office of Personnel Management (OPM), as well as within the various agencies of government. State and local governments have many human resources positions as well, often within a department of civil service or personnel. Human resources staff within government may work within complex civil service hiring procedures, run apprenticeship and training programs, and handle labor relations with unionized employees.

Nonprofit organizations also offer human resources positions. Small nonprofits might not have a human resources staff, but midsized or larger ones tend to have at least one human resources generalist who manages all the functions of an HR department. Larger nonprofits have more specialized positions.

The job of a volunteer coordinator exists mainly within nonprofit groups. Volunteer coordinators manage the challenge of recruiting, training, and coordinating the schedules of today's busy volunteers, who provide some of the services in many nonprofit organizations.

Median salaries for state government HR professionals were $48,480 in 2008, $52,080 for local government, and $40.35 an hour for nonprofits. HR is a field which is expected to grow much faster than average.

PROFILE: JOHARI M. RASHAD, PHD

EPA National Telework Coordinator, Human Resources Policy Division, U.S. Environmental Protection Agency

What is your brief career history?

I started working for the federal government in July of 1976, right after I graduated from Howard University. I started my career as a GS-4 clerk-typist [see Chapter 11 for more on GS levels]. I knew it wasn't going to be my permanent job, but it gave me a foot in the door. I immediately started looking for other opportunities where I could use some of the things I had gone to school for. It took me about six months, but I found a new job in what was then the U.S. Civil Service Commission, working on personnel data standards for the central personal data file system. I stayed in that position for two years.

Then I found out that the Civil Service Commission had a competitive intern program, but I found out about it too late to apply that year. I spoke to the coordinator of the internship, and I credit this person, as an HR person, for being the linchpin for the career I now have, because she sat down with me and answered all the questions I had. The next year when the internship came up, I applied and was selected. When I was selected, I could pick which part of the Civil Service Commission I wanted to work in. I spent a year as an intern rotating through different offices in the Bureau of Training. At the end of the one-year internship, I decided I wanted to be an instructor. In 1980, I became a GS-9 instructor, teaching equal employment opportunity and personnel management courses for federal employees.

(continued)

(continued)

I got my master's degree and my doctorate while working full time as a federal employee. One of the great things about being a fed is that many agencies have tuition assistance. My agency, OPM, couldn't pay for the whole degree, but it would pay for the portion that was related to the work I was doing.

What do you do on a typical day?

I am in an HR policy division, and I write the human resources policy for the entire organization. Specifically, I deal with telework, which is a very big issue right now in the federal government. I also have to draft policy on how to help people get professional credentials by reimbursing them for some of the cost. I'm also working on the Family Medical Leave Act and how we provide for employees to take leave to deal with family medical issues. I'm involved in an onboarding or orientation task group. I am also working on pandemic issues, specifically for emergency telework in case of a pandemic crisis.

What do you like the most about this career?

Although I'm not in a training position per se, one of the things I love the most about it is being able to teach people. My background in HR is employee development. My favorite thing is helping people manage their careers.

My favorite accomplishment was creating a course for the U.S. Coast Guard called the Career Enrichment Seminar. There were about 5,000 civilian employees of the Coast Guard at the time, and I trained 10 percent of them.

What are some of the challenges about this career?

There are people who come to work in one specific agency, and they stay there their whole careers. That's never been me. The challenge for me is not how long I will be here, but how long will the work be interesting enough for me to continue to grow. I believe in taking my career temperature every three to five years and asking whether I am learning anything. If the answer is no, my responsibility is not to stay at the agency and complain, but to find out where the new opportunity is.

What skills, education/training, abilities, values, or personality are needed to succeed in this field?

First, you need to like people and have good interpersonal skills. You need the ability to provide answers and resources; to come up with different ways to do things; to research, analyze, and collect information; and to defend recommendations. If you have a good business case for doing something, then you have to be willing to stand up and represent what you're presenting. You need to have computer skills; you can't function if you're not computer literate. We need HR people who can be internal consultants, who can think outside the box, and who have an understanding of organizational development or organizational communication.

Fundraising and Development

Development or fundraising exists in nearly every nonprofit organization. Because most nonprofits are not lucky enough to be able to rely on a large endowment, they must continually solicit donations from donors and grant makers.

Fundraising is usually structured in two ways: asking people for money and asking organizations for money. Those who ask people for money are usually involved with individual wealthy donors and may also run direct-mail campaigns soliciting donations from large numbers of smaller donors.

Essential qualities in a good fundraiser include creativity and excellent interpersonal skills, as well as the ability to be a great salesperson on behalf of an intangible product. After all, donors do not receive anything except the satisfaction of helping a worthy cause and maybe their names on the side of a building. In addition, a new trend in fundraising is *customer relationship management,* where data about donors is captured in a database and analyzed to determine typical donor profiles (for seeking new and similar donors) and estimate how much different donor profiles are likely to give so that you can make a reasonable and targeted request. Skills relevant to this task include data analysis and database management.

Another aspect of fundraising is grant writing (one way of asking organizations for money). Most organizational donors, otherwise known as philanthropies, foundations, government agencies, or corporate donors, need to see an application in a format they prefer, explaining the following points:

- Why the grant-seeking organization needs their funding
- Why there is a need for the service the grant seeker will provide
- How the grant seeker is qualified to provide the needed service
- What measurable outcomes the grant seeker will produce if the funding is given

In a smaller organization, one person may have to solicit donations and write grants, but larger organizations may have several people working in a fundraising department, each specializing in different types of giving, such as corporate and foundation giving, individual donors, special events, direct mail, or bequests.

Some jobs in the private sector also involve influencing decision makers to give funds towards a project. For example, many companies that obtain government contracts spend a good deal of time marketing their services to gain these government contracts. There are also individuals who focus on government relations or government affairs, in both the private and nonprofit sectors, though these roles are more related to some of the communications and outreach work or advocacy work described in other parts of this chapter.

PROFILE: AMY WHIPPLE

Midwest Regional Coordinator, ALS Therapy Development Institute (photo: Amy, right, with her mother, Bernadette Cooper, left, and her aunt, Mary Lou Krauseneck, center)

What is your brief career history?

I graduated from Saint Mary's College in Notre Dame, Indiana, with a bachelor of arts degree. My major was mass communications, with minors in marketing and Spanish. After graduation, I worked for Compuware Corporation in Detroit in a number of marketing-related roles, such as project manager in the creative services department and marketing manager. I then became a sales representative for NewPage Corporation.

How did you enter your current profession?

My aunt, Mary Lou Krauseneck, was diagnosed with amyotrophic lateral sclerosis (ALS, more commonly known as Lou Gehrig's disease) when she was only 44 years old. She inspired her family and friends to raise awareness and support to fuel research. Shortly after her diagnosis, we learned about the research being done by the ALS Therapy Development Institute (TDI) in Cambridge, Massachusetts.

Supporting ALS TDI gave our family hope and enabled us to channel our frustrations with Mary Lou's declining health in a positive way. As volunteers for ALS TDI, my mom and I led a committee of passionate supporters to host an annual event (A Passion for Life); publish cookbooks (*Recipes for Life,* three editions are now available); and handle fundraising walks, wine tastings, and more. Through our efforts over the years, we raised more than $1,600,000 to fuel research at ALS TDI. Mary Lou lost her valiant battle with ALS. However, her passion for life and her vision of a world free from ALS inspired me in my mission to continue to raise the desperately needed funds and awareness to support the research efforts of ALS TDI.

At this time, I was working as a sales representative for NewPage and traveling to customers all around the Midwest. In addition, I was a new mom. Balancing the travel for my job, volunteer efforts for ALS TDI, and responsibilities as a mom and wife was becoming difficult. I was approached by ALS TDI to become its midwest regional director. I was absolutely ecstatic and jumped on this opportunity.

What are some of the things you do on a typical day?

My responsibility is to connect patients living with ALS to the work our team is doing in the lab to discover a therapeutic to slow or stop this devastating disease. I travel to Muscular Dystrophy Association support groups being hosted in my states (Michigan, Illinois, Ohio, Indiana, Kentucky, Kansas, Oklahoma, Missouri,

Wisconsin, Minnesota, North and South Dakota, Nebraska, and Iowa). At these meetings, I educate patients, supporters, and medical professionals on the research being done by our team of 30 scientists. At my home office, I connect with patients on a daily basis to answer questions about research, provide resources in their community, and extend knowledge and hope in the face of this insidious disease.

Furthermore, I work with families, patients, and supporters to help them initiate grassroots fundraising activities to support ALS TDI. I serve as a fundraising consultant and help committees in their execution of initiatives to support our research. I also work on cultivating "major donor" relationships, foundation and grant support, and corporate sponsorships.

What do you like the most about this career?

Serving as an employee for the ALS Therapy Development Institute enables me to combine my life's mission while still supporting my family. I am so passionate about our research and putting an end to this disease that I never feel like my job is done. I know there are so many people depending on me and our entire team to bring therapeutics to patients as quickly as possible.

Today, ALS TDI is the world's largest research effort focused on developing effective therapeutics for patients living with ALS. More exciting is that our team is making amazing strides in the lab.

What are some of the challenges about this career?

Given the current economic challenges, fundraising is especially difficult. Major donors, events, and other revenue-generating activities have taken a significant hit.

Beyond the fundraising challenges, I am dealing with patients and families who are facing a devastating diagnosis and disease. I have become friends with so many amazing people who bravely face a daily decline in their physical abilities. Serving as a source of emotional support is both amazing and exhausting.

What skills, education/training, abilities, values, or personality are needed to succeed in this field?

Some of the qualities that are necessary in a career like this are passion, commitment, dedication, optimism, faith, organizational skills, interpersonal skills, being hardworking, and having the ability to travel.

Any other advice for people who want to enter this field?

My only advice to someone entering into a nonprofit organization would be to have a true passion and belief in what the organization is looking to accomplish. If I didn't believe 100 percent that my hard work and investment (emotional, physical, and spiritual) was going to translate into something that could help ALS patients, it would be much more difficult to meet the daily demands of the job.

Contracting, Grants Management, and Consulting

On the other side of the aisle from fundraising is the job of giving money away or investing it in the public good. Government agencies have outsourced or contracted out much of the work they do for the last several years, and so overseeing and supervising contracts is a very important role in government. This role cannot be taken lightly because it can involve millions of taxpayer dollars.

Skills needed in the field include understanding the contracting or purchasing process for the agency, evaluating bids and contracts, researching new sources for suppliers or contracts, keeping track of inventory, and supervising contractors. A related role in government is that of grants administration, which involves overseeing funds given to states, local governments, or nonprofit organizations. Strong attention to detail, combined with some business or public administration background, is important for these roles. According to the most recent data, contract and purchasing managers earned a median of $51,870 in local government and $73,520 in federal government. Job growth is expected to be flat.

There are some related roles in grant-making philanthropies. For example, in grant-making foundations, employees determine which organizations should receive grants and oversee grants that have been given out to ensure the funds are used properly and the grantee organization has the support it needs to implement the program (more details on philanthropy are in Chapter 6).

In addition, you can find many public service jobs in private sector consulting firms with government or nonprofit contracts. Many of these positions allow consultants to work directly in their client organizations and conduct work ranging from writing emergency management plans, to creating cost-benefit analyses, to providing technological services. Such jobs tend to have higher salaries and simpler hiring processes than government jobs, but job security and benefits may be less.

Finance, Accounting, and Budgeting

Nearly every organization needs an accountant or bookkeeper. Related positions include auditing and fiscal analyst roles. Most organizations require a strong academic background in accounting, finance, or a related field; knowledge of financial statements and generally accepted accounting principles; and excellent organizational skills. Some positions require a CPA (certified public accountant) license as well. Accountants in the public and nonprofit sectors are quite similar in many respects to those in the private sector, but the accounting techniques can be quite different. For more detail, read Chapter 6's section on auditing.

According to the most recent data, the median salary for accountants in the federal government was $78,655. Junior accountants and auditors earned from $28,862 to

$43,731 as a starting salary, depending on experience and education. In local government, the median salary for accountants was about $53,660, and in state government, it was $51,250. In nonprofit organizations, the average was $25.25 per hour. Job growth is expected to be faster than average.

Administration

Even though some administrative tasks have been automated in recent years, there is a continuing need for detail-oriented and organized people throughout both government and the nonprofit sector. Every organization needs administrative staff to keep the organization running, including answering phones, ordering supplies, arranging meetings, filing, and managing other details. These people are the backbone of an organization, the glue that holds everything together.

In addition to general administrative positions, some organizations also offer positions for people providing direct service to the public. Positions in local government range from claims processing to temporary election workers. Salaries of administrative staff in local government averaged from $32,610 to $41,880 in 2008. The salary was $29,850 for administrative staff in elementary and secondary schools, and $31,530 to $39,200 for administrative staff in colleges and universities.

Information Technology (IT)

Every government agency and nonprofit organization needs technical support. This support can range from an outsourced IT consultant who comes in to set up a network to the most involved programmer who designs management software for a large government agency. Technology positions are some of the most in-demand jobs in the public service field. Positions range from network technicians, to IT application specialists, to systems analysts.

IT managers may work with vendors and end users to ensure systems are functioning, handle risk management, design data models, and create written documentation. There are IT positions within every mission area—for example, an emerging career field within international development is focused on how to best utilize technology to help people in the developing world.

Requirements and skills are likely to be similar to those needed in the private sector. Earnings vary based on the type of position and the type of employer. For example, systems analysts in state government earned a median salary of $61,340 in 2006. Computer support specialists working in colleges earned a median salary of $40,130, those working in schools earned $37,880, and those in nonprofit organizations earned $32 per hour. Job growth in this field is expected to be much faster than average.

PROFILE: CRAIG NEWMARK

Customer Service Representative and Founder, craigslist

Can you tell me a little about yourself and how you started craigslist?

The craigslist site started by using email log files as a database, and I rewrote the code using MySQL. That occurred late in 1999, which means I haven't done anything technical for almost 10 years. In craigslist now, my primary job is customer service.

In September I suddenly realized that my job over all, beyond craigslist, is to be a kind of a community organizer, or a community meta-organizer. You do customer service for 14 years or so, and that changes you. You interact with thousands of people, and you have to handle a lot of negative situations. But you do see that people are overwhelmingly good. You do see that people normally want to give each other a break.

What do you think of the new idea of Government 2.0—more "transparent" government through interactive technology?

They're off to a really great start. There's a lot more to go. There's a lot happening, and my role seems to be just pointing to it happening, encouraging people, and being some combination of encouraging and annoying.

The idea is that whenever you run things a democratic way, in fact it does provide opportunities for bad guys. That's not only true on the Web, but in everyday life. That's one of the problems with democracy. The good news that I observe when dealing with bad guys—which is part of the customer service job—is that there aren't that many bad guys out there. They're busy, they're noisy, and we perceive them out of proportion to reality. But to deal with them, you've got to give some power to everyone else. On our site, it's called "flag for removal." On other sites, it's called "report for abuse." And for the most part, American culture and places like craigslist are self-policing. Sometimes you need to have cops, but, you know, things only work if the majority of policing is done by citizens. Now, there are some other kinds of sites, for example, the Sunlight Foundation. It's more and more stuff online that may expose information some people won't want to be in the public eye, but that's good for the country.

I think we have to get together to figure out how to better implement this national pull to service. We need to get word out better for full-time service, like military, Peace Corps, or federal webmasters. We need to help build and focus on mechanisms that have people volunteer, either on an ongoing basis or just for the day, like to help clean out a river. It goes on from there. That's the craigslist for service metaphor.

Policy Positions

> *"Ideas are great arrows, but there has to be a bow. And politics is the bow of idealism." —Bill Moyers*

In addition to the management and support roles that focus on keeping an organization running, there is another important career field in public service: making, researching, and influencing policy. For every major issue area, whether it is improving housing for low-income people, finding new ways to build energy-efficient transit systems, or providing national security, there are a host of opportunities to

- Research and evaluate the policy issues involved.
- Serve on a legislative branch committee analyzing solutions to the issue.
- Lobby or advocate to legislators to push a certain solution to the issue.
- Run for office on a platform related to the issue.
- Support an elected official's work on the issue.

These tasks can be grouped into three main career fields that span across all possible issue areas: policy analysis and research, advocacy, and elected office (including the many roles that support elected officials).

Policy Analysis and Research

Governments and nonprofits need to know whether their efforts are paying off and whether their proposed policy (or the policy they are advocating for) will have its intended consequences. For-profit firms that consult for the government or the nonprofit sector also need this information. That's where policy researchers and analysts come in.

Policy analysts research policy problems and alternatives, determine criteria for selecting solutions to problems, handle statistical models to forecast the impacts of various policy decisions, and conduct reviews of the literature on certain subjects. They may write memos to synthesize their analysis of problems and present them to decision makers within their agencies or to elected officials considering various legislative options. Some policy analysts also focus on tracking legislative proposals and budgets to assess their impact.

This profession is good for individuals with strong analytical, writing, statistical, and interpersonal skills. Sometimes, strong statistical knowledge is required, as is an advanced degree such as a Master of Public Administration (MPA) or Master of Public Policy (MPP). A good understanding of politics is essential as well, because a certain policy may make perfectly logical sense on paper but be politically unfeasible.

Think tanks are research organizations that produce policy research. In addition to hiring policy analysts with MPAs, think tanks also look for individuals with PhDs.

In addition, many nonprofit organizations and government agencies seek program evaluators, whose role is to collect and analyze data to determine whether the program has reached its goals or is producing the outcomes it expects. These reports help the organization improve its programs for the future and can also be helpful when the organization reports to donors about how funds were used. Although this role is not usually as technical as policy analysis, it is an essential function in many organizations.

PROFILE: RICHARD HENDRA, PHD

Senior Research Associate, Low-Wage Workers and Working Communities Policy Area, MDRC

What is your brief career history?

I majored in Economics at the College of New Jersey (then Trenton State College). I focused on econometrics and economic forecasting and took several courses in advanced mathematics and statistics. At my first job, I was a data analyst at a compensation analysis firm. While this used my technical skills (head), it didn't give me a sense that I was contributing to the betterment of those in need (heart). This led me to Milano The New School for Management and Urban Policy. I did my Masters in Public and Urban Policy while continuing to take statistics classes and got my PhD.

Today, I am a senior research associate at MDRC, a think tank created in 1974 by the Ford Foundation and several federal agencies to assess the effect of policy on low-wage earners. I have also taught several statistics classes at Milano The New School for Management and Urban Policy for the past 10 years. This work has given me great pleasure.

How did you enter this profession?

The focus of my whole career has been on using technical skills toward a good end. So the first thing I did was to relentlessly try to improve my skills by taking difficult classes in fields such as mathematics, economics, and statistics. I have also worked hard to pick up data management and computer programming skills over the years. Fortunately, the social policy field is not crowded with people with these kinds of skills, so it has been relatively easy to find work in this area. I had been interviewing for quantitative jobs in the city or federal government, but when the MDRC opportunity came along, I jumped on it. I found the position through my graduate program's career services.

What are some of the things you do on a typical day?

Most of my time is ultimately dedicated to producing high-quality research reports that I hope are used by policy makers to help form sound, evidence-based, public policy decisions. In the initial phases of a project, I am involved in a lot of statistical and data management design work to help set up the methodology and the data collection systems that will be used to evaluate a program. During the middle phase, I oversee the work of technical analysts, who process the data and perform statistical analysis to determine whether a given program or policy achieved its goals. During the later stages, most of my time is spent writing up the results and giving presentations to policy makers and at the key conferences in my field.

What do you like the most about this career?

Without a doubt, the most gratifying aspect of my work is that it is for a good cause. Ultimately, this work is designed to help find programs that will enable at least some low-income people to escape from the vicious cycle of poverty. This is government at its best: trying something new, testing it, and refining the model based on the results. MDRC was at the forefront of bringing science and experimentation to government.

What are some of the challenges about this career?

Doing nonpartisan science in a political field can sometimes be difficult. The needs of the researcher are not always in alignment with the needs of policy makers. The policy-making landscape changes quickly, while knowledge builds slowly and methodically. Having a strong set of ethics and working at a nonpartisan organization are important.

What skills, education/training, abilities, values, or personality are needed to succeed in this field?

To be successful in a think tank, you need to have hard skills. These can be in quantitative methods, qualitative methods, mixed methods, policy design, survey, or operations areas. Simply an interest or passion for public policy is not enough. To break into this area, you have to show that you can do the work—that you have passion not only for the "big picture," but that you also have the ability to get the little things right as well—being good with details, being a careful analyst, being a good writer. A unique aspect of think tanks is that the methodical, systematic workers ultimately do better than the fast workers who make mistakes. You also need to be able to work well in teams and to be able to handle criticism of your work.

People who are interested in research jobs should take as many methods courses as possible. Take the hard courses. Substantive knowledge of a particular policy area is less important than being able to do research. A key conference in this area is the Association for Public Policy Analysis and Management (APPAM) conference. This conference gives you a nice sense of the key issues researchers are grappling with at any given point in time.

Advocacy and Lobbying

While certain nonprofit organizations focus heavily—or entirely—on advocacy work (such advocacy and civil rights organizations are explored in more depth in Chapter 4), many other nonprofit organizations have a role for at least one advocacy person, community organizer, or lobbyist.

Nonprofits that file under the 501(c)(3) tax exemption are not allowed to lobby directly for particular legislation or to help elect a specific candidate. However, they may still conduct community outreach and advocate more generally for certain policies. They can organize petitions and ask their members to write or call their elected representatives about certain issues, which can have a major impact on policy decisions. Some nonprofit organizations also choose to have a separately incorporated lobbying affiliate that is not a tax-exempt entity and can more directly work to influence legislation.

Community advocates (sometimes called field organizers, campaign managers, or community organizers) often work directly with the clients of an organization and help them advocate for themselves. They typically also conduct significant outreach to the community, offer advocacy training for community members, organize awareness campaigns, recruit and organize volunteers, develop and implement grassroots campaigns, and handle other field operations work.

Community advocates may start as canvassers, going door to door to make people aware of certain issues and raising money for a cause. As they progress and gain experience, they may lead additional organizing efforts. Advocacy positions are also sometimes closely related to "citizen outreach" or communications positions. An ability to be extremely outgoing, persistent, and passionate about a cause is essential for this career. Average salaries for community organizers tend to be between $27,000 and $37,000 (according to Salary.com).

Some nonprofit organizations also produce research (described in the previous policy analysis and research section) to help influence policy. Often, the research is designed to ensure that the organization's messages are persuasive and backed with facts.

In addition to advocacy performed by nonprofit organizations that have a more general mission, there are numerous organizations whose entire function is influencing legislation. For example, according to the U.S. Federal Election Commission, there were more than 4,200 political action committees listed in 2007, of which 1,600 represented corporations; 273 represented organized labor; 925 were trade, membership, or health-related organizations; and 1,300 were independent. These organizations made $141 million in campaign contributions in 2006.

The term *lobbyist* may have some negative connotations, but lobbyists can serve an important role in representing the views of the organizations or industries they represent. (Supposedly, the word *lobbyist* refers to the fact that a lobbyist often spends a lot of time waiting in lobbies to speak to elected officials or at committee hearings.) Many lobbyists are self-employed individuals who are hired as consultants to help a particular organization's cause. There are regulations covering lobbying activity, and most lobbyists must register with the government. Some organizations, such as the Center for Responsive Politics, track financial contributions by lobbyists.

Federal, State, and Local Elected Office

Many people serve the public in elected office, which requires a passion for improving the world, a thick skin, and political savvy. There are opportunities to be an elected official at all levels, including city or county councils, regional councils or planning commissions, state legislatures, or on the federal/national level as a member of the House of Representatives or Senate. There are also opportunities in the executive branch, as an elected official such as a county executive, mayor, governor, or even the President of the United States. Some people focus instead on becoming leaders of political parties.

Getting elected to nearly any position in government requires significant energy, perseverance, interpersonal connections, and financial backing. (Additional details on the "job search" of getting elected are described in Chapter 11.) Once in office, the hours of an elected official may be quite long and the challenges daunting, but the chance to create change can be profound.

Salaries of elected officials range tremendously. Some local government elected offices are unpaid, and the salary of the mayor of a small town may be less than a living wage. The President of the United States earns about $400,000.

Legislative Staff

Many people employed in the legislative branch are not legislators. Most elected officials have a number of individuals who work directly for them. These careers sit at the junction of politics and policy and at the interface of elected officials' work and their relationship with the people who elected them. For the right person—one who understands politics and can be part of an often fast-paced environment—these careers can be exciting and fascinating.

Campaign Work

Every elected official depends on significant support in the community, usually starting with grassroots campaigning and get-out-the-vote work. Working on a campaign is, of course, an excellent way of making political connections for the future and is almost a prerequisite for future political positions.

Legislative Staffers, Constituent Relations

Once a candidate is elected, there are positions working as staffers, researchers, or supporters of the elected official. Numerous individuals work to respond to the requests of the electorate by providing what is known as *constituent relations*—responding to questions, concerns, emails, phone calls, and letters of citizens. Other staffer roles include chiefs of staff, press secretaries, schedulers, and administrative staff.

Legislative Research

In addition to policy analysis positions, which may exist in various agencies, there are also research positions within the legislative branch. At the state level, some state legislatures have a research service whose role is to analyze proposed legislation to determine its potential impact. These researchers must be nonpartisan in their work, conducting research for any legislator regardless of that legislator's party affiliation. Of course, the number of legislative staff and their level of specialization vary state by state, especially because some states are part-time legislatures that meet only a few months of the year.

Individual state representatives each have a legislative assistant who conducts research on proposed legislation and handles constituent relations. A legal or public affairs background is an asset in these positions.

On the federal level, positions exist at legislative branch agencies such as the Congressional Research Service and Congressional Budget Office, as well as for specific elected officials. Some individuals who are policy experts on certain issues become legislative researchers for particular legislative subcommittees.

In state legislatures, as well as the federal government, additional research positions exist in the party-affiliated caucus—for example, the House Democratic Caucus or Senate Republican Caucus. Those in the executive branch (including mayors, governors, and the President of the United States) also employ policy or legislative researchers as advisors.

PROFILE: JILL RAYNOR LANE

Instructor of Political Science, North Seattle Community College; formerly held several legislative positions

What is your brief career history related to political/legislative/policy work?

I am currently an Adjunct Instructor for Political Science for North Seattle Community College and Central Texas College. Prior to that, I was the Manager of Legislative Affairs for the Water Environment Federation, where I researched, wrote, and edited weekly and monthly newsletters focusing on state and national legislative news, presented articles on state and federal requirements for wastewater facilities and on clean water issues, and organized congressional educational briefings on water and environmental issues.

My legislative experience includes working as a Federal Liaison for the North Carolina Department of Environment and Natural Resources (DENR) in the Washington, DC, Office of the Governor under governors Jim Hunt and Mike Easley. I wrote and edited weekly briefings for senior staff at DENR, fostered relationships among the North Carolina Congressional delegation, and worked on policy issues affecting the state.

I also worked as a Legislative Specialist for Wilmer, Cutler, and Pickering and as a Fellow/Fundraising Assistant for U.S. Senator Bob Kerrey (D-NE).

How did you enter this profession?

I have an MA in Political Science from North Carolina State University and a BA in Political Science, with a minor in Sociology from the University of North Carolina at Greensboro. I liked political science from my very first course. My professor, Jeffrey Colbert, was absolutely brilliant. This interest, coupled with my desire to effect change for the better, led me to the goal of working in politics.

When I finished undergraduate work, I did not feel quite prepared in how to start in politics, so I went to graduate school. While there, I interned for U.S. Congressman Richard Gephardt (D-MO, House Minority Leader). While in DC, I learned some tips from other political staffers about where to live, how to enter the field, and the importance of networking.

After graduate school, I moved to the metropolitan DC area. I hand-delivered my resume to every Democrat in the U.S. Senate, offering to work for free to get "in the loop." Everyone had stressed the importance of being employed and present within the system to get news of jobs first. Some congressional offices got thousands of resumes for one job. Having contacts helped get my resume out of the stack. I had to attend as many functions as possible and work hard to create contacts. I also worked a paying job at night until I found a full-time job with an elected official.

What were some of the things you did on a typical day when you worked with elected officials?

As a fundraising assistant, I attended hearings and wrote summaries, researched and summarized legislative histories, organized a presidential fundraising event, and researched and edited correspondence for the senator's signature. I also maintained and tracked political action committee and individual contributor efforts and managed volunteers and interns.

As a federal liaison, I advocated for the governor of North Carolina's environmental agenda. I wrote and edited weekly congressional briefings for senior staff at DENR; organized and facilitated federal information briefings on environmental issues; coordinated efforts between the governor's office, DENR, and the North

(continued)

(continued)

Carolina Congressional delegation to maximize opportunities; oversaw intern staff; and developed and maintained contacts to provide advanced intelligence on key legislative issues.

What did you like the most about this career?

I enjoyed working on behalf of the public. My proudest accomplishment was being able to be on the Senate floor. I also really felt good about working on behalf of the state of North Carolina, the state where I grew up, especially after Hurricane Dennis. The 100-year and 500-year flood plains flooded, and money was needed. The governor's office and other branches of the state government worked hard to help the citizens of the state.

What are some of the challenges about this career?

The pay is low, and the hours are long when you work for an elected official. Also, you must realize that you do not represent your own interests. You represent the interests of the elected official—while at work and after hours. That does not mean that you always agree personally with the elected official, but it is very important to keep personal opinions to yourself while in public (unless providing a disclaimer or replying to the elected official's request for your opinion). If you are lucky, then you share many viewpoints with the elected official for whom you work.

What skills, education/training, abilities, values, or personality are needed to succeed in this field?

A working knowledge of government is helpful, but not essential (it can be learned). Also needed is the art of diplomacy, patience, tenacity (policy is a slow, incremental process), and the ability to research and assess complex information and communicate its impact effectively to key audiences in order to achieve goals.

I recommend a graduate degree or law degree. Policy in particular has a language of its own. Many folks who work in the field now have advanced degrees.

I recommend that people who go into politics know who they are and have a strong value system. The work can be high pressure and highly visible, and there are temptations, too. It's also important to be able to interact well with many different types of people. It can take a while to get your first job in politics, but once you do, you will hear about a lot of opportunities that are never published.

Professional organizations to join include the political party of your choice (sometimes, they have seminars and networking events—particularly at the local level). If you want to lobby, join the group that you are targeting (for example, The Sierra Club). However, if you want to work for an elected official, you may want to put off joining special interest groups so that you may appear fair and impartial.

I had a college professor who said to me once that if you worked in politics in DC, you can eat free every night. I had no idea what he meant until I worked in Congress. There is a dinner, happy hour, or fundraiser every day in Washington, and a lot of information is exchanged at these events. Go to as many as possible—especially when first looking for a job.

References and Resources

For more information on the topics presented in this chapter, refer to the following sources.

The Public Sector

Bureau of Labor Statistics; "Federal Government," *Career Guide to Industries, 2010–11 Edition;* www.bls.gov/oco/cg/cgs041.htm
Mannion, James; *The Everything Guide to Government Jobs* (Adams Media, 2007)
U.S. Census Bureau, *Statistical Abstract of the United States 2010,* www.census.gov/prod/www/abs/statab.html
U.S. Office of Personnel Management, www.opm.gov/feddata

The Nonprofit Sector

Bureau of Labor Statistics; "Advocacy, Grantmaking, and Civic Organizations," *Career Guide to Industries, 2010–11 Edition;* www.bls.gov/oco/cg/cgs054.htm
Cryer, Shelly; *The Nonprofit Career Guide: How to Land a Job That Makes a Difference* (Fieldstone Alliance and American Humanics, 2008)
IRS, www.irs.gov/charities
National Center for Charitable Statistics (Urban Institute), http://nccs.urban.org/

Executive Positions

Idealist.org, "Professionals for Nonprofits Salary Survey 2005," www.idealist.org/en/career/salarysurveys.html
Professionals for Nonprofits, www.nonprofitstaffing.com

Communications and Outreach

National Association of Government Communicators, www.nagc.com
Public Relations Society of America, www.prsa.org

Human Resources (HR) and Volunteer Coordination

American Society for Training and Development, www.astd.org
International Public Management Association for Human Resources, www.ipma-hr.org
National Association of State Personnel Executives, www.naspe.net
Society for Human Resource Management (SHRM), www.shrm.org

Fundraising and Development

American Grant Writers' Association, www.agwa.us
Association of Fundraising Professionals, www.afpnet.org
Certified Fund Raising Executive (CFRE) International, www.cfre.org

Contracting, Grants Management, and Consulting

National Institute of Governmental Purchasing, Inc., www.nigp.org

Finance, Accounting, and Budgeting

American Accounting Association, Government and Nonprofit Section, aaahq.org/GNP/index.htm
Association of Government Accountants, www.agacgfm.org
Government Finance Officers Association, www.gfoa.org

Information Technology (IT)

Digital Government Institute, www.digitalgovernment.com
Government Technology magazine, www.govtech.com

Policy Analysis and Research

Association for Public Policy Analysis and Management (APPAM), www.appam.org
Policy Jobs, www.policyjobs.net
Policypointers, list of think tanks, www.policypointers.org/Links

Advocacy and Lobbying

American Association of Political Consultants, www.theaapc.org
American League of Lobbyists (ALL), www.alldc.org
American Society of Association Executives, www.asaenet.org
Association for Community Organization and Social Administration, www.acosa.org
Center for Responsive Politics, www.opensecrets.org
Lobbyists.info, http://lobbyists.info
Lobbyist Finder, www.lobbyistfinder.com
Public Affairs Council, http://pac.org/jobs
Salary.com, www.salary.com

Legislative Staff

The Hill, http://thehill.com
Library of Congress, THOMAS legislative information, http://thomas.loc.gov
Roll Call, www.rollcall.com
The Washington Post, www.washingtonpost.com
The White House, staff salaries, www.whitehouse.gov/blog/Annual-Report-to-Congress-on-White-House-Staff-2009

CHAPTER 3

Helping People Through Human Services and Health

"Nothing liberates our greatness like the desire to help, the desire to serve." —Marianne Williamson

One of the most pressing issues we face today is how to help the 39.8 million people in our nation who struggle with poverty (U.S. Census Bureau, 2008 data). Millions of people also face homelessness, child abuse and neglect, and illness. And behind this struggle are many related injustices—racism, sexism, discrimination. At the same time, there are tremendous opportunities to solve these problems, both by directly providing essential services to people as a social worker, manager of a human services organization, health-care provider, or health-care researcher or by advocating for long-term solutions to underlying issues.

You can be part of the solution by pursuing a career that helps people lead healthy lives. This chapter notes some of the organizations involved in the issues of human services and health care at the federal, state, or local government or nonprofit levels and highlights some of the typical jobs in each field.

Human/Social Services

"I have found the paradox that if I love until it hurts, then there is no hurt, but only more love." —Mother Teresa

The extremely broad category of human and social services covers services to individuals who have various needs. This section describes organizations according to the population they serve: youth, children, and families; elderly individuals and people with disabilities; people who struggle with poverty; and various groups such as immigrants, ethnic and racial groups, women, and veterans.

Of course, many human services organizations provide a variety of services to many different populations of people. For example, the Salvation Army provides human services such as finding missing persons, coordinating disaster relief, conducting prison rehabilitation and drug rehabilitation programs, fighting human trafficking, hosting youth camps, providing elderly services, and supplying international aid.

Many organizations that provide direct service for people also advocate for the rights of those served, either by helping individuals secure their own rights, or by working to change policies that affect the population they serve. Those organizations that focus mainly on advocacy are described in the Civil Rights section of Chapter 4.

Children/Youth, Parents, and Families

> *"There is always one moment in childhood when the door opens and lets the future in."* —*Graham Greene*

Because they cannot advocate or care for themselves, infants, children, and youth are vulnerable populations that need special attention and service. To survive and flourish, children need a safe and caring environment to grow up in that is free of abuse, neglect, hunger, and crime. Sometimes government or nonprofit agencies step in to ensure children get what they need.

One of the federal government agencies that focuses on helping children and youth is the Administration for Children and Families (ACF), a division of the U.S. Department of Health and Human Services. ACF focuses on adoption and foster care issues and also provides the following:

- A national directory of adoption agencies
- Child welfare
- Research and statistics into issues affecting children and youth
- Lists of toll-free crisis hotlines
- Child care information
- Child support and enforcement assistance (including a federal parent locator service)
- Funding for community initiatives

- Youth services
- Health insurance for children
- Early childhood education programs for low-income children (such as Head Start)
- Child health guidelines
- Temporary assistance for needy families

It also gives both funding and technical support to state and local government human services agencies and nonprofit organizations that provide services in the community.

State agencies that focus on children and youth are usually housed in a department of health and social services, human resources, children and families, or family and protective services. Services they provide include adoption and foster care referrals; child protective services, which send social workers to investigate reports of child abuse; and public education on child safety.

Local government provides resources and support services to help families, including those with special issues such as teenaged parents, homeless families, and families with members who have disabilities. People working at the local level may distribute clothing, food, and school supplies or conduct parenting education classes or life skills training. Cities may also offer youth services, such as youth employment opportunities, youth violence prevention programs, and academic enrichment.

Much of the hands-on support to children and families is provided by nonprofit organizations (over 8,000 youth development nonprofits filed with the IRS in 2009), often with some of the funding coming from government. Families and individuals in crisis rely on nonprofits for essential services. For example, children's aid organizations such as Children's Aid Society, The Home for Little Wanderers, and Children's Home Society provide adoption assistance, family support, counseling, legal help, food, and advocacy for abused children. These organizations strive to help keep families together and help parents be better at raising their children. Other organizations, such as the YWCA and YMCA, provide direct youth and children's services such as summer camps, after-school programs, and day care.

On the lighter side, many organizations encourage children to become strong adults, train them with leadership skills, and provide recreation opportunities. Examples include the Boy Scouts, Girl Scouts, Camp Fire USA, Girls Incorporated, Boys' and Girls' Clubs, Police Athletic Leagues, and Big Brothers and Big Sisters mentoring programs. Other types of youth organizations include the following:

- Development programs such as YouthBuild USA, Prep for Prep, and the Posse Foundation
- Community service clubs such as Youth Service America

- Religious leadership programs
- Civic education programs such as the Center for Civic Education and Junior State of America
- Programs that help young adults pursue careers in business, such as INROADS, which matches minority students to paid internships in corporations, and Students in Free Enterprise, which runs business competitions for kids
- Programs that inspire youth to understand farming and agriculture, such as 4-H and Future Farmers of America

NOTE

> If you are interested in working with children, also check out the Education section in Chapter 4. Teachers and educators on the "front lines" provide many services and interventions that help children, and many programs that benefit children are provided through schools and other educational institutions.

Elderly/Seniors and Individuals with Disabilities

"Cast me not off in the time of my old age; forsake me not when my strength faileth."—Psalms 71.9

As the Baby Boom generation ages and longevity increases, the need for services that ensure dignity, health, and care for senior citizens and individuals with disabilities will continue to grow. (According to the U.S. Census, there were 36.3 million people over age 65 in 2004 and 49.7 million people with disabilities in 2000.) Although individuals with disabilities and senior citizens are two distinct groups with different issues and identities, some human services agencies tend to serve both populations.

On the federal level, the Administration on Aging (AoA) of the Department of Health and Human Services has the mission of "helping elderly individuals maintain their dignity and independence in their homes and communities through comprehensive, coordinated, and cost-effective systems of long-term care and livable communities across the U.S." Some of their programs include implementing improvements to Medicare; offering a clearinghouse of information on long-term care; giving grants to states for services such as legal assistance and disease prevention; and providing oversight, funding, technical assistance, and leadership to a network of 29,000 state, local, and nonprofit service organizations in the United States. The AoA also provides an Eldercare Locator call center to link older adults and their caregivers with local resources. Other federal agencies that provide services related to the aging include the Federal Transit Administration (part of the Department of Transportation), which funds transit programs to serve the elderly and people with disabilities; the Department of Housing and Urban Development, which provides funding to build accessible housing; and various regulatory agencies that ensure that senior citizens are not targeted by mail fraud and other scams.

In addition to providing services for the elderly, the federal government has many agencies that provide assistance, benefits, and equal opportunities for individuals with disabilities. These include agencies at the Departments of Health and Human Services, Education, Transportation, and Justice. The Department of Labor has an Office of Disability Employment Policy, and the Social Security Administration offers benefits to individuals with disabilities. The federal government also offers waiver programs that provide funds to nonprofits for people with developmental and other disabilities.

On the state level, numerous agencies on aging (with various names such as Office of Services to the Aging or Department of Aging) provide information and referrals to health-care-related resources such as home-delivered meals, home health-care agencies, or adult day care. Most states also have agencies that serve people with disabilities (usually called the Department of Vocational Rehabilitation). Often these agencies focus on helping individuals with disabilities to enter or re-enter the workforce by providing training or assistance with finding adaptive equipment. These agencies also work with a statewide, federally funded Independent Living Council to create a plan and implement programs for independent living services and Centers for Independent Living that provide services to people with disabilities to help them live on their own.

On the local government level, older Americans maintain independence through the help of various programs such as senior centers. In addition, local governments also often have Americans with Disabilities Act (ADA) compliance officers or programs for people with disabilities. Local governments also usually have programs within their public transportation departments and public works departments to ensure that buses and other transit systems are made accessible and that sidewalks and other public works have wheelchair cutouts and other features to accommodate individuals with disabilities.

Nonprofit organizations, often with funding from both government and private donors, provide direct care to seniors and individuals with disabilities. For example, in Seattle, Senior Services offers adult day programs, a caregiver outreach and support program, community food programs such as Meals on Wheels, social activities, fitness and exercise classes, outreach to seniors who live alone, education about retirement planning, consumer and legal rights advice, a law clinic, information on Medicare and other health-care coverage, and transportation programs. Half of their funding comes from government sources; the other half comes from sources such as United Way funds, individual donations, corporate and foundation grants, and fees. There are also some retirement communities run by nonprofit organizations.

Residential care and adult day programs for individuals with disabilities and centers for people with developmental disabilities, deafness and hearing impairment, and blindness are also often run through various nonprofit entities.

PROFILE: LOREEN LOONIE

Director of Community Relations, Independence Care

What is your brief career history?

I have a bachelor's degree from State University of New York, Plattsburgh, in mass communications and a master's degree in public administration from the School of Public Affairs at Baruch College.

I have worked with people with disabilities for my entire career, beginning in 1991 at the Capital District Center for Independence, an independent living center in Albany. I moved from there to the Eastern Paralyzed Veterans Association (now called United Spinal Association), a nonprofit that helps veterans and all people with disabilities. There I was a regional advocate and later, the director of advocacy. Next, I worked at the YWCA-NYC as the director of the Angela Perez Center for People with Disabilities, working with young people with disabilities. Currently, I am the director of community relations at Independence Care System, a Medicaid managed care plan for people with disabilities.

How did you enter this profession?

I found my first job working with people with disabilities through an advertisement in the *Albany Times Union.* I knew that I wanted to work at a nonprofit, and I was hoping for a job in development. (I had never heard of an advocate before.) I remember doing the research for the interview and being amazed that during the four years I was in college, I somehow missed a major civil rights movement. The issue of equality for people with disabilities made sense to me right away, and helping people understand their legal rights and getting people what they need provided me with a great way to channel my values about the world into my work.

What are some of the things you do on a typical day?

My job entails outreach to get more people interested in joining my organization, communications to internal and external audiences, and advocacy for the organization and its members and programming. On a typical day, I write and edit publications, create strategies with staff to get more members, help members to solve problems, and attend meetings on many issues, including internal issues and processes to improve work methods and the direction of the organization. I also spend some time on administrative issues (such as timesheets, invoices, supplies, etc.).

What do you like the most about this career?

I love that I was able to find something that I feel passionate about. I feel very lucky that my job allows me to use my strengths to help people live a better life and to make a real difference in the lives of many people.

What are some of the challenges about this career?

For many years, I worked for very little money. Advocacy can be draining—it often takes a long time to see the results of your work. Sometimes you have to help a lot of people with the same problem before you can figure out that there is a system problem and find a way to deal with the system causing the issue. Many people with disabilities in New York City live in poverty and have all of the same issues other people living in poverty face—low wages, poor health care, substandard housing—but these difficult issues are compounded by having a disability, making the challenge of overcoming the issues that much more difficult. This situation can often feel incredibly overwhelming.

What skills, education/training, abilities, values, or personality are needed to succeed in this field?

The first thing that is helpful is to think about people with disabilities as equals—not someone you are taking care of. If you can get to a point where you do not like an individual with a disability and do not censor your feelings because of the disability, then you have accomplished true disability competence. I have had job applicants tell me they cannot spend all day with people with disabilities because it makes them too sad. Once you understand that people with disabilities, like all of us, are complex people that may on a given day be heroes or goats, you can begin to have real conversations with people and figure out what they need and want. It also helps to have a strong sense of justice and to find real joy in meeting and helping people. Having a sense of humor is helpful, because whenever you are dealing with people, government agencies, and other nonprofits, there is bound to be a day when you want to pull out your hair. On that day, you have to find something to laugh about.

Any other advice for people who want to enter this field?

I felt very lucky to come to the disability rights field right when the ADA (Americans with Disabilities Act) was being implemented. I was able to work alongside many of the advocates who pushed and pushed to get that law passed. Now it is normal to have a person with a disability in your Psych 101 class, and a person in a wheelchair getting on the bus seems like no big deal. I think it is important to read some history to understand how hard people had to fight to be considered a first-class citizen [see the list at end of the chapter for her suggestions].

Being able to live my beliefs and values every day of my 18-year career has made me very happy. The great thing about advocacy and communications is you get paid to be a big mouth, to point out what is wrong, and to try to fix it. It still gives me a charge to help people, to fight for someone's rights, and to right a wrong.

Poverty Alleviation

"Poverty is now an inhuman anachronism." —*Hubert Humphrey*

Underlying the many struggles of people who utilize human services programs is poverty. Hunger, homelessness, unemployment, financial stress, and lack of health care compound other problems people face. Many organizations focus on providing the basic essentials of life (housing, food, and medical care) to people who face economic disadvantages. In fact, most social service agencies, even if their focus is on a particular population, work to provide these essentials.

NOTE

> Other important ways to help people rise from poverty in the long term include education and advocacy (described in Chapter 4) and community and economic development (described in Chapter 6).

Some agencies provide direct financial benefits for people who live in poverty. Federal programs include the Social Security Administration (SSA), which provides benefits to individuals through the Social Security Disability Insurance and the Supplemental Security Income programs as well as retirement benefits, and the Temporary Assistance for Needy Families (TANF) program through the U.S. Department of Health and Human Services. State agencies coordinate with the federal government to provide benefits. Local government agencies may also provide subsidized assistance with child care, reduced energy bills, food, and health care for low-income residents. Among nonprofit organizations providing general direct services, some of the largest include such institutions as Catholic Charities, Goodwill, and the YMCA. The rest of this section focuses on specific ways that the public and nonprofit sectors work to help people with some of their most immediate needs.

Homelessness

Agencies work on the issue of homelessness in two ways—providing emergency shelter to homeless people and helping people in the longer term to find employment and affordable housing. (While these two areas are interrelated, low-income housing development and management are covered in Chapter 6 in the Community and Economic Development section.) Numerous nonprofits, including many religious organizations, run shelters and residences for homeless people, such as Covenant House, which helps homeless youth; shelters organized by Catholic Charities missions; and various Travelers Aid agencies. More than 17,000 nonprofits focused on housing and homelessness in 2009.

Hunger

Helping people get enough nutritious food to eat is another major part of fighting poverty. Federal agencies involved with this issue include the Food and Nutrition Service of the USDA (U.S. Department of Agriculture), which provides the Supplemental Nutrition Assistance Program (SNAP, formerly known as food stamps); the Women, Infants, and Children (WIC) program; the national school lunch program; and food assistance during disasters, among other things. Most of these programs are administered by state governments and implemented by local governments, including WIC, school lunch, school breakfast, and after-school and summer feeding programs. States also appropriate additional funds for these programs and to fund food banks.

There are also numerous nonprofit food banks and soup kitchens, including the Feeding America food bank network, City Harvest, Food Lifeline, and meal delivery programs such as God's Love We Deliver and Project Open Hand. Many other broad-based nonprofit social service organizations also provide food aid, such as Volunteers of America and the American Red Cross. Other organizations focus on ensuring better nutrition.

Employment

A major cause of poverty is unemployment, underemployment, or low-wage employment. To help people find better employment opportunities, various organizations provide training and job-search skills, and others provide unemployment benefits.

On the federal level, the U.S. Department of Labor's Federal-State Unemployment Insurance Program establishes the guidelines for the unemployment insurance programs administered by state governments. The Department of Labor also sponsors the CareerOneStop program, which offers "career resources and workforce information to job seekers, students, businesses, and career professionals" through a network of local career centers. The Employment and Training Administration "administers federal government job training and worker dislocation programs, federal grants to states for public employment service programs, and unemployment insurance benefits."

The actual administration of unemployment benefits is usually handled on the state government level, through agencies with names such as the Employment Security Department or Commission, Workforce Office, or Department of Labor and Workforce Development. These agencies also offer vocational rehabilitation programs for individuals with disabilities, labor market research and information, worker's compensation claims, financial aid and grants for career-related education, and resources for employers who want to hire workers in the state. Similarly, there are workforce development agencies on the local government level as well, and many cities offer resource links to career resources for local residents. Many state-funded community colleges also provide significant resources for individuals wishing to build skills to enter the workforce.

More than 4,000 nonprofits focus on employment in the U.S. (as of 2009). These nonprofits offer employment training and support, especially for individuals who have disabilities or barriers to employment. Examples include Federation Employment and Guidance Services (FEGS), Philadelphia Workforce Development Corporation, and Goodwill Industries, as well as vocational counseling services, sheltered employment programs for individuals with disabilities, and vocational rehabilitation services.

Specific Populations

A number of organizations work with specific groups of people who often face discrimination or particular challenges, such as immigrants or refugees; Native Americans, African Americans, and other ethnic and racial groups; people who are gay, lesbian, bisexual, and transgender; women; and veterans. Many of these same organizations also advocate for the rights of these groups.

- **Immigrants:** The United States offers refuge and asylum to thousands of people fleeing war and persecution each year. Federal agencies that work with refugees and immigrants include the Office of Refugee Resettlement of the Department of Health and Human Services; U.S. Citizenship and Immigration Services of the Department of Homeland Security; and the State Department's Bureau of Population, Refugees, and Migration. State governments may offer a Refugee Bureau or Bureau of Refugee and Immigrant Assistance, usually within a larger human services agency. Local governments also may have special programs for immigrant and refugee family support within the Human Services Department. Some nonprofits that work directly with immigrants to help them resettle and adapt to their new country include the International Rescue Committee, Hebrew Immigrant Aid Society, and the U.S. Committee for Refugees and Immigrants.
- **Ethnic groups:** Some organizations focus their work on specific ethnic or racial groups, such as the NAACP, which advocates for civil rights of African Americans, and the ASPIRA Association and the Hispanic Scholarship Fund, which work with Hispanic/Latino populations (others are mentioned in the Civil Rights section of Chapter 4).
- **Native Americans:** A number of federal organizations work specifically with Native American populations, such as the Administration for Native Americans and the Indian Health Service (IHS) of the Department of Health and Human Services, the Office of Public and Indian Housing of the

Department of Housing and Urban Development, and the Bureau of Indian Affairs (BIA) in the Department of the Interior. State agencies may have an Office of Indian Affairs as well, and a wide variety of nonprofit organizations focus on Native American issues.

- **Gay, lesbian, bisexual and transgender individuals:** Various community centers offer services for gay, lesbian, bisexual, and transgender individuals and others advocate for their rights (see Civil Rights section in Chapter 4).
- **Women:** Though women have gained many rights, they still disproportionately face challenges such as domestic violence and discrimination in the workplace, still earn less than men, and typically have more child-care responsibilities. Many organizations focus on improving the lives of women through health-care services and advocacy to ensure gender equality; and many nonprofits such as the YWCA and Girl Scouts provide services that especially empower and benefit women and girls.
- **Veterans:** A variety of services and programs are offered to people who have served their country in the military. Of course, the federal agency most involved is the U.S. Department of Veterans Affairs (VA), which provides health services through the Veterans Health Administration and the VA hospitals; education through the Veterans Employment and Training Service; and numerous benefits through the Veterans Benefits Administration, which provides compensation, pensions, education, home loans, vocational rehabilitation, and more. State and local governments provide services through veterans' affairs offices. In addition, veterans (and sometimes their spouses) are given strong preference in hiring for federal government jobs and often in state or local government jobs. Nonprofits that provide care to veterans and advocate for them include Army Emergency Relief, Air Force Aid Society Inc., Paralyzed Veterans of America, and Navy-Marine Corps Relief Society.

Volunteers

Some organizations focus on harnessing the resources of volunteers to solve community problems. On the federal level, the National Corporation for Public Service funds and promotes many of the large-scale volunteerism promotion efforts in the United States, such as AmeriCorps.

Many nonprofit organizations utilize volunteers to support their missions, but some focus on matching volunteers with suitable projects at other organizations. Examples include Volunteers of America and women's and men's volunteer organizations such as the Junior League. There are also community service clubs such as the Lions Clubs, as well as organizations that find volunteers for short- or long-term projects, such as City Year, Points of Light Foundation, and New York Cares.

Human/Social Services Jobs

Some of the most common jobs in the social and human services field include direct care providers, social workers, and counselors, as well as specialized positions such as homeless shelter managers. Many positions that are common to most nonprofit and government agencies (including those in the human services field), such as program management, research, fundraising, communications, and budgeting, are described in Chapter 2. Note that the numbers in the following descriptions reflect the most recent government data available (2008), as collected in the Department of Labor's *Occupational Outlook Handbook.*

Social and Human Service Assistants

At the entry level in human services are human service assistants, who help social workers and other professionals. This type of job goes by many different titles:

case management aide	life skills counselor
client advocate	mental health aide
community outreach worker	psychological aide
community support worker	social services aide
gerontology aide	social work assistant
human service worker	youth worker

The job involves working directly with clients or patients through such activities as running a group home, supporting people at a homeless shelter, helping people find out how to apply for benefits, or helping them take medication or get dressed. Often, people start out as aides and then pursue further education to become social workers, case workers, or administrators.

About 352,000 people work as human and social service aides, and demand for more workers in this field is growing, especially as the population ages. Median salaries range from $23,580 for residential treatment center workers to about $32,560 for local government staff.

Social Workers

Most human services agencies employ social workers, who provide a broad array of services to clients, manage programs, and perform advocacy work. Of the 642,000 social workers in the United States, 5 of 10 social work positions are in health-care and social assistance organizations, and 3 in 10 are in state or local government agencies.

Social workers often work on the front lines of society's problems. They help people with substance abuse problems, homelessness, and physical and mental illnesses, and intervene in families with domestic or child abuse. Some focus on mental health or substance abuse treatment, and others work in public health settings to help people find the care they need to cope with life-threatening illness. Some social workers also manage human services agencies, work on policy analysis, or conduct research to create better solutions for societal problems. Social workers who provide counseling or therapy services can also work in private practice as therapists.

A bachelor's degree is the minimum requirement for this field, but a growing number of positions require a Master of Social Work (MSW) and a license or certification. Master of Social Work programs allow for certification as a social worker and often require extensive internships of up to 900 hours. Coursework typically covers the history of the social welfare system, human behavior, social work practice, clinical practice, group work, community organizing, and administration.

Median salaries for child, family, and school social workers were $46,650 for those who work in local government, $39,600 for state government workers, and about $34,450 for those working in individual and family services and residential treatment programs. Social workers in medical and public health settings earned from $38,370 to $51,470, and median salaries for mental health and substance abuse social workers ran from $33,950 to $36,660. Job growth is expected to be faster than average.

Counselors

The 665,500 counselors in the United States range from education, vocational, and school counselors; to rehabilitation counselors, mental health counselors, and substance abuse counselors; to marriage and family therapists. Counselors work in many of the same types of agencies as social workers, though only 11 percent work for government agencies and 47 percent work for human services nonprofits. Counselors also work in educational settings (such as career counselors in colleges and universities) and in private practice. Salaries range from $35,220 for vocational rehabilitation counselors to $57,800 for school counselors. Job growth is expected to be faster than average.

Most counselors need to have at least a master's degree to be certified or licensed, and some agencies require supervisors to have a PhD. Master of Counseling Psychology and other psychology programs provide training on counseling and therapy to help people with life adjustments and can certify individuals as school counselors or rehabilitation counselors.

Health

"The greatest wealth is health." —*Virgil*

Health care is the single largest industry in the United States, employing 14 million people. It is also one of the fastest-growing fields in terms of employment, largely due to the aging of the population. The United States has about 580,000 health-care institutions, including doctors' and dentists' offices, hospitals, diagnostic labs, home health-care services, psychiatric hospitals, nursing homes, residential care facilities, and outpatient care centers. The government and nonprofit sectors make up a large portion of the field, providing research, benefits, and health-care services to patients.

Among federal agencies, the U.S. Department of Health and Human Services is the largest related to health care, employing about 61,000 people in 2007. According to the U.S. Office of Management and Budget, the U.S. government spent about $728 billion on direct health-related benefits to individuals in 2008, including $459 billion on Medicare, $203 billion on Medicaid, $35 billion on veterans' health, and smaller amounts on state children's health insurance, Native American health-care programs, and substance abuse and mental health services. It also spent $29 billion on health research and training and $3.1 on consumer safety. In contrast, state and local governments spent $247.6 billion on health care in 2006.

The numerous areas within the health-care field include public health, direct care through health-care facilities, mental health and substance abuse treatment, health benefits, and research. The following sections describe these areas in more detail.

Public Health

Broad-based disease prevention in communities is the focus of public health. To create healthy living conditions for people, public health agencies work behind the scenes to accomplish the following tasks:

- Identify causes and sources of community-wide diseases and find ways to prevent them
- Ensure that food and water are safe to consume and that consumer products are safe to buy
- Educate people about how to prevent communicable diseases
- Create new prevention strategies, such as vaccines
- Intervene in health emergencies

Various agencies are involved in this work at the federal, state, local, and nonprofit levels. Federal agencies that are involved include the following:

- The Department of Health and Human Services' Centers for Disease Control and Prevention (CDC), which provides public information on disease and focuses on disease prevention and control
- The Agency for Toxic Substances and Disease Registry of the CDC
- The Food and Drug Administration (FDA), which tests food, drugs, medical devices, cosmetics, and more for safety
- The Office of Healthy Homes and Lead Hazard Control of the Department of Housing and Urban Development, which focuses on preventing lead poisoning

State health agencies offer public health education programs, community wellness and prevention programs, environmental health protection programs, public health labs (which provide services ranging from newborn screening to testing water for chemical pollution), and public health emergency preparedness and response programs. Local health departments provide health education as well as birth and death certificates, local health codes, environmental health services, and public health clinics. Nonprofit organizations providing public health services include local health clinics and public health education and research groups. Philanthropies such as the Robert Wood Johnson Foundation also provide funding for public health.

PROFILE: DR. NGOZI OLERU, PHD

Division Director, King County Department of Public Health, Environmental Health Services Division

What is your brief career history?

I have worked for public health, in government, all through my career. I started work at a state health department, as a field person, an environmental health specialist. About two years after that, I moved up to unit supervisor and became the chief of toxicology for the State of Massachusetts Public Health Department. I then became the director of public health for the City of Boston Public Health Commission. I then moved to the federal level to work as the environmental justice coordinator for Region 1 EPA in Boston. That job didn't have the same level of activity I enjoyed at the local level, so I left it for the one that I'm in right now.

(continued)

(continued)

I have a bachelor's in pre-med biology and a master's in public health, with an environmental health concentration, from the University of Massachusetts, and a PhD from the University of Oklahoma.

How did you enter this profession? What led you to get into this field?

I had been on my way to medical school, but changed my mind, because the medical route would have led to me making a difference in people's lives only one person at a time. I just didn't have the patience to save the world one person at a time, so public health provides me with the avenue to achieve change at a population level and a community level.

What do you do on a typical day?

My day could be determined by something that came out in the paper. For example, the EPA did some sampling of air quality in schools around the country, one of which was in my jurisdiction. The researchers found some extraordinary levels of a chemical that they were not expecting. That became the agenda for the day. I checked in with the EPA and other local or regional agencies in charge of air quality.

What do you like the most about this career?

What I find exciting about the work I do is that I directly touch the lives of people, that I can see the difference my efforts make. My career is very much anchored in the philosophy of equity and social justice—the idea that all people should be treated fairly and have a fair chance at actualizing themselves; I'm proudest of anything I have done to further this goal.

What is a challenge of your position?

The challenge I face is the lack of flexibility with financial resources to embrace the comprehensiveness of my field. Philosophically, I can't look at what I do in a siloed way. For me, the definition of environment is very broad: it's social, physical, economic. You don't stop being in one arena just because you're talking about toxics. I'm constantly struggling, whether with budget or my peers and colleagues, in having to convince people to practice this profession in a more holistic way.

What skills, personality, and education would you suggest for someone entering this field?

Cultivate the spirit of open-mindedness. To go into this field, you have to come at it from a philosophy of "both/and," not "either/or." If you have the approach of "both/and," you will be able to entertain other people's perspectives. Be humble enough to accept that other people have good ideas. They may not put them in the same technical terms or jargon you do, but that doesn't make them any less of a good idea.

What kinds of positions are available in your field?

The vehicle of 21st century public health practice is policy. Up to now, we have done a lot of programming. Programs are great, but they have not been the answer to what is wrong. We need to step back now and look at real primary prevention, and the way to get there is through policy.

In environmental health right now, there are a lot of technical people with bachelor's degrees in environmental health or science, working in regulatory programs that have been the mainstay of public health practice. In the past few years, public health is on its way to branch out into more broad areas. I actually created some new positions with not a strict public health background, but a planning background.

The major issues that produce health problems and costs are chronic disease related to nutrition, physical activity, and smoking. Yes, there are a lot of programs that teach people to eat well and exercise to encourage them to change behavior. But you can go a step further and put a land-use policy in place that requires builders to have amenities that naturally encourage people to be physically active. Walking trails, sidewalks, grocery stores in the neighborhood that people can walk to that have fresh, healthy foods—all that is in place already. Over time that becomes the norm. You don't then have to change behavior, because the good behavior would already be there.

Any other advice for people wanting to enter this field?

William Foege [former director of the CDC] said that the philosophy of public health is social justice. Ground yourself in that philosophy. Urban planners are public health people. People in transportation are public health people. People in economic development are public health people. Look at what these people do and how it affects human beings—these are the things that affect health. Unfortunately, we tend to look at health from a disease perspective. The things that produce health are a good job; a good, affordable roof over your head; and a safe neighborhood. If you have these things, I guarantee you will be healthier than someone who only has great health insurance. As Dr. Foege said, all social policy is health policy.

What organizations should people who work in public health join?

Organizations to join include the American Public Health Association. Another organization for someone in local health—though people don't join as individuals, it's an organization of local government—is the National Association of County and City Health Officials. Also look at the National Environmental Health Association.

Direct Care in Hospitals and Other Facilities

In the United States, most of the responsibility for healing the sick and running large health-care facilities falls to nonprofit hospitals, with support from government. Some of the largest nonprofits in the country are nonprofit hospitals and health insurers, such as the Kaiser Foundation Health Plan Inc., Children's Hospital Inc., Cleveland Clinic Foundation, New York–Presbyterian Hospital, and Memorial Sloan-Kettering Cancer Center. Other direct health-care nonprofits include community clinics, family planning centers, rehabilitation medical centers, blood and tissue banks, nonprofit ambulance companies, nursing homes, hospital volunteer organizations, visiting nurses' associations, and hospices for terminally ill individuals. Universities also run large teaching hospitals.

The federal government does provide some health care to people directly through its various agencies. The Indian Health Service, for example, provides direct health services to American Indians and Alaska Natives, and the U.S. Department of Veterans Affairs runs numerous VA medical centers nationally. In addition, the federal government's Health Resources and Services Administration provides funding to states to help build community health centers for low-income individuals without health insurance.

State governments often run state hospitals, which provide service to the public, especially lower-income or psychiatric patients. States also may run emergency medical systems and rural health programs to fund clinics in underserved areas. Local governments fund local nonprofit health clinics or may run their own; they also offer child immunizations and other disease prevention programs.

Mental Health and Substance Abuse Treatment

The federal agency most involved with mental health is the Substance Abuse and Mental Health Services Administration (SAMHSA) of the Department of Health and Human Services, which runs the Center for Mental Health Services, the Center for Substance Abuse Prevention, and the Center for Substance Abuse Treatment. These centers offer funding and support for local efforts to provide community care for people with mental illness. They also provide emergency mental health treatment in the case of traumatic disasters and offer mental health block grants to states.

State agencies, through the mental health divisions of state health departments, run state hospitals, which may offer psychiatric care to children, and forensic psychiatric facilities for incarcerated mentally ill populations. Local governments may offer crisis services and treatment to low-income individuals, including community mental health treatment, housing programs, crisis interventions, and case management.

Nonprofit mental health providers include the following types of organizations:

- Substance abuse prevention organizations such as Partnership for a Drug-Free America

- Treatment centers such as the Hazelden Foundation and Betty Ford Center
- Mental health treatment facilities such as the Devereux Foundation or Community Care Behavioral Health Organization
- Psychiatric hospitals such as McLean Hospital
- Community mental health centers
- Group homes and residential care facilities
- Hotlines and crisis intervention organizations
- Rape crisis centers

In addition, organizations that focus on specific mental illnesses, such as the Hope for Depression Research Foundation or Anxiety Disorders Association of America, help perform research and offer support for people suffering from these disorders.

Health Benefits

Who should pay for the skyrocketing cost of health care? This has been a hot topic lately, but in fact the public sector and nonprofit organizations already provide a large portion of the payment for medical care for millions of Americans.

For example, the Department of Health and Human Services' Medicare and state funding of Medicaid are huge programs. According to the Department's website, the Medicare program "is the nation's largest health insurer, handling more than one billion claims per year. Medicare and Medicaid together provide health-care insurance for one in four Americans." Hospitals also receive federal funding through the Agency for Healthcare Research and Quality (AHRQ), Centers for Medicare & Medicaid Services (formerly the Health Care Financing Administration), and the Health Resources and Services Administration (HRSA).

The Medicaid program offers insurance to the most low-income citizens and is run by state governments. A few state governments also supplement the insurance for many of their low-income residents who live above the Medicaid income threshold, and many state governments provide insurance to children.

Health Research

Another important part of the health-care field is medical research, which focuses on finding causes and cures for various illnesses. The federal agency most involved with health research is the National Institutes of Health, which conducts and finances research to lead to medical discoveries such as disease causes, prevention methods, and cures. This agency employs about 6,000 scientists who conduct the agency's own research; it also provides about $28 billion per year in funding to universities and independent health research facilities and organizations that conduct the majority of the research. State health agencies typically gather statistics related to disease and health within their states.

Much of the advocacy, research, and care for specific diseases is performed by nonprofit organizations. Famous examples are the American Cancer Society, American Heart Association, Leukemia and Lymphoma Society, Muscular Dystrophy Association, and the March of Dimes. Thousands more focus on finding cures for specific diseases such as HIV/AIDS, Alzheimer's disease, autism, or epilepsy.

Health-Care Jobs

The majority of jobs in the field are in professional and service occupations requiring specialized training, including doctors, nurses, social workers, physical therapists, and technicians. About 18 percent of workers in health care are in service positions requiring less training, such as home health aides, nursing aides, and medical assistants. Other positions include paramedics and emergency medical technicians.

- **Direct care providers (doctors, nurses, technicians):** Medical doctors diagnose and treat diseases and help patients heal from injury. They range from family practitioners to very specialized surgeons. Doctors must be licensed and complete an MD or a DO and an internship. Job growth in this profession is faster than average.

  Of the 661,400 doctors working in 2008, 53 percent worked in doctors' offices; 12 percent were self-employed; 19 percent worked in hospitals; and many more worked for government, universities, and outpatient centers. Salaries ranged from $186,044 for a primary care practitioner to $339,738 for a specialist.

- **Epidemiologists, statisticians, and medical researchers:** Medical scientists conduct research to find causes and cures of diseases and to understand disease patterns and incidence. Many work in laboratories as part of universities or university hospitals or independent research centers, and some work for government agencies such as the National Institutes of Health or a state health agency. Some also work for pharmaceutical companies or biotechnology companies. Most medical scientists and researchers hold a PhD or an MD, or sometimes both.

  There were 109,400 medical scientists in 2008, not counting numerous university faculty. Earnings for medical scientists ranged from $44,600 for scientists in universities to $82,640 for those in industry.

  Epidemiologists focus on researching the incidence and causes of diseases on a statistical level, and usually hold a Master of Public Health degree. Fifty-seven percent of epidemiologists work for government. There is strong demand for this profession, especially for individuals with both an MD and PhD; though there is also tough competition for research grant funding. Job growth is expected to be faster than average.

- **Public health occupations:** A variety of other careers exist in the realm of public health, such as health inspectors, public health educators, health research coordinators, and health-care program and project managers. For example, there were 66,200 health educators in 2008, earning a median of $44,000 per year; and there were 55,800 occupational health and safety specialists, earning a median of $62,250.

  Public health specialists at the state level often train local health-care managers how to prevent various illnesses, collect specimens to track disease outbreaks, develop clinic policies and procedures, or conduct outreach and education programs to inform the public about healthy living as well as health threats. A Master of Public Health degree is useful in the field. This degree program focuses on teaching people how to build healthier communities, and such a program can cover areas such as environmental health, international health, health services management, and epidemiology.
- **Health administrators:** A variety of other careers exist in the administration of health-care programs, such as supervision of staff, program management, human resources, research grants management, health services consulting, and benefits or claims management.

References and Resources

For more information on the topics presented in this chapter, refer to the following sources.

Human/Social Services

American Public Human Services Association, www.aphsa.org
Association of Social Work Boards (has licensing information), www.aswb.org
Coalition on Human Needs, jobs page, www.chn.org/jobs
Human Services Career Network, www.hscareers.com
Jebens, Harley; *100 Jobs in Social Change* (MacMillan Publishing Company, 1996)
National Human Services Assembly, www.nassembly.org
SocialService.Com (job site), www.socialservice.com
Social Work Job Bank, www.socialworkjobbank.com

Children/Youth, Parents, and Families

Administration for Children and Families, www.acf.hhs.gov
National Association of Youth Service Consultants, www.naysc.org

Seniors/Elderly and Individuals with Disabilities

Administration on Aging, www.aoa.gov
Fleisher, Doris Zames, and Zames, Freida; *The Disability Rights Movement: From Charity to Confrontation* (Temple University Press, 2001)
Linn, Barbara; *Ode to a Diet Coke: Disability, Choices and Control* (JimSam Inc. Publishing, 2008)

National Association of Area Agencies on Aging, www.n4a.org
Rousso, Harrilyn; *New York Activists and Leaders in the Disability Rights and Independent Living Movement, Volume III;* http://bancroft.berkeley.edu/collections/drilm/collection/items/rousso.html
WorkWORLD Help/Information System, State Vocational Rehabilitation Agencies list, www.workworld.org/wwwebhelp/state_vocational_rehabilitation_vr_agencies.htm

Poverty Alleviation

CareerOneStop, www.careeronestop.org
The Congressional Hunger Center, www.hungercenter.org
Emergency Food and Shelter National Board Program, www.efsp.unitedway.org
Employment and Training Administration, www.doleta.gov
National Alliance to End Homelessness, www.endhomelessness.org
National Association of Workforce Development Professionals, www.nawdp.org
U.S. Census Bureau, Poverty page, www.census.gov/hhes/www/poverty/poverty.html

Specific Populations

African American Nonprofit Network (AANN), www.aannexchange.org
Association for Refugee Services Professionals, www.refugeeprofessionals.org
Blacks in Government, www.bignet.org
Hispanic Federation, www.hispanicfederation.org
National Council of La Raza, www.nclr.org

Social Workers

Council on Social Work Education, www.cswe.org
National Association of Social Workers, www.socialworkers.org

Counselors

American Counseling Association, www.counseling.org
National Board for Certified Counselors, Inc., www.nbcc.org

Public Health

American Public Health Association, www.apha.org
Association of Schools of Public Health, jobs page, www.publichealthjobs.net
Association of State and Territorial Health Officials, www.statepublichealth.org

Direct Care in Hospitals and Other Facilities

American Hospital Directory, www.ahd.com
American Medical Association, *Health Care Careers Directory,* www.ama-assn.org/ama/pub/education-careers/careers-health-care/directory.shtml
Bureau of Health Professions, http://bhpr.hrsa.gov

Health Benefits

Centers for Medicare and Medicaid Services, www.cms.hhs.gov

Health Research

Centers for Disease Control and Prevention, www.cdc.gov
Infectious Diseases Society of America, www.idsociety.org
National Institutes of Health, www.nih.gov

CHAPTER 4

Educating People and Defending Their Rights

"Education remains the key to both economic and political empowerment." —Barbara Jordan

Like human services and health care, education helps people lead better lives. Individuals improve their well-being and prosperity through better education, and societies that focus on educating their citizens well are able to produce innovations, improve their economies, and have a better functioning government.

Making sure people have equal rights also improves society. Groups of people form organizations that advocate for the rights of those who have been left out, left behind, or discriminated against, with the goal of forming a society that can meet its full potential. This chapter highlights educational, labor, and civil rights organizations.

Education

"If you think education is expensive, try ignorance." —Derek Bok

The education of children and adults is a huge aspect of both the public and nonprofit sectors. Although the first education career that might come to mind is a teacher—and, in fact, the great majority of individuals who work in education work as teachers—there are thousands of other careers in education, including education administrators, child-care workers, librarians, psychologists, and researchers.

Federal agencies involved with education include, of course, the U.S. Department of Education. The role of the U.S. Department of Education is to ensure that people have access to education and to help states and local school systems improve the quality of education by acting as a clearinghouse for education information and research.

In particular, the U.S. Department of Education manages federal financial aid for higher education and for students with disabilities, performs research on education trends, recommends reforms, works to prohibit educational discrimination, and provides funding to state-level educational agencies such as libraries, museums, and universities. Other federal agencies are also quite involved with education, including the National Science Foundation, which invests substantial grant funding into math, science, and engineering education, and the Department of Defense, which often hires teachers and instructors.

However, unlike in many other nations where educational programs are centrally controlled, in the United States, much of the actual work in the education field happens at the state and local levels, and state and local governments maintain significant control over their schools. The following sections divide the education field into categories based on the people being educated: early childhood, K–12, higher education, special education, and vocational and continuing education. Also included are sections on libraries and the types of jobs that are available in education.

Early Childhood

Early childhood education refers to the education and care of children under the age of five. As more families are unable to provide traditional unpaid child care to their children, the demand for day-care/child-care services has increased tremendously. According to the U.S. Census (2006 data), more than 12 million 3- to 5-year-olds attend preprimary education programs (preschools, nursery schools, and so on), and millions more infants and toddlers are in other day-care programs.

Much of the care and education for children younger than five is provided by either day-care centers (often nonprofit, sometimes for-profit) or family child care (offered in the provider's home). Some of the more formal day-care establishments offered by nonprofit organizations include those offered by YMCAs and similar community and recreation centers, by religious organizations, and within schools or social service agencies.

One federal early childhood educational program is the U.S. Department of Health and Human Services' Head Start program for children from low-income families. State governments often have an Office of Early Childhood Education within their Education or Health and Human Services departments. Local Human Services departments may offer professional development for early childhood educators, preschool programs, and child-care assistance to low-income families.

K–12

K–12, probably the largest subsection of the education field, includes the education of children from kindergarten through high school. During the 2005–2006 school year, nearly 49 million U.S. children attended 97,300 different public schools, which employed more than 3 million teachers at a median salary of $49,000. Another 9,200 private schools enrolled more than 5 million children and employed 435,000 teachers. In addition, more than 16 million children took part in after-school activities such as arts, sports, or tutoring.

Federal organizations related to K–12 education include the Department of Education's Elementary and Secondary Education unit and the Office of English Language Acquisition. The U.S. Department of Agriculture is also involved through its National School Lunch and School Breakfast programs.

State and local government, however, are the entities primarily responsible for funding and managing education at the elementary and secondary level. Every state has its own Department of Education, Board of Education, or Superintendent of Public Instruction. Many states run programs that gather statistics on how various school districts are performing, set standards for graduation requirements for high school, provide teacher resources, assist with career and technical education, and manage the certification of teachers in the state. States also provide child nutrition programs and assist with student transportation (school buses). And most K–12 education is delivered at the local level.

Although most K–12 schools are public institutions, some are nonprofits, such as private and religious schools. Nonprofits such as Teach for America encourage people to consider becoming teachers, while others focus on school reform. Some philanthropic organizations provide funding related to education. The Bill and Melinda Gates Foundation, the Lumina Foundation, and Broad Foundations, for example, are putting a huge amount of funding into improving teacher quality and educational outcomes.

Special Education

Special education is a subset of education that focuses on helping students with learning disabilities, speech or language difficulties, mental retardation, emotional disturbance, orthopedic impairments, autism, vision and hearing problems, and other health issues to achieve academically. The Individuals with Disabilities Act (IDEA) authorizes the U.S. Department of Education to provide grants to states and nonprofit organizations to support special education, serving about 6.8 million children and youth with disabilities.

Special education encompasses numerous programs and specialized jobs in all sectors of education. The jobs include teaching positions at schools and administrative and other positions at the local and state levels, within higher education, and within the Department of Education's Office of Special Education and Rehabilitative Services. For example, there were about 473,000 special education teachers in the United States in 2008, and the field is growing. Special education teachers work to create an Individualized Education Program (IEP) for their students to tailor educational goals to each student's abilities.

PROFILE: HILLARY TABOR

What is your brief career history?

In high school, I tutored students to save money for college. During college, I taught part-time at religious schools to help pay my bills and sometimes substituted at a private school. I also stumbled onto a college class that involved working with individuals with disabilities and really enjoyed it.

After working in corporate communications, I realized that I missed being in the classroom, so I found a part-time position teaching in a private religious school (in addition to working full-time doing communications for a nonprofit organization). I considered returning to graduate school to become a full-time teacher, but I quickly realized that I didn't have the patience that I knew was necessary to be an excellent teacher. Instead, I decided to attend graduate school so that I could pursue special education policy and law, thereby advocating for individuals with disabilities.

In graduate school, I pursued a dual degree (a master's in education policy and administration and a law degree) and a certificate (disability policy and services) so that I could learn as much as possible about special education. At the same time, I began substituting in the local public schools in special education classrooms. This work helped me to better understand the coursework I was taking, as well as the difficulties faced by special educators.

When I offered to volunteer with a group that advocated for individuals who were deaf and blind, the group referred me to the Department of Health, where I was immediately offered a part-time position working on universal newborn hearing legislation—a perfect fit for me because I also studied sign language and deaf culture during college. I also volunteered at the Minnesota Disability Law Center. Later on in my graduate work, I worked as law clerk for a special education (parent advocate) attorney. I also participated in my law school's special education clinic, providing legal advocacy for children with disabilities.

This period of my life was a whirlwind. I was attending class and studying multiple hours a day, and then working and networking in the field. This sleeves-rolled-up, hands-on, can-do attitude landed me each subsequent position, including my current position—the people I met and worked with would recommend me to someone else in the field, and another opportunity would open up.

During my last year of graduate school, I applied for and obtained a two-year Presidential Management Fellowship. Through the fellowship, I submitted my resume to the U.S. Department of Education and asked that it be directed to the Office of Special Education and Rehabilitative Services (OSERS). It turned out that one of the supervisors in that office had previously worked for the Minnesota Disability Law Center, and we knew many of the same people. I was offered a position as an education program specialist in the Office of Special Education Programs, Monitoring and State Improvement Planning, doing a combination of special education monitoring and technical assistance at the state level. After the fellowship is complete, I will convert to a regular government employee in the same position.

What are some of the things you do on a typical day?

Among many roles, my agency works to ensure access to educational opportunity for all individuals. The states are the primary player in the education field; however, the federal government tries to help supplement the state's efforts by providing additional money, research, and other support.

I work with the states' Departments of Health and/or Education to ensure that they are in compliance with the Individuals with Disabilities Education Act (IDEA). I may help them determine whether a policy is consistent with the IDEA or help them determine an appropriate resolution to a problem they are facing. I also do a lot of reading to ensure that I understand current best practices so that I can be a resource for the states with which I work.

What do you like most about this career?

I like that my work is challenging. Every day, I face new questions and new obstacles. I like working directly with the states because I am able to see the impact of statutory and regulatory changes, as well as of judicial decisions, on the functioning of the education system.

(continued)

(continued)

My proudest accomplishment was helping a parent who was frustrated and angry about some difficulties she was facing in the special education system. Instead of just pointing her to a website for information, I provided her with information about resources that were available within her state. The parent thanked me for providing her with information, but also for listening to her concerns. Sometimes just taking the time to listen can make a big difference to a parent.

What are some of the challenges about this career?

One challenge is that there isn't always a clear answer to the questions people face. Sometimes the laws are unclear, and my agency is unable to give an answer. Or the laws may be clear, but the answer doesn't make sense given the situation. Another challenge is that I may not always agree with the policy decisions that have been made, but it is my job to ensure the states abide by them and to enforce them.

What skills, education/training, abilities, values, and personality traits are needed to succeed in this field?

You have to be able to clearly explain difficult concepts because states frequently make their own statewide policy decisions based on the agency's guidance. You also have to be very analytical. States frequently present complex scenarios and need guidance disentangling the problems and determining workable solutions. You have to understand the way the special education system operates, including the moving pieces related to (just to name a few) personnel, funding, data, research, and privacy concerns.

Any other advice for people who want to enter this field?

Contact people in the field and talk to them about what they do. I learned a lot about what I did and didn't want to do just by talking with people about their jobs. In addition, it gave me a leg-up when I was looking for jobs because everyone already knew who I was and how energetic I was about the work. Don't be afraid to ask people to talk to you—as I learned, most people are glad to do it.

Volunteer with special education–related organizations whenever you can. When you put yourself out into the field and show that you are passionate about the work, opportunities will quickly emerge.

Read as much as you can about education. The more you understand about the issues relevant to special education, the more of an asset you will be to the special education field.

Higher Education

Higher education refers to college and university education. Recent data reveals that more than 18 million students are enrolled in colleges and universities in the United States. To meet the needs of these students, the 4,352 different universities and colleges employ about 3.6 million people, of whom about 1.37 million are professors, 329,000 are research or instructional assistants, 711,500 are other professional staff, and 932,000 are nonprofessional staff (as of 2007).

A college or university may be a public, state institution (such as the University of Michigan) or a private nonprofit (such as Duke University). In fact, some of the largest nonprofit organizations are private universities, such as the Massachusetts Institute of Technology, Yale, Stanford, New York University, and Harvard.

Funding for higher education may come from the state or federal government, tuition, research grants, and private donations. State and local governments spend between 2.6 and 12.8 percent of their appropriations on public higher education, totaling over $69 billion in 2006. In 2007, higher educational institutions received an additional $29.7 billion in donations and voluntary support. Some of this money comes from large organizations such as the Nellie Mae Foundation, College Success Foundation, United Negro College Fund, and Education Resources Institute, all of which raise money for college scholarships.

NOTE

Federal involvement in higher education comes from Department of Education agencies. For example, the Office of Federal Student Aid manages Pell Grants, Stafford loans, PLUS loans, Federal Work Study, Perkins loans, and Federal Supplemental Educational Opportunity grants totaling over $90 billion in aid each year. The Office of Postsecondary Education creates federal higher education policy, improves access to higher education for disadvantaged students, and provides teacher development resources.

Other affiliated nonprofits work in tandem with higher education, such as fraternities and sororities, campus religious programs, and student-run bookstores and businesses. In addition, some educational testing services, such as the Educational Testing Service or ETS (creators of the SAT), are nonprofit organizations.

Vocational and Continuing Education

Vocational and continuing education includes both training programs to help adults find specific careers and opportunities for adults to continue their studies or develop useful skills. (Chapter 3 has additional details on this field in the Human/Social Services section titled "Employment.") Federal agencies related to this area are the Department of Education's Office of Vocational and Adult Education and the

Department of Labor's Employment and Training Administration. Numerous community and technical colleges are funded or run by state governments. Nonprofits include technical training schools, such as auto mechanics schools; high school vocational programs; enrichment programs such as yoga centers; and trade schools.

Libraries

Libraries are another important component of the education sector and exist at K–12 and postsecondary educational institutions, government agencies and corporations, and as public and privately owned libraries. The American Library Association counts more than 122,000 libraries of all types in the United States, of which about 3,600 are housed in universities and colleges and 9,200 are public libraries.

The federal government maintains the National Archives and Records Administration and the Library of Congress. The federal government also provides national support to libraries and museums through the Institute of Museum and Library Services.

Public libraries are typically funded by local governments, with some supplement from private and federal funds. Nonprofits associated with libraries include organizations that raise money for public libraries as well as privately owned libraries that are open to the public, such as the Morgan Library and Museum.

Libraries these days offer a variety of services to their visitors. Of course, they house books and other written materials and provide research assistance, but they also usually provide free Internet access to the public, music CDs and videos, workshops, and cultural performances.

Jobs in Education

Teachers are by far the largest occupational group in the field of education, numbering 3.5 million in 2008. This total breaks down into 179,500 kindergarten teachers, 1.5 million elementary school teachers, 659,500 middle school teachers, and 1.1 million secondary school teachers. Median annual earnings of kindergarten, elementary, middle, and secondary school teachers range from $47,100 to $51,180, but this number varies greatly by school district and level of experience. This field is always in demand, though some subfields (such as special education) are more so than others.

Master of Education programs typically prepare their recipients to be elementary, secondary, or special education teachers and can offer courses in teaching methods, curriculum and instruction, classroom management, and specific topics such as mathematics education. These programs typically also offer practical experience and internships. Other possible areas of focus include educational psychology, educational administration and policy, curriculum design, and so on.

Other jobs in education include the following:

- **Preschool teachers and child-care workers:** The United States has about 457,200 preschool teachers and 1.3 million child-care workers. Many positions in child care are available to individuals with minimal education, and many positions are part-time. The median salary for child-care workers is $18,970. Preschool teachers often have higher education requirements, such as an associate's or bachelor's degree, and make a median salary of $23,870. The demand for preschool teachers is expected to grow in the coming years. A small percentage of people in this field are program administrators, who run centers or preschools, supervise staff, and manage financial and marketing tasks.
- **School administrators:** Administrative and managerial opportunities also exist at school boards and school districts as program managers, evaluators, budget analysts, facilities managers, auditors, labor negotiators (as most public school teachers are unionized), curriculum designers, grant writers, and much more. Median wages are about $83,880 for principals, and job growth is expected to be steady (neither increasing nor decreasing).
- **Guidance counselors:** Guidance counselors work in K–12 settings to help students plan for college and postgraduate jobs, as well as to ensure they meet the requirements to graduate. They also provide counseling to students in general. In the United States, about 260,000 people work as educational and guidance counselors. Most states require certification or licensing for guidance counselors. The median salary of counselors working in K–12 education is $57,800 (2008 data), and employment for counselors is expected to grow faster than average.
- **Other opportunities in K–12 education:** Other opportunities at the K–12 level include teacher's aides and assistants; support functions such as food service, school transportation, or building maintenance; and professional positions such as school social workers, psychologists, and nurses.
- **College and university professors:** Most college and university professors must have a PhD in their discipline, and to find positions in more competitive disciplines or certain universities, they also must have been published in academic journals. Many university professors must be willing to relocate to get good positions. The academic job search is different in many ways from a typical job search, and most PhD programs should provide advice to their students about how to conduct such a specialized search.

  In addition, obtaining a "tenure track" (permanent) position does not, in itself, guarantee job security. New professors must prove to their departments that they are worthy of tenure. If they do not achieve tenure within a certain time frame, they typically must leave that university and seek positions elsewhere. Professors who obtain tenure, however, have virtually unparalleled job security.

Average salaries of college professors were $77,009 for public universities or colleges and $92,257 for private universities or colleges. Requirements for community college professors are sometimes similar to those for university and four-year college professors, but many community colleges also seek instructors who have a master's degree and some years of practical experience in their subject area.

- **Higher education administrators and student services professionals:** Colleges employ numerous professionals to provide services to students, from admissions counselors and financial aid staff to career counselors and alumni relations officers. Some positions are more administrative in nature, such as registrars, who organize class schedules and maintain student records; financial aid officers, who work with students to help them afford college; and facilities managers, who manage university buildings.

  Other positions are more involved with helping students get through college emotionally and have a good experience while there, such as residence life directors, athletics program officers, student life program managers, and psychological counselors. Career counselors help students build successful careers upon graduation. People in these fields have a variety of backgrounds; no one course of study is required. However, some may pursue a Master of Higher Education Administration, which can prepare professionals for careers in higher education student services and other fields.

- **Vocational and adult educators:** Vocational education teachers train students for specialized occupations, and adult education teachers provide both remedial courses in reading or writing and adult enrichment classes and continuing education. Many adult education or enrichment teachers are self-employed and teach subjects such as cooking, computer skills, arts and music, or fitness.

  In the United States, there are about 112,300 vocational education teachers and 96,000 adult literacy and remedial education teachers, with job growth expected to be faster than average. Average salaries for vocational education teachers are about $23.63 per hour. For adult literacy teachers, they are $23.95 per hour (according to 2007 data).

- **Librarians:** A Master of Library Science (MLS), Master of Library and Information Studies (MLIS), or Master of Librarianship is required to work as a librarian. Such degrees focus on information management and organization, information science, training and instruction methods, reference services, research, and management.

There were about 159,900 librarians in the U.S. in 2008. Median salaries for librarians ranged from $47,940 for local government/public librarians to $55,250 for librarians at junior colleges. Because many librarians are expected to retire in the coming years, job growth should remain steady.

Workers' Rights

"The labor of a human being is not a commodity or article of commerce. You can't weigh the soul of a man with a bar of pig iron."
—Samuel Gompers

In addition to careers in educating people, many careers exist in defending people's rights. One of the larger areas in this field is workers' rights.

For many years, workers did not have protection from dangerous work conditions, unfair wages, and unreasonable hours. Children were often exploited as cheap labor. These conditions remain in many areas of the world. In the United States, there is an ongoing effort to ensure that conditions for workers are fair and safe. The two main groups involved in this effort are the government, which enforces labor laws, and unions, which represent groups of workers in job-related disputes.

Labor Rights and Relations in Government

On the federal level, the Department of Labor has several agencies that ensure laws regarding wages, hours, equal employment opportunities, and safety issues are followed; that people have the right to join unions; and that workers have opportunities for employment:

- The Wage and Hour Division focuses on laws regarding minimum wage, overtime pay, family leave, youth employment, and migrant workers.
- The Occupational Safety and Health Administration (OSHA) ensures safe working conditions.
- Offices such as the Veterans' Employment and Training Service, Women's Bureau, and Office of Disability Employment Policy ensure that certain populations have resources to obtain employment and are not discriminated against.
- The Mine Safety and Health Administration protects miners by enforcing mining safety laws.

The federal government often has positions for inspectors for these agencies that ensure that labor laws are enforced.

Positions in labor relations and negotiation are available in federal agencies that focus on these areas. These agencies include the Federal Labor Relations Authority, Federal Mediation and Conciliation Service, Merit Systems Protection Board,

National Labor Relations Board (NLRB), and the National Mediation Board. The Department of Labor's Office of Labor-Management Standards focuses on ensuring that unions representing private sector workers maintain democracy and fiscal responsibility.

State and local government agencies have Equal Employment Opportunity Offices and similar agencies to protect workers. In addition, because state and local government employees are often unionized, labor relations is a function with state and local government. Many states have a labor relations board, and human resources staff must take collective bargaining agreements into consideration when hiring or promoting workers.

PROFILE: TOM MELANCON

Technical Writer, U.S. Department of Labor, Office of Worker's Compensation Programs

How did you start in federal service?

I finished a master's in counseling and started as a basic orientation specialist at a Job Corps [a federal vocational training program] center in Reno, Nevada. I stayed for eight years, working my way up to program director. I worked for a few years as a career counselor in private practice and came back to Job Corps as a consultant. Then I went to work at the Job Corps in Astoria, Oregon. During my time in Oregon, I met the people working in the Seattle office of Job Corps, and they recruited me to work as a project manager. I had to fill out that very long federal job application form, which was followed by a lengthy phone interview. I didn't get the position at that time, but a year later I got a call from the same office, and I was hired based on the previous application.

What is your role with the Department of Labor (DOL)?

I currently have two jobs. Tuesday through Friday, I serve as the Manager for the Seattle Federal Executive Board's (SFEB) Alternative Dispute Resolution (ADR) Program. This assignment is a "detail," which means that the Department of Labor is essentially loaning 80 percent of my time to the Seattle Federal Executive Board.

Here is how it works. An agency with employees in a conflict contacts me. I get some preliminary information from the agency liaison, and then I contact the parties in conflict by phone. I ask questions such as, "How would you describe the nature of your relationship with the other party?" and "What are you hoping to achieve by mediating this situation?" After talking with all parties, I send an email out to the mediators asking for volunteers. I select the mediators and work with the agency liaison to ensure that there is an adequate space for the mediation to take place. I then send out a mediation confirmation document to all of the parties involved.

In my other position, I work for the Division of Energy Employees' Occupational Illness Compensation Program (DEEOICP). This division obtains compensation and benefits for federal and contract employees who became ill as a result of their employment at the sites where nuclear weapons were developed in this country. My role is to keep the office's employment and physician databases up-to-date and to train staff members on how to utilize DEEOICP's automated data systems.

The regional office has 100 staff. Some of the other positions are claims examiners, senior claims examiners, and fiscal officers—quite a few attorneys are claims examiners. It's a GS-11 to GS-12 and a good position for people entering the government.

How did you get into this job?

As a project manager for Job Corps in Seattle, I was a consultant; I worked with three Job Corps centers to improve their performance and make sure they had funding. I loved the job, but the administration of the office changed and closed the Seattle regional office. I was recruited into my current position because I was a Job Corps program director and the DOL regional office needed someone with center experience.

The way I got into the mediation detail was circuitous. While working for Job Corps, I came across a scholarship application from the Seattle Federal Executive Board's ADR Program (the one I currently manage) offering to pay for the cost of basic mediation training to those who qualified. I applied for the scholarship, but didn't get it. I told my supervisor in the Job Corps office about it, and she agreed to get the agency to pay for the training and to allow me to go to the training on agency time. For the next several years, I picked up the additional training I needed by paying for the training and getting my agency to allow me to attend the training on work time. I observed six mediations, and I co-mediated 12 sessions. It took over three years, but I finally received my certification as a mediation practitioner from the Snohomish and Island Counties Dispute Resolution Center and the Seattle Federal Executive Board.

I ran into the former SFEB ADR program manager at a mediation training we were both attending at Seattle's Antioch University. She informed me she was retiring, and I told her I was very interested in applying for the job. The next step was to get the Department of Labor to agree to an 80/20 detail. DOL was amazingly supportive, and the nomination panel at the SFEB thought my program management and mediation qualifications made me a perfect match for the job.

(continued)

(continued)

What is a typical day like for you?

A typical day involves answering email messages and phone calls in the morning and then scheduling mediation sessions in the afternoon. I attend meetings with the King County Inter-local Conflict Resolution Group and the NW ADR Conference Planning committee, as well as quarterly meetings of my consortium and occasional subcommittee meetings. On the one day a week I spend at the DOL office, most of my time is spent updating the employment database and office templates. I also help staff members with issues they are having with their computers and assist them in utilizing the DEEOICP automated data systems.

Unions

Unions themselves offer a variety of opportunities in public service. More than 16.1 million American workers, or about 11 percent of the workforce, were union members in 2008. Unions are numerous and represent many different types of workers, ranging from the United Farm Workers, to the American Federation of Television and Radio Artists, to Public Services International, to the AFL-CIO.

A variety of positions are available in unions, such as accounting, administration, communication, education or training, legal, legislative relations, management, and research. One of the most important union positions is that of a union organizer. In many respects, this position is quite similar to that described in the Advocacy section of Chapter 2, and includes empowering workers to take part in union activities and negotiating with management to ensure workers' rights.

Civil Rights

"Get up, stand up, stand up for your rights." —*Bob Marley*

Many people who pursue a public service career are motivated by a need to bring justice to the world or to advocate for people who do not have much power in society. "Making things right" is a motive behind many other careers throughout this book. Advocacy is also described in Chapter 2, because it is possible to find an advocacy role within most public service organizations. In addition, some organizations have the main purpose of advocating to further the rights of particular groups.

Within the federal government—not counting the elected officials who make policy—there are certain agencies that exist to protect people's rights:

- The Equal Employment Opportunity Commission enforces federal employment laws against discrimination.

- The Commission on Civil Rights investigates complaints concerning voting rights and collects information concerning discrimination throughout the country.
- The Office for Civil Rights within the Department of Education helps resolve discrimination issues in school systems.
- The Office of Fair Housing and Equal Opportunity within the Department of Housing and Urban Development works to ensure that people have equal access to housing choices.

State governments also have Civil Rights Commissions, Human Rights Commissions, and other civil rights offices, which focus on issues such as eliminating racial profiling at traffic stops, ensuring equal opportunity in employment, and ensuring equal treatment in public accommodations and housing. They also provide training to the public. For example, they may provide training to landlords on how to avoid housing discrimination or training to supervisors and managers on how to avoid hiring discrimination. Local governments may have an office for civil rights to enforce civil rights rules within a local jurisdiction. Such an office may handle discrimination cases based on housing, employment, contracting, or public benefits.

Nonprofit organizations also vigorously work to advocate for the rights of certain populations or for civil liberties in general. Some organizations that work to ensure individual liberties and civil rights range from the American Civil Liberties Union (ACLU) and Americans United for Separation of Church and State to the Catholic League for Religious and Civil Rights. Groups that focus on censorship, freedom of speech, and a free press include the John S. and James L. Knight Foundation, People for the American Way, and the Center for Democracy and Technology.

Many groups focus on advocating for the rights of particular populations of people or minority groups. Some examples focused on minority groups include the NAACP, Southern Poverty Law Center, ACCION USA, the Lawyers' Committee for Civil Rights, and Native American Rights Fund. Others focus more on intergroup and race relations, such as Facing History and Ourselves, Search for Common Ground, and the Anti-Defamation League.

Organizations that advocate for the rights of people with disabilities (most of which also provide services to people with disabilities) include The Arc, Independence*First*, Center for Disability Rights, and Autism Society of America. Those focused on seniors' rights include Alliance for Retired Americans and Medicare Rights Center.

Women's rights organizations include the Ms. Foundation for Women, Family Violence Prevention Fund, National Partnership for Women and Families, and National Women's Law Center. Organizations focused on reproductive rights include Planned Parenthood, Center for Reproductive Rights, and NARAL Pro-choice America; and those which focus on the right to life include the National

Right to Life Committee. Yet others focus on the right to die, such as Compassion and Choices and Death with Dignity.

Organizations focused on the rights of lesbian, gay, bisexual, and transgender people include the Pride Foundation, the Gay and Lesbian Alliance Against Defamation (GLAAD), Human Rights Campaign, Astraea Foundation, National Gay and Lesbian Task Force, and Parents, Family, and Friends of Lesbians and Gays (PFLAG).

Numerous organizations also organize people to get them involved politically. For example, coalitions of organizations might run "get out the vote" campaigns to support a particular initiative. Others encourage general civic involvement, such as the League of Women Voters. Some focus on government accountability, such as Common Cause, and others advocate on a broad array of issues, such as U.S. PIRG.

Most of the positions in advocacy organizations are similar to those described in Chapter 2, especially under advocacy. Federal, state, and local governments have opportunities for equal opportunity specialists and complaints processors and in public education or outreach. Claims investigators and enforcement positions typically require a law degree, as do prosecution and judicial appeals positions.

PROFILE: ED BAROCAS

Executive Director, American Civil Liberties Union (ACLU) of New Jersey

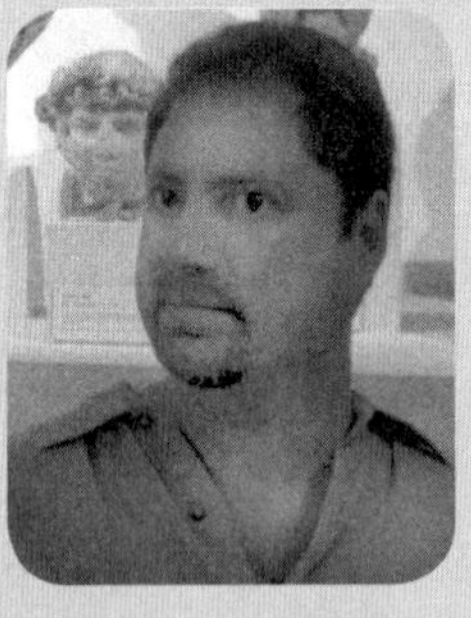

What is your career history?

I think I always knew I would end up as a civil rights lawyer because I had empathy for others, a questioning of authority or rules that didn't make sense, and love of debate. I went to law school thinking I wanted to do international human rights, but in my third year of law school, I took criminal law and constitutional law and started getting really excited about making a change locally rather than globally. I also interned with a prosecutor's office in the major crimes unit.

While I studied for the bar, I donated my time providing legal support to residents of the Jericho Project, a nonprofit housing organization for formerly drug-addicted homeless people. I provided advocacy services for people who had problems with their housing or had a child in foster care or the like.

At the time, the Mental Health Division of the Public Advocate's Office needed help in representing psychiatric patients, so I became a per diem attorney for them. I was handling cases of patients who were committed to psychiatric hospitals and who were seeking to get out against the doctor's orders. That really fit in with who I was, helping people who couldn't help themselves, helping the underdog, and ensuring Constitutional rights were being protected. It became my full-time job. I spent the next two years representing mental health patients.

In 1994, New Jersey passed Megan's Law, where sexual offenders would be tracked; and the big issue to determine was the level of dangerousness of these offenders (which determined who in the community was notified of their presence). The Public Advocate's Office decided it would select four people from the Mental Health Division to handle these cases because we were the experts on defending people on the issue of whether they were dangerous or not. I was selected (partly because other people didn't want the job) to handle Megan's Law in the special hearings unit.

My first client had already brought a federal challenge to Megan's Law. As his lawyers, my boss and I represented him in his federal court hearing and became the two lead counsel in the statewide class-action lawsuit challenging the constitutionality of Megan's Law.

During this case, I worked alongside the ACLU because it was supporting our case. The legal director for the ACLU also happened to leave around this time, so I applied for the job and ultimately got it.

What do you do on a typical day?

I manage the legal department (7 people) of the ACLU of New Jersey, which has a total staff of 16. I deal with administrative and managerial tasks. I also meet with either staff or cooperating attorneys (who work with the ACLU free of charge) and supervise all the cases on the docket, which covers freedom of speech; freedom of religion; reproductive rights; students' rights; discrimination cases including racial discrimination; lesbian, gay, bisexual, and transgender rights; police misconduct; and more. I review and rewrite briefs, and handle a few of the cases myself.

This office receives more than 2,000 requests for assistance a year. We take on maybe 50 matters; we provide advocacy for about 25, and take on 25 new cases (actually filing them in court). Every day we figure which cases we should spend our time on and which requests for assistance we can't handle. There are a number of areas where people's rights may have been violated, but it's not an ACLU matter. We might consider cases if it's a particularly interesting issue of employment discrimination or if there's a question of law, of how the law applies.

(continued)

(continued)

What stands out as your most proud accomplishment?

At 27 years old, I argued the issue of Megan's Law in the New Jersey Supreme Court. One of the justices, Marie Garibaldi, asked me, "What do you think the process should look like, and why?" That moment was what every lawyer loves to do, which is to create law through an explanation of an argument. I explained to Justice Garibaldi exactly what the process should be and, more importantly, why I thought the Constitution required it to be that way. A number of months later, the case was decided. As soon as I saw that Justice Garibaldi was the author of the decision, I smiled, because I knew without reading anything else that I'd been successful.

What is your biggest challenge?

We take a number of cutting-edge cases, so we lose some cases. What's hard for me is not so much the cases I handle and might lose, but the cases where I know people have been wronged, and yet I have to turn them down for representation because I know that based on the law, there's no remedy.

My goal has always has been bettering the world, and specifically getting to the point where society accepts differing ways of thought and being. When that happens, individuals are allowed to flourish, and society will flourish as well.

What skills/abilities are needed to succeed in this field?

The most important thing is showing a constant interest in the area of law that the organization you're applying with is involved in. Without that, to me it doesn't matter how many years you've been a lawyer or how many cases you've been engaged in. If you've always been involved in contract law and have never shown any interest in civil rights, then I'm not going to look upon you as positively as someone who is less experienced, but has experience in the civil rights field and has shown dedication to that area. (We post our lawyer searches on Idealist.org.)

Even if you're a lawyer in another area, there's an individual rights section of the New Jersey Bar—and getting involved in that will help you meet people in that area. You also can contact the ACLU and volunteer your time. We only handle a third of our cases in-house, but the others we supervise are private attorneys donating their time.

In addition to lawyers, we also have two development (fundraising) people, a communications director, a field director, a grassroots organizer, and an outreach person. We do public education. We also have an intake manager who's in charge of our volunteers and is our first point of contact with potential clients. Our executive director is actually not a lawyer. She started 20 years ago as an intake manager with the ACLU of Washington State. A number of different skills can transfer.

References and Resources

For more information on the topics presented in this chapter, refer to the following sources.

Education

Department of Education, www.ed.gov
National Education Association, www.nea.org

Early Childhood

Center for the Child Care Workforce, www.ccw.org
National Association for the Education of Young Children, www.naeyc.org
National Child Care Information and Technical Assistance Center, http://nccic.acf.hhs.gov/
National Institute for Early Education Research, http://nieer.org

K–12 Education

Department of Education, State Contacts and Information, www.ed.gov/about/contacts/state
National Association of State Boards of Education, http://nasbe.org
National Center for Education Statistics, Search for Public School Districts, http://nces.ed.gov/CCD/districtsearch/

Special Education

Association on Higher Education and Disability, www.ahead.org
National Association of Special Education Teachers, www.naset.org

Higher Education

American Association of University Professors, www.aaup.org
The Chronicle of Higher Education, http://chronicle.com
HigherEdJobs.com, www.HigherEdJobs.com

Vocational and Continuing Education

American Association for Adult and Continuing Education, www.aaace.org
Association for Career and Technical Education, www.acteonline.org

Libraries

American Library Association, www.ala.org; career information at http://librarycareers.org

Jobs in Education

Teachers:

American Federation of Teachers, www.aft.org
EnCorps Teachers Program, www.encorpsteachers.com
Teach for America, www.teachforamerica.com

School administrators:

American Association of School Administrators, www.aasa.org

Guidance counselors:

American School Counselor Association, www.schoolcounselor.org

Higher education administrators:

American Association of Collegiate Registrars and Admissions Officers, www.aacrao.org
American Association of University Administrators, www.aaua.org
NASPA—Student Affairs Administrators in Higher Education, www.naspa.org
National Association for College Admission Counseling, www.nacacnet.org
National Association of Colleges and Employers, www.naceweb.org
National Association of Student Financial Aid Administrators, www.nasfaa.org

Workers' Rights

Association of Labor Relations Agencies, www.alra.org/lablinks.htm
Labor and Employment Relations Association, www.lera.uiuc.edu
National Public Employer Labor Relations Association, www.npelra.org
Union Jobs Clearinghouse, www.unionjobs.com
Unions.org, www.unions.org

Civil Rights

Alliance for Justice, www.afj.org
FindLaw, State Civil Rights Offices, public.findlaw.com/civil-rights/civil-rights-resources/state-civil-rights-offices.html
National Organizers Alliance, www.noacentral.org

CHAPTER 5

Protecting the Environment and Managing Infrastructure

"Conservation is a state of harmony between men and land."
—Aldo Leopold

The number of issues threatening our planet is staggering: reduced biodiversity, climate change, water and air pollution, soil erosion, ozone depletion—the list goes on. These problems were caused by humans, and you might just be the human to solve them. As awareness of the environmental issues grows, so do the number and types of jobs devoted to protecting the environment. "Green jobs" have come to be defined very broadly, ranging from the more classic environmental careers, such as cleaning up toxic waste and managing national forests, to newer careers, such as developing more sustainable business practices and trading carbon credits.

A number of public service careers also exist in the area of infrastructure: the design and maintenance of transportation facilities (roads, bridges, railways, bus lines); the production and conservation of energy; and the protection of clean water and air. Because the protection of the environment is intertwined with decisions about infrastructure, these careers are included in this chapter as well.

The Environment

To get a sense of the scope of the environmental field, think about the fact that the federal government spent more than $35 billion on natural resources and the environment in 2008. This number includes $8.7 billion on water resources, $9.7 on conservation and land management, $3.4 on recreational resources, and $7.8 on pollution control and abatement. Some of the federal agencies most involved with the environment are the Environmental Protection Agency, the Department of the Interior, the Department of Agriculture, the Department of Commerce, the Department of Energy, and the Department of Transportation, among many others.

State agencies spent a total of $12.7 billion on environmental programs in 2008, and employed about 52,000 staff, according to the Environmental Council of the States. Although state governments vary in the types of environmental services they provide, most have departments for natural resources, fish and wildlife, agriculture, parks and recreation, and conservation. Others have departments with names such as Environmental Management, Environmental Quality, or Environmental Conservation. Some states have other related departments. For example, Washington has the Department of Ecology, Biodiversity Council, Conservation Commission, Environmental Hearings Office, Puget Sound Partnership, and Salmon Recovery Office. Many states also have offices that focus heavily on environmental issues such as permitting, regulations, air quality, hazardous waste, solid waste, public drinking water, land surveying, *brownfields* (polluted areas), environmental education, and soil and water conservation.

Local governments' environmentally related jobs include many that are covered in the Infrastructure section in more detail, such as those related to solid waste, utilities, transportation, and water quality. Many of the decisions that directly affect how a city manages its environmental impact, such as whether it will recycle its solid waste or use electric vehicles in its city-owned car or bus fleet, are made at the local level. Determining where business and housing can be built through zoning regulations is typically a local government job, and such decisions can have great environmental impacts. Local governments also maintain city and county parks and sometimes have Natural Resources Departments.

In addition, according to the National Center on Charitable Statistics, the 13,028 environmental nonprofit organizations that filed with the IRS in the United States had $20.6 billion in assets in 2009. These organizations include broad-based groups such as the Natural Resources Defense Council (NRDC), Environmental Defense Fund, and Earthjustice; those providing technical assistance, such as the Environmental Careers Organization (ECO); and those that raise funds, such as the Sierra Club Foundation (with total assets of over $107 million) or Greenpeace Fund (at $38 million).

The environmental field has numerous subareas and opportunities, including

- Teaching the public about the environment and facilitating their ability to enjoy nature through parks and recreation
- Managing natural resources and lands
- Protecting and managing animal and plant species
- Enforcing environmental laws
- Researching and monitoring the environment (ranging from studying invasive plants to taking samples of Arctic ice in order to understand global warming)

These and other environmental subareas are highlighted in the sections that follow.

Parks, Recreation, and Environmental Education

> *"Climb the mountains and get their good tidings. Nature's peace will flow into you as sunshine flows into trees. The winds will blow their own freshness into you...while cares will drop off like autumn leaves."*
> *—John Muir*

Parks and recreation is a broad field, ranging from the management of spectacular national and state parks to recreation activities provided by the YWCA. It could even include private health and fitness centers and sports organizations. (For the purpose of this book, I'll focus on the public parks and recreation sites provided by government and nonprofit organizations.)

The most well-known federal agency that is involved with parks is the Department of the Interior's National Park Service, which maintains the nation's 391 national parks, 40 national heritage areas, and 582 national natural monuments on 84 million acres of land, employing 28,000 paid workers and nearly 2.5 million volunteers. Several other federal agencies also manage lands that may be used for recreation. For instance, many campers and outdoor sports enthusiasts enjoy the national forest lands of the Department of Agriculture's Forest Service. The U.S. Fish and Wildlife Service manages 150 million acres of wildlife refuges, some of which are open to public use. The military also sometimes has recreational sites for its members.

All states have state parks and recreation areas; however, the names of the agencies that manage these areas and run related programs differ from state to state. Local governments also manage city and county parks and provide recreation activities to their residents.

Certain nonprofit organizations also manage private land that may be open to the public, such as wildlife refuges or nature centers. Other nonprofits raise money to supplement the funding of public parks. For example, the Central Park Conservancy, a nonprofit that contracts with the City of New York to maintain Central Park, provides 85 percent of the funding to maintain the park. Similarly, the National Parks Conservation Association advocates for the National Park System.

Environmental education is also provided by federal, state, and local agencies and nonprofit organizations, environmental science programs in schools and universities, and by corporations. This education can range from creating pamphlets that help consumers determine how to save electricity or reduce their carbon footprint to teaching children about ecology. Many environmental nonprofit organizations combine an environmental education component with trips to wilderness areas, such as the Sierra Club, Appalachian Mountain Club, or Outward Bound. These organizations often provide their members with opportunities to enjoy nature by organizing trips to wilderness areas.

Natural Resources Management and Conservation

> *"We abuse land because we regard it as a commodity belonging to us. When we see land as a community to which we belong, we may begin to use it with love and respect."* —*Aldo Leopold*

In addition to maintaining and preserving parks and wild areas for public enjoyment, the government and certain nonprofit organizations also own and manage a huge amount of land. The way these lands are managed differs according to the mission of the organization that manages the land—and can sometimes be controversial, with some parties wanting more resources to be exploited and others wanting resources to be conserved.

About 20.7 percent of the entire land area of the United States (401.9 million acres), including national parks and historic areas, is managed by the federal government. The Department of the Interior, in particular, has the mission to protect and allow access to public lands and honor federal commitments to American Indian tribes and island communities through resource protection, resource use, and recreation, among other goals. As part of the Department of the Interior, the Bureau of Land Management (BLM) is in charge of 253 million surface acres (mostly in western states and Alaska) and 700 million acres of subsurface mineral estate. The Bureau of Reclamation manages dams and reservoirs and supplies water to millions of people. It also produces energy through hydroelectric projects.

The Department of Agriculture (USDA) manages national forests through the USDA Forest Service. The USDA also maintains the Agricultural Research Service, which it describes as "one of the world's premier scientific organizations." Agencies involved with protecting soil and land include the USDA's Natural Resources Conservation Service.

State governments manage their public lands and parks, and they are involved with state land use planning issues. Increasingly, local governments are also considering conservation efforts to maintain urban green spaces. The field of urban forestry is a development in this area.

Nonprofit organizations establish land trusts to protect large portions of wild land to prevent them from being developed or work in other ways to prevent lands from being developed. Some of the larger examples include The Nature Conservancy, Trust for Public Land, The Conservation Fund, Open Space Conservancy, and the Wilderness Society. There are nonprofit organizations focused on saving specific resources such as forests (American Forest Foundation, Save the Redwoods League, and Rainforest Alliance) and wetlands (Ducks Unlimited) or natural resources in general (Conservation International).

Wildlife and Fisheries Management and Animal Welfare

Closely aligned with the field of natural resources management is species protection and wildlife management. Maintaining the earth's biodiversity in the face of a growing human population is a huge challenge; as of 2008, 357 species in the world are listed as endangered. In addition to protecting wild and endangered species, many organizations are also involved in the humane treatment of domestic animals.

Conservation of natural resources and species is part of the work of several federal entities. Examples include the National Atmospheric and Oceanic Administration's National Marine Fisheries Service, which is part the Department of Commerce; and the Fish and Wildlife Service within the Department of the Interior.

States also usually maintain a fish and wildlife agency, wildlife management agency, or a game commission. Local government also often helps provide for animal welfare, employing people to help run animal shelters and sometimes run zoos and aquariums.

Many nonprofits work to protect threatened species and animals. These range from the American Bird Conservancy, which is devoted to conservation of wild birds, to People for the Ethical Treatment of Animals (PETA), which focuses on animal rights. Some nonprofits provide training or technical assistance to other organizations in the field, as in the following examples:

- Veterinary societies
- Research institutes (such as the Jane Goodall Institute)
- Animal protection organizations and animal shelters (such as the Humane Society)
- Bird or other wildlife sanctuaries (such as the Wildlife Alliance)
- Fisheries management councils or fish hatcheries

Others focus on the protection of a specific species or group of animals, such as the Xerces Society, which protects invertebrates.

Zoos and aquariums also protect endangered animals, and provide education to the public so people can better understand their relationship with wildlife. Some zoos, such as the Los Angeles Zoo, are entirely owned by a city, but have an adjunct nonprofit organization (the Greater Los Angeles Zoo Association) that exists solely to raise funding for the zoo and coordinate its volunteer programs. Others, such as Seattle's Woodland Park Zoo, are nonprofits, but receive some financial support from city taxes.

PROFILE: GIOVANNINA SOUERS

Seattle Aquarium, Interpretive Training Supervisor

What is your brief career history?

Before my current position, I was the director of summer art and science camps for teens at Alki Community Center in Seattle, where I developed and coordinated a collaborative group of educators to work with multicultural teens making science-based art in the environment. I was also director and lead teacher of the pottery program at Alki Bathhouse Art Studio. Prior to that, I was the project and volunteer coordinator at the University of Hawaii's Service Learning Program, where I organized special events, restoration projects, and local trail rebuilding and recruited and organized hundreds of volunteers.

I have a bachelor's in environmental science from the University of Washington and a bachelor's in fine arts, sculpture, from the University of Hawaii at Manoa. I also have long-term volunteer experience teaching environmental science and sailing for all ages at Sound Experience in Port Ludlow, Washington, and as a restoration and trail work volunteer for Seattle Parks and Recreation. I was also a volunteer at the Waikiki Aquarium, interpreting about the animals, giving presentations and tours, and teaching classes for aquarium visitors.

How did you enter this profession?

Growing up in Wisconsin, my two passions in life were the outdoors and art. I attended the University of Hawaii at Manoa to pursue a degree in fine arts, specializing in pottery and glass blowing. While in school, I also ran many outdoor environmental programs for children with disabilities. I was an avid scuba diver, volunteered at the Waikiki Aquarium, and for a short time worked as a Sierra Club canvasser to support myself in college and fulfill my need to be working for the environment. When I graduated, I moved to Seattle to find a career in the arts.

While searching for a job, I began volunteering at the Seattle Aquarium as an educator. Soon after, I was hired part-time at the aquarium to teach outdoor educational programs. Over the next four years, I worked part-time at the aquarium and part-time teaching pottery. I was hired full-time at the Seattle Aquarium to work in the interpretation department to redevelop and manage the interpretive volunteer training program. The training program needed to prepare our volunteers for the opening of a new hands-on tide pool exhibit, "Life on the Edge." Volunteers were trained to interpret the animals on display and ensure the safety of the animals. The most recent opening was "Window on Washington Waters," a 120,000-gallon local tank that features an underwater diver who can talk with visitors.

What are some of the things you do on a typical day?

I could be supervising or checking in with the interpretive volunteers and divers for the day, training new volunteers, giving talks or presentations for visitors (dry or from underwater), or developing new programs and trainings for exhibits. Although my main priority is training and supervising volunteers, I also get the chance to be involved in research and animal husbandry from time to time.

What do you like the most about this career?

Many of the volunteers I work with have years of experience in the field of marine science, and I learn something new from them every day. One of my proudest accomplishments at the Seattle Aquarium has been the development and success of the underwater interpretation program. The aquarium opened an exhibit that was specifically designed to have volunteer and staff divers talking with the visitors from underwater.

What are some of the challenges about this career?

One of my biggest challenges is keeping up with the research and new information that is coming out every day about the marine environment. As an educator and trainer of volunteers who will be talking with the aquarium's visitors, I want to make sure everything I am passing along is up-to-date and accurate. Continuing my education is key, and continuing to offer updated and fun trainings for volunteers is a never-ending process.

What skills, education/training, abilities, values, or personality are needed to succeed in this field?

In order to work with volunteers and train and supervise them, I feel you should first be one. Many volunteer supervisors have started their careers as volunteers themselves. A degree in a related field like marine biology, environmental science, or oceanography is helpful in knowing the content you will be sharing with the visitors and your volunteers. A degree and/or experience in education and interpretation are extremely useful and will help you to relate to your audience. You must be a sociable and communicative person who is flexible and considerate with volunteers and visitors of all ages, cultural backgrounds, and knowledge levels.

Pollution Prevention and Control

"The activist is not the man who says the river is dirty. The activist is the man who cleans up the river." —Ross Perot

Here's a sobering thought: The U.S. generated 38 million tons of hazardous waste in 2005 and 251 million tons of general solid waste—totaling 4.6 pounds of solid waste per person per day. Some of that waste is collected in the more than 1,300 different hazardous waste sites throughout the United States.

Federal agencies that focus on pollution control, prevention, cleanup, and enforcement include the Environmental Protection Agency (EPA), which has the mission "to protect human health and the environment." In 2007, this agency employed more than 19,000 people from across the country. The Department of Energy includes the Environmental Management unit, which cleans up nuclear waste; and the Federal Energy Regulatory Commission (FERC), which regulates energy industries such as gas, oil, and electricity. The Department of Justice also has an environmentally focused unit that helps prosecute EPA lawsuits.

The federal government is not alone in fighting pollution. State governments maintain their own pollution control initiatives. Some local governments also have climate change initiatives and other pollution control efforts on the local level. Nonprofit organizations that focus on pollution prevention include organizations such as the Climate Trust and Clean Air Campaign.

A number of for-profit corporations provide environmental consulting services. According to the *Environmental Business Journal,* the environmental industry had $295 billion in revenue in 2007. This industry includes analytical services, wastewater treatment, solid and hazardous waste management, remediation, consulting/engineering, air pollution control equipment, prevention technology, water utilities, resource recovery and clean energy systems. Some examples of environmental consulting firms include Brown and Caldwell; CH2M Hill; Ecology and Environment, Inc.; ENTRIX; Environmental Resources Management (ERM); ICF International; Jacobs; and Tetra Tech.

Many times, these companies have government clients and manage projects such as helping a state government develop a wastewater permitting process for businesses, bringing various organizations together to decide on a climate change policy, or overseeing the technical details of a toxic site cleanup. Some even work on "forensic chemistry" to determine which company is responsible for which toxic emissions at a certain site. These companies also help with project planning and communications or serve as expert witnesses in lawsuits.

PROFILE: KRISTEN TADDONIO

Lead, Strategic Climate Projects, Climate Protection Partnerships Division, EPA

What is your brief career history?

After college, I started as a technical writer for a software company. Then I found a position with the EPA as a marketing associate for the ENERGY STAR for New Homes Program. Later, I moved into the Strategic Climate Projects area of the EPA, which led to my current position.

How did you enter this profession?

Growing up in a rural community, I saw the impact that people had on the environment all around me: Urban sprawl, roadside litter, and agricultural run-off into the lake I swam in were perennial problems. I attended a charter high school, the Washtenaw Technical Middle College (WTMC), the goal of which was to increase the pool of technology-savvy job seekers in the Michigan marketplace. At WTMC, I had the freedom to pursue my academic interests; however, in return for permission to take college classes, I had to earn a technical degree. At the time I wasn't too keen on this, but it turned out to be one of the best things that ever happened to me. I begrudgingly embarked upon a degree program in scientific and technical communication and, in the process, learned the vital role that science and technology plays in society in general, and in environmental protection in particular.

I moved to Washington, DC, to pursue a degree in International Affairs at the George Washington University. Later, I started both a master's degree program in international science and technology policy, with a concentration in environmental protection, and a job with the EPA's ENERGY STAR program, which promotes cost-effective products and technologies that reduce air pollution. In my academic program, I learned a lot about economics, the environment, and the way that Washington creates policies that impact science and technology; however, environmental progress and economic progress were always portrayed as opposing goals. I didn't believe that to be true—programs like EPA's ENERGY STAR were proving that environmental protection and economic progress could go hand-in-hand. By employing efficient technologies and practices, companies and individuals were able to reduce their impacts on the environment and save money.

An opportunity arose shortly thereafter. Dr. Stephen O. Andersen and Durwood Zaelke came to my office to present the findings of their new book, *Industry Genius* [Greenleaf Publishing, 2003], about people and companies that were protecting the climate and the ozone layer and prospering. I attended the presentation and

(continued)

(continued)

introduced myself to the coauthors afterwards, telling them that I'd like to work with them someday. Less than a month later, Dr. Andersen had an opening, and I became manager of Strategic Climate Projects, working to create public-private partnerships to accelerate the development and adoption of technologies that reduce greenhouse gas emissions and protect the ozone layer. When Dr. Andersen retired, I took over for him.

What are some of the things you do on a typical day?

One of the benefits of my job is that there is a lot of variety. One day I may be researching new standards that are being developed to test a new technology; another day I may be researching international regulations on chemicals that have strong global warming potentials. I attend a lot of conferences and meetings, so travel and the telephone take up a sizeable chunk of my time as well. One thing is always consistent, however: Environmental protection is the first priority.

The individual tasks that take up my day always add up in the pursuit of a larger goal. No matter if I'm helping remove barriers to a particular technology or researching refrigerant regulation, I know that it's all part of the bigger picture: clean air and a cooler climate.

What do you like the most about this career?

I'm very proud to have coauthored a book on technology transfer to protect the climate and ozone layer, and I'm also very proud to have helped the automotive industry transition to refrigerants that are better for the climate. However, the thing that makes me most proud is the knowledge that I'm helping to make this planet one that is healthier for us and for future generations. I couldn't think of a job I'd be happier doing.

What are some of the challenges about this career?

Even though I'm working to make a difference, sometimes it is overwhelming to think of the size of the environmental challenges we face. Getting up each day and finding the motivation to come in and tackle those issues is challenging and downright intimidating sometimes, but it is also what makes the job worth it in the end.

What skills, education/training, abilities, values, or personality are needed to succeed in this field?

Engineering and other technical knowledge is a big bonus. In the 21st century, the way we design things will determine how sustainable our society can ultimately become. Yet few students interested in the environment think to study engineering, architecture, or other technical disciplines so critical to environmental protection.

In addition to technical knowledge, business savvy and interpersonal skills are also key—environmental topics impact a lot of different groups, and it is critical to be able to communicate (speak and listen) effectively with them all.

Any other advice for people who want to enter this field?

Read! Read as much as you can about the topics you're interested in—find out who the major players are, what the latest technical developments have been, and where the stumbling blocks are. By reading as much as you can about what's happening in the field, you'll get a sense for where the most exciting work is going on and who the most influential people are. Make an effort to reach out to them. Who knows? You might even land a job with them if you do.

Sustainable Business

Aside from companies that provide environmental consulting, many corporations have discovered that using environmentally sustainable products or producing their products and services in a sustainable manner is good business sense. For example, the green building movement, which aims to make buildings more environmentally sound, seeks people who are "LEED certified" (Leadership in Energy and Environmental Design) and who understand how to build buildings that meet requirements set by the U.S. Green Building Council.

Cap and trade of pollutants and "carbon credits" is another emerging field with implications for many corporations. How this field works is that government sets a limit on the amount of pollution that can be emitted, and companies can obtain permits to emit a certain amount. These permits can then be traded, creating a market value on the pollution, which is an incentive to reduce pollution.

Environmental Research

In order to know which species need protection, which chemicals should be controlled, and how the environment works in general, accurate scientific research is needed. Numerous federal agencies produce environmental research, including the National Oceanic and Atmospheric Administration (NOAA), which is part of the Department of Commerce. NOAA forecasts weather (through the National Weather Service) and monitors marine ecosystems to provide accurate and useful information to businesses, the government, and the public. The U.S. Geological Survey (USGS) of the Interior Department investigates natural hazards, such as earthquakes and wildfires, and collects information on natural resources. Additional opportunities exist in agricultural development research. Numerous environmental organizations also have a research or scientific unit. For example, the EPA has a research unit, as do many state and federal agencies.

Examples of nonprofit research institutes include Resources for the Future and Cary Institute of Ecosystem Studies. Many other broad-based environmental nonprofits also conduct environmental research. Corporations also are involved with environmental research to help companies comply with environmental regulations and to develop new environmental technologies and programs. Significant research is also conducted at colleges and universities.

Environmental Jobs

A wide variety of opportunities exist in the environmental field. A science or engineering background is often helpful, but not always essential. Public affairs, public information, and policy analysis positions are available; and nonprofits have positions in advocacy and fundraising. The following sections highlight jobs specific to environmental organizations.

Park Rangers and Naturalists

Occupations in parks and recreation include park managers, park regulation enforcement, park rangers, guides, naturalists, scientists, facilities management, archeologists, historians, ecologists, and more. Although many positions are seasonal or temporary and often require physical exertion, they can also offer the chance to work in beautiful settings and so can be quite competitive.

Park rangers and naturalists interact with park visitors to educate them about the natural environment, lead tours, run events, manage campgrounds, or sell tickets or gift items. They also are responsible for ensuring the park is protected from damage from visitors and enforcing regulations and laws, and they may be involved with search and rescue or other emergency duties. Some of their responsibilities are similar to those of foresters and natural resource managers.

NOTE

The Association of National Park Rangers (www.anpr.org) publishes *Live the Adventure: Join the National Park Service,* a book that has detailed information on becoming a park ranger. If you are a college student, another great way to find out if you would enjoy working at a national park is to become involved with the Student Conservation Association (www.thesca.org).

About 18,000 people worked as park naturalists in 2008, with median wages of about $28.23 per hour. Wages in this occupation vary and can be seasonal. Employment is predicted to be growing at an average rate.

Environmental Educators

Environmental educators make up one of the largest groups of environmental professionals. Among the 1.67 million postsecondary teachers and professors in the nation, thousands are environmental science teachers, and many more work in K–12 education. At the postsecondary level, their work may include research, mentoring of new faculty, grant writing, and teaching. Visit the Education section in Chapter 4 for more details.

Foresters, Natural Resource Managers, and Fish and Game Wardens

Foresters, fish and game wardens, and other resource managers have hands-on, outdoor jobs, though some positions are more analytical and "indoors" in nature. Foresters may write plans to replant trees, supervise harvesting of trees, check for disease in forests, and ensure that habitat is protected and important ecosystems preserved. Some conduct research on policy and scientific issues affecting forests and rangelands, and many interface with private landowners to plan for forest or agricultural use. They may use Geographic Information Systems (GIS) to map large areas. Soil conservationists focus on erosion and educate landowners on its prevention.

There were 29,800 foresters and conservation scientists in 2008, most of whom worked in government. Average earnings were between $42,980 and $73,280. Growth in the field is expected to be as fast as average.

Environmental Scientists

Thousands of scientists were employed in environmentally related jobs in 2008, including

- 85,900 environmental scientists and specialists
- 91,300 biological scientists (including 19,500 zoologists and wildlife biologists)
- 9,400 atmospheric scientists
- 33,600 geoscientists and 8,100 hydrologists
- 35,000 environmental science and protection technicians and 34,000 forest and conservation technicians

Affiliated with this field are individuals who enforce compliance with environment regulations and investigate incidences of environmental misconduct.

Technicians require less education and training, and conduct hands-on work such as monitoring pollution levels and collecting samples to measure water quality. Forest technicians, for example, gather data about populations and sizes of trees. In 2008, hourly wages for environmental technicians averaged $19.34 (with fast job growth) and forest and conservation technicians averaged $15.39 (with little change in job growth).

Scientists and other "-ologists" often require more advanced training, up to and including a PhD. Environmental scientists earned salaries ranging from about $45,340 to $78,980 in 2008. Hydrologists earned about $71,450, and atmospheric scientists earned from $55,140 to $101,340 (with employment expected to be growing at a faster rate than average). Most zoologists and wildlife biologists earned between $43,060 and $70,500. There will continue to be demand for zoologists and biologists, but opportunities are limited by the small number of openings in the field.

For many of these careers, an environmental science education might be helpful. Programs cover a range of specializations such as marine affairs, fisheries biology, toxicology, environmental science and policy, environmental health, forest resources/forestry, environmental engineering, biochemistry, ecology, plant biology and conservation, natural resources management, sustainable development, GIS (geographic information systems) mapping, plant and soil sciences, water resources, oceanography, industrial/environmental hygiene, earth and atmospheric sciences, geology, crop science, life sciences, and even geography. These programs range from highly technical ones focusing heavily on research and science to those that are more policy-oriented.

PROFILE: FRED HENSON

Aquatic Biologist, New York State Department of Environmental Conservation

What is your brief career history?

My first full-time professional job after graduating with my BS was as a research technician at a biological field station operated by my alma mater. I then completed an MS, which helped me land my next job as a fisheries specialist with the Minnesota Department of Natural Resources. After that, I accepted a position as a biologist with the New York State Department of Environmental Conservation.

How did you enter this profession?

I was always interested in plants and animals. In school, I enjoyed the study of biology, but I was also very interested in history and public policy. I hoped that a career in natural resources management would allow me to combine those interests in an exciting way while helping to ensure that future generations inherit a functioning ecosphere.

What are some of the things you do on a typical day?

My current responsibilities are related to fish health. I diagnose sick fish and recommend courses of treatment to fish hatchery managers. I also conduct inspections of samples of hatchery fish prior to stocking to ensure that my agency is not inadvertently spreading serious fish pathogens around the state.

What do you like the most about this career? What's your proudest accomplishment?

I am most satisfied with my career when I am able to work with other biologists, engineers, or members of the public to solve or cope with a difficult problem in a way that has a positive impact for the long term. Probably my proudest accomplishment was being a member of a team assigned to ensure that a contaminated aquifer was cleaned up in such a way as to adequately protect the spawning areas used by a rare strain of brook trout. The collegial interaction between the biologists, hydrologists, and engineers was wonderful, and we got the job done for a reasonable cost.

What are some of the challenges about this career?

There is always more work to do than there are material and human resources with which to do it, and I don't foresee any change. Because natural resource issues usually involve multiple jurisdictions and stakeholder groups, you have to be willing to spend a lot of time on developing informed consent from the people who decide whether your proposals will be acted upon. A lot more people skills are required than most people would suppose, and while I still consider myself to be an introvert, I have become a facultative extrovert out of necessity.

What skills, education/training, abilities, values, or personality are needed to succeed in this field?

You need a strong background in the appropriate applied sciences, in my case, biology, ichthyology, ecology, and statistics. You also need a high level of commitment and motivation because many more people want to be a part of this field than there are positions that pay a living wage. Patience is also important because you will need to build your resume with internships, seasonal jobs, and volunteer work before you have a chance at a full-time gig.

Any other advice for people who want to enter this field?

Speaking narrowly of fisheries and aquatic science, aspiring fisheries professionals should join the American Fisheries Society and consider attending the annual meeting of their nearest active chapter. An even better idea for college seniors or graduate students is to present their research at such a meeting. If your specialty is in another area of natural resource management or conservation, then search out an equivalent professional society and become active.

Infrastructure

"You and I come by road or rail, but economists travel on infrastructure." —Margaret Thatcher

People who work in the field of infrastructure keep the trains running on time, the water running from the taps, the garbage collected, and the electricity flowing to homes and businesses. Energy, transportation, water supply systems, and management of sewerage and waste are all part of infrastructure. Most people never think about these services until a disaster strikes and wipes them out or until they travel to a country without such services.

Because these services are considered so vital to the public good, most utilities and infrastructure-related services are provided by companies that are heavily regulated by government or by government directly or through quasi-governmental agencies (agencies that are publicly owned or chartered by government, but operate separately). A large percentage of the overall number of jobs in this field are in hands-on production or installation areas, with about 14 percent being professional positions (largely engineering) and 12 percent in business, management, or finance. Most positions in infrastructure reside in government or corporations, though there are some organizations in the nonprofit sector that advocate for better infrastructure or alternative energy policy.

Energy

During a blackout, people discover that there are few ways to light up the night, refrigerate food, or use computers or appliances without access to electricity. Yet using oil and gas (a major part of the energy field) to create electricity or heat buildings creates ongoing issues for national security as well as the tremendous problem of global climate change. At the same time, complex issues arise from using alternate fuels as well, such as the risk of nuclear proliferation when countries build nuclear plants to generate power or the use of land to create wind farms or biofuels instead of to produce food.

Energy utilities create electrical power or heat, which may be generated from coal, nuclear power, gas, or water or renewable sources such as geothermal, solar, or wind energy. According to the American Public Power Association, the 2,000 community-owned electric utilities in the United States serve about 45 million people. Public utility commissions heavily regulate the industry, which is also regulated by the Energy Policy Act to promote cleaner technology.

A large part of the recent federal stimulus bill has been to push energy efficiency initiatives. The largest agency involved in this area is the federal government's

Department of Energy. Its mission is to "advance the national, economic, and energy security of the United States; to promote scientific and technological innovation in support of that mission; and to ensure the environmental cleanup of the national nuclear weapons complex." Its offices include the Office of Energy Efficiency and Renewable Energy, which has the role of reducing America's dependence on foreign oil and developing energy-efficient technologies. It produces research and encourages the production of new and more efficient energy sources. Much of the research work is done in partnership with universities and the various National Labs. The Department of Energy and the EPA are also the creators of the ENERGY STAR label, which indicates energy efficiency on refrigerators and other appliances. The Department of Energy also works on nuclear security by managing the nuclear weapons stockpile (another agency, the Defense Nuclear Facilities Safety Board, provides oversight into this process). The Nuclear Regulatory Commission (NRC) is another independent agency that regulates nuclear power plants. Lastly, the Federal Energy Regulatory Commission regulates the distribution of natural gas, oil, and electricity between states.

State governments have departments called Public Utilities Commissions, Public Service Commissions, or Utilities Boards that deal with regulating and managing the provision of power throughout the state. Their work includes interfacing with federal agencies relating to energy; offering energy efficiency programs for state residents' homes, businesses, and industry; managing and enforcing energy-related building codes; managing fuel supplies and distribution; and handling energy-related emergency preparedness. According to the National Association of State Energy Officials, "States manage and invest more than $3 billion of their own funds derived from appropriations and system benefit charges each year."

In some areas, local governments actually produce needed energy (or oversee heavily regulated utilities companies) and manage billing for customers, provide assistance programs for low-income individuals, and maintain the physical infrastructure of electricity delivery, such as power cables and power generation. Local governments also enforce energy codes, ensuring that new buildings and homes are energy efficient.

There are some nonprofit public utilities, such as the California Independent System Operator Corporation, New York Independent System Operator, and Cascade Water Alliance. Various organizations also advocate for alternative or efficient energy use, such as the Alliance to Save Energy and professional associations such as the American Solar Energy Society or the U.S. Green Building Council. Many of the large environmental nonprofits have an energy program as well.

Corporations also are heavily involved in the energy industry. Although most provide energy from conventional sources, some are involved with new and renewable energy technologies or improvements on the disbursement of energy through programs such as a "smart" electric grid.

PROFILE: HUGH HO

U.S. Department of Energy, Program Analyst
(Presidential Management Fellow)

What is your brief career history?

I have an undergraduate education in science, engineering, and the social sciences. Eight years later, I started my graduate program in public administration at the Evans School of Public Affairs at the University of Washington.

Prior to my current analyst position at the U.S. Department of Energy, I did basic science research at Sandia National Laboratories, handled materials engineering at a U.S. Navy contractor, taught English in the Peace Corps, and administered clinical trials at the University of Washington.

How did you enter this profession?

I was searching for a career field that took advantage of my scientific background and also applied the tools I learned in my public administration graduate program. I knew that I wanted to be in a position to provide advice to policy makers, but I did not restrict my search to a specific sector (such as health, transportation, or community services).

I learned about the U.S. government's Presidential Management Program through my graduate program, and my acceptance into the program shortly before graduation was the catalyst for me to consider several federal offices, including the Department of Energy's Office of Program Analysis and Evaluation.

What do you like the most about this career?

I enjoy seeing some of my work appearing in policy makers' briefs and decisions, sometimes hours and sometimes months after my input. Because my work is focused on producing advice for internal decision making, I don't see my work on the news, but I enjoy the relatively peaceful space that I have to do my research, talk with experts, and generate recommendations that are backed by good reasoning and analysis. I also enjoy doing my work independently of the political process. Some people are surprised by the intellectual freedom that I have, but the popular perception of what happens inside of government is often skewed by exceptional anecdotes.

My proudest accomplishment has been to compile guidance to departmental offices on implementing the Recovery Act of 2009. The time pressure to act quickly and the number of offices involved made these few months some of the most intense in my life. I took on responsibilities that were unusual for my seniority level and made my share of mistakes, but the exposure that I had to other parts of the department was invaluable. I am proud of my small role in my department's many successful actions in the past year.

What are some of the challenges about this career?

Working in the federal government has well-known challenges that accompany the considerable benefits. Job security means that you sometimes work with those who, to put it nicely, have lost the spark of curiosity and camaraderie that they may have had when they first started working. Most of the policy-related jobs at the federal level are in the Washington, DC area, which can be good or bad, depending on your tolerance for a generally high-stress lifestyle. Also, the immense size of federal agencies often means that even trivial administrative changes take months of frustration to work through the system.

What skills, education/training, abilities, values, or personality are needed to succeed in this field?

To work effectively as a federal analyst, you should have a solid understanding of how government works, both in theory and in reality. Rigorous policy analysis skills and related quantitative skills, such as statistics or computer modeling, are becoming more valuable as many agencies are moving towards increasingly complex decision-making processes. A strong motivation towards public service, a sense of curiosity, and the willingness to network are also especially valuable as an ambitious federal employee. You should also have a thick skin and the ability to be patient with others, balanced with an ability to be assertive and forceful when necessary. Finally, given the level of scrutiny placed on government decisions, you should constantly work toward ethical actions.

Do you have any other advice for people who want to enter this field?

In Washington, DC, there is no shortage of networking opportunities through professional organizations. For example, an active Young Professionals in Energy group in DC hosts happy hours and other meetings for people from government, industry, and nonprofits. As with any profession, it helps to ask around for how others continue their professional development, which may be through conferences, courses, journals, general news, or rotations to other offices.

The most ambitious analysts also tend to have some Capitol Hill experience at some point in their careers. You should also keep an open mind about lateral moves between executive branch offices and agencies. There is often something interesting that doesn't make the news but could help expand your knowledge or skill set. Many career paths also move between government, contractors, other industry, and nonprofits such as universities or think tanks.

Transportation

Without roads, rails, flight paths, and bike routes, society as we know it would come to a grinding halt. Government at all levels is heavily involved in maintaining the infrastructure needed to get people from point A to point B, from keeping roads paved and bridges maintained to running public transit systems and ensuring planes don't crash. Both regulation and provision of transportation can be part of government.

Also, more people are starting to agree that car-oriented building and development, while an American tradition, is not the best for the health of people and communities. The design of new developments centered on public transit and alternatives to cars is a growing field, and mass transit is becoming more popular because of skyrocketing gas prices and the difficult economy. According to the American Public Transportation Association, 7,700 separate organizations provided public transportation during 2007 and spent a total of $48.4 billion.

The federal government's Department of Transportation is the agency most involved with transportation. It includes the Federal Aviation Administration (FAA), Federal Highway Administration, Federal Transit Administration, and a number of other subagencies involved with ensuring safe transportation, providing funding to states to construct national highways and roads in national lands, and conducting research into innovations in transportation. The National Railroad Passenger Corporation, better known as Amtrak, provides passenger train service nationally.

State governments also have Departments of Transportation (DOT) that maintain state highways and roads and conduct research. A state DOT's work may vary significantly by the state. For example, Washington's DOT runs an extensive ferry system, something you would not find in Iowa. Other transportation modalities range from aerial tramways to cable cars, from monorails to van pools.

Local governments also help maintain local roads and provide transit systems, such as buses, subways, and light rail systems. In fact, the great majority of transit systems are provided by local governments or quasi-government agencies such as transit authorities or transit corporations. Nonprofits are mainly involved as advocates for better transportation and transit systems.

NOTE

> Government at the federal, state, and local levels often contracts with private sector companies to maintain transportation infrastructure. Such companies maintain roads, build buses, or provide consulting services on transportation planning.

PROFILE: STEVE SCOFIELD

Superintendent, Track Access, NYC Transit Authority

How long have you been in this position?

I've had this job and title for 5 years. I've been at the Transit Authority for 27 years and have worked in this department doing this kind of work for 23 years.

What is your brief career history?

When I was in my 20s, I tried to make a living as a musician (flute and saxophone). This was a pretty futile pursuit, and I usually paid the rent working for bicycle messenger services, either making deliveries or dispatching.

How did you enter this profession?

I had always had a fascination with the subway system ever since I was a little kid. A married couple I knew were both urban planners; he worked for New Jersey Transit. They convinced me that I would be good at this, and at the time, the Transit Authority was hiring. The path was to get a master's degree in urban planning.

I gathered my transcripts from college, took the GSATs, and was accepted at Hunter College. While at Hunter, I began working as an intern at New York City Transit as a traffic checker. By the time I graduated, I was a full-time traffic checker.

When I graduated, I was hired into a full-time professional position in a department that was supposed to analyze the efficiency of various departments. The job was a nightmare; I worked for a lunatic (a former drill sergeant). After six months, I was ready to quit and go back to messengering when I heard of an opening in my old department (Operations Planning or OP). I was selected for that opening and did bus route planning for three years. After three years, OP was given the job of scheduling and planning service diversions to accommodate construction. It was conceived as a part-time job for three people, and they would give us other stuff to do to fill the time. Well, I now run the Track Access Group, and it's an extremely full-time job for 17 people.

What are some of the things you do on a typical day?

I generally get in at 8 a.m. It's an early culture—lots of people arrive at 6 or 7 a.m.—so things are already hopping when I arrive. Sometimes I have to meet with night shift track superintendents, so for that I have to get in at 6 or 7 a.m. When I get in, there's frequently an emergency repair that has to be done that night. If it's not too complicated, my immediate reports deal with it, but if it's really complicated or needs some negotiating, I get involved.

(continued)

(continued)

I spend a lot of time in meetings. Most are devoted to short-term planning—I have to meet with different groups to get their input and approval on that week's service plans. On top of this, there are lots of other meetings about upcoming projects or crises that need to be resolved. I answer a lot of phone calls—there are always problems, details to be worked out, angry people to placate. Occasionally, I have to do some research or number-crunching. I rarely take a lunch hour, but I usually can leave by 4:30, because a lot of the early arrivers are gone by 2 or 3 p.m.

What do you like the most about this career?

The best thing is that what I do is about as real-world as you can get. My team and I come up with a complicated week-by-week schedule of track work and diversions, and the trains run according to our plan, and the work gets done. For the most part, I also work with an incredible group of people from all over the world, with backgrounds as varied as you can get, from PhDs to former track workers who didn't graduate high school. My proudest accomplishment over the years is the fact that I've been a part of bringing the subway system back from the brink of disaster in the early '80s to a system that is now far from perfect, but it runs pretty well and is in a state of good repair. My proudest short-term accomplishment was getting the subway system up and running again after 9/11.

What are some of the challenges about this career?

The toughest thing about this job is dealing with organizational dysfunction—contracts are awarded with no concept that the jobs are supposed to work together; senior management sets organizational goals that conflict with each other; and there are difficult personalities to deal with. I feel like every day I have to pull a rabbit out of a hat.

What skills, education/training, abilities, values, or personality are needed to succeed in this field?

What you need is a thorough knowledge of the subway system, a good sense of how the different pieces interact with each other. You need a good sense of spatial relationships and should probably either have "road" experience or have been a subway buff since you were five. I've hired really smart people who never figure it out, and otherwise dysfunctional people who grasp this in two days.

Although these days you need a college degree to get the job, it is of absolutely no use once you get here. I can honestly say that there is not a single thing that I learned in grad school that has been of any use whatsoever on this job, but without the MUP degree, I would have never been hired. The guy who taught me my job didn't graduate high school, but he had 44 years of experience.

Having a good deal of patience helps; an ability to multitask and a photographic memory of the system are essential. You have to be a good negotiator and get along with people, and try not to take stuff personally. Most importantly, you have to be able to put all this stuff in a little box at 4 p.m. and wipe the slate clean until you have to reopen the box the next morning.

Water Quality and Waste Management

Clean water is essential to life. Water treatment operators make water safe to drink, and wastewater operators remove pollutants from water before it is discharged into the environment. An entire system of sewers and pipes must function for this to happen. According to Kevin Lee Doyle's *Complete Guide to Environmental Careers in the 21st Century*, "water quality management employs more environmental professionals than any other field." Subsections of the field include drinking water supply, wastewater treatment, protection of groundwater, and management of wetlands. Increasingly, water professionals look at entire watersheds to maintain clean water and prevent toxic runoff. Water quality also can include the protection of ocean areas.

Federal agencies are involved in this area in many ways:

- The Environmental Protection Agency enforces water quality regulations.
- The U.S. Fish and Wildlife Service protects animals and plants from waterborne pollution.
- The U.S. Army Corps of Engineers considers environmental effects when building public works.
- The National Forest Service protects water affected by logging on public land.
- The U.S. Department of Agriculture works with farmers to prevent agricultural pollutants.
- The U.S. Geological Survey researches water flows.

State governments typically have a Clean Water Commission or a department within their Environmental Protection Agency or Department of Natural Resources that manages statewide water quality and control, handles federal funding and aid for water systems, offers financial assistance to localities (through a Clean Water State Revolving Fund), and manages watershed protection. Local governments manage the majority of actual water quality and treatment. Most water treatment plant employees typically are local government employees, though many are also privatized. Local government employees may also be involved with watershed protection and management, mapping of watersheds, interaction with farmers to reduce pesticide emissions, and outreach and communication with individuals owning land sitting atop groundwater sources.

In addition, local governments also manage solid waste removal, snow removal, and other utilities. These services are sometimes grouped in to the Water Quality Management Department of a city under the public utilities area. Handling waste and managing recycling programs are other major undertakings of cities and municipalities.

The nonprofit sector has a large and active group of water protection–related organizations that advocate for clean water and protection of rivers and oceans. Many large nonprofits such as the Natural Resources Defense Council and Earthjustice have a water-related subfocus; whereas others, such as the Water Environment Federation, Clean Water Action, and the River Network, focus entirely on water protection issues.

Public Works

Public works focuses on the actual construction of roads, bridges, drainage systems, and public buildings such as schools. In some cities, the term also refers to water treatment, sewerage, and garbage removal, as well as other infrastructure-related services. Examples of agencies involved include the Army Corps of Engineers as well as state and local Public Works Divisions.

Infrastructure Jobs

A huge number of opportunities exist within this field for people with hands-on skills, such as bus drivers, electricians, cable splicers, mechanics, construction workers, wastewater treatment operators, and street cleaners. To enter such fields, you typically need to complete an apprenticeship program in the skilled trades and obtain relevant licenses (such as an electrician's license or commercial driver's license). Also, a good number of opportunities exist in the "behind the scenes" planning activity that gets this vital work done. The following sections highlight additional occupations in this area.

Urban and Regional Planners

Planners help determine where and how to build infrastructure. The majority of urban planners work for local governments, providing recommendations for land use and building, taking into consideration the projected population growth of a city, needs for recreation and open space, and environmental concerns. A planner might work on a broad array of issues, from building new schools and communities, to mapping out the most efficient bus routes, to planning where a sidewalk should go.

In order to make informed decisions, planners analyze a broad array of data on existing infrastructure and often use geographic information systems (GIS) and other mapping and statistical software. Strong communications skills are also important, such as the ability to conduct outreach to citizens who will be the end users of public projects to ensure their input is heard on issues such as where a road or bus station will be built.

Master of Urban Planning (MUP) programs certify their students as urban planners, who focus on helping make decisions about zoning, building projects, road construction, and community development. MUP programs are sometimes housed in a school of architecture or built environments.

In 2008, 38,400 worked as urban and regional planners. Earnings for planners averaged from $47,050 to $75,630. The field is expected to grow faster than average.

Civil Engineers

Civil engineers focus on the more technical aspects of building major projects such as bridges, roads, dams, and public buildings. The many technical specializations within civil engineering include transportation engineering, surveying, and construction engineering. Many engineers receive a Bachelor of Engineering degree and are further certified through experience and exams. The 278,400 people employed as civil engineers in 2008 earned a median of about $74,600 per year. Employment for this job is growing much faster than average.

Water Treatment Specialists

Water treatment professionals must ensure that water meets the requirements of the Clean Water Act and the Safe Drinking Water Act. Water treatment operators must pass certifying exams and may need to be licensed by their state. In addition, the water quality field employs hydrologists, hydrogeologists, toxicologists, engineers, chemists, and scientists.

Water treatment and sewage utilities employ thousands of people. In the United States, there are 111,000 water treatment operators and 45,000 water resource specialists. Salaries for water treatment operators average $36,000 and can go up to $112,800 for water resource specialists who oversee water quality monitoring and conduct technical studies of watershed improvement projects. Projected job growth is much faster than average.

Other Jobs

The infrastructure field also includes these jobs:

- **Utilities rates analysts** produce forecasts and analysis of how much to charge consumers for utilities, examining the cost of providing service. A background in economics, mathematics, engineering, or business is preferred.
- **Safety and environmental coordinators** ensure compliance with regulations, provide safety training to staff, and report on any problems that arise. Familiarity with regulations set by the Environmental Protection Agency, state pollution control agencies, and the Occupational Safety and Health Administration combined with an environmental or health background is helpful in this career.
- **Management and program analysts** evaluate the effectiveness of programs and operations, ensuring that they are managed efficiently. A background in project management or budget analysis combined with long-range planning skills is essential. Skills in GIS mapping or land management are also important. (See Chapter 2 for details on this career.)

- **Scientists** hold a variety of jobs in the energy, water quality, and other utility areas. In particular, chemists, hydrologists, geologists, and other researchers are needed to produce the information necessary to assess whether a pollutant is being released, whether groundwater is at risk, or whether environmental regulations are being fulfilled. (See the section on Environmental Research in this chapter for more details.)
- **Community outreach workers** communicate with the public about public works projects, road construction, traffic systems, and so on.

References and Resources

For more information on the topics presented in this chapter, refer to the following sources.

The Environment

Doyle, Kevin Lee; *Complete Guide to Environmental Careers in the 21st Century* (Island Press, 1998)
EcoIQ Magazine, www.ecoiq.com
eco.ORG, www.eco.org
Environmental Business Journal, www.ebiusa.com
Environmental Career Opportunities, www.ecojobs.com
Environmental Council of the States, list of state programs, www.ecos.org/section/states
Environmental Jobs.com, www.environmentaljobs.com
EPA, State Environmental Agencies, www.epa.gov/epahome/state.htm
Green Careers Center, www.environmentalcareer.com
Office of Management and Budget, President's budget for fiscal year 2009, www.whitehouse.gov/omb/budget

Parks, Recreation, and Environmental Education

Association of National Park Rangers, www.anpr.org
Cornell, Joseph; *Sharing Nature with Children* (Dawn Publications, 1998)
EPA, Environmental Education, www.epa.gov/education
Ham, Sam H.; *Environmental Interpretation: A Practical Guide for People with Big Ideas and Small Budgets* (Fulcrum Publishing, 1993)
National Association for Interpretation, www.interpnet.com
National Recreation and Park Association, www.nrpa.org
North American Association for Environmental Education, www.naaee.org

Natural Resources Management and Conservation

Agricultural Research Service, www.ars.usda.gov
Association of Partners for Public Lands, www.appl.org
Department of the Interior, www.doi.gov
Forestry USA, www.forestryusa.com
National Association of State Foresters, www.stateforesters.org
Public Lands Information Center, www.publiclands.org/agencies.php
Society for American Foresters, www.safnet.org

Society for Range Management, www.rangelands.org
Soil and Water Conservation Society, www.swcs.org

Wildlife and Fisheries Management and Animal Welfare

American Fisheries Society, www.fisheries.org
Association of Zoos & Aquariums, www.aza.org
U.S. Fish & Wildlife Service, Species Reports, http://ecos.fws.gov/tess_public/Boxscore.do
U.S. Fish & Wildlife Service; USFWS Management Offices—State, Territorial, and Tribal; www.fws.gov/OFFICES/STATELINKS.HTML
Woodland Park Zoo, www.zoo.org
World Association of Zoos and Aquariums (WAZA), www.waza.org

Pollution Prevention and Control

Association of State and Interstate Water Pollution Control Administrators, www.asiwpca.org
National Association of Clean Air Agencies, www.4cleanair.org
National Pollution Prevention Roundtable, www.p2.org

Sustainable Business

GreenBiz.com, www.greenbiz.com
International Business Leaders Forum, www.iblf.org
SustainableBusiness.com, www.sustainablebusiness.com
U.S. Green Building Council, www.usgbc.org

Environmental Research

American Institute of Biological Sciences, www.aibs.org
Association of Environmental Engineering and Science Professors, www.aeesp.org
Association of Environmental Health and Sciences, www.aehs.com
Botanical Society of America, www.botany.org
Commission on Professionals in Science and Technology, www.sciencemasters.org
Ecological Society of America, www.esa.org

Energy

American Public Power Association, www.appanet.org
Association of Energy Services Professionals, www.aesp.org
Department of Energy, www.energy.gov
Greenjobs, http://greenjobs.com
National Association of State Energy Officials, www.naseo.org
The Utility Connection, www.utilityconnection.com

Transportation

American Association of State Highway and Transportation Officials, www.transportation.org
American Public Transportation Association, www.apta.com

Water Quality and Waste Management

Air & Waste Management Association, www.awma.org
American Water Resources Association, www.awra.org
American Water Works Association, www.awwa.org
Clean Water Network, www.cleanwaternetwork.org
National Association of Clean Water Agencies, www.nacwa.org
Water Environment Federation, www.wef.org

Public Works

American Public Works Association, www.apwa.net

Infrastructure Jobs

American Planning Association, www.planning.org
American Society of Civil Engineers, www.asce.org

CHAPTER 6

Managing and Developing Financial Resources

"Business underlies everything in our national life, including our spiritual life … No one can worship God or love his neighbor on an empty stomach." —Woodrow Wilson

People with business-related, finance, accounting, and economics backgrounds are always in demand in the public service arena. Government agencies and nonprofits are often heavily involved with business. Some of these organizations increase economic opportunities and build new businesses to help bring in more employment opportunities for communities. Other government agencies regulate aspects of business to ensure that the public good is not harmed by business activity. Nonprofits also advocate for corporate responsibility.

Also, although government and nonprofit organizations are not in business to make a profit, they still need money to function, and they need contract managers, accountants, and other financial professionals to keep track of that money. Bringing in tax dollars or donations, investing funds to achieve public goals, and ensuring that the money is well spent and efficiently used are all essential aspects of public service. This chapter is an overview of the public service opportunities that are available for those with financial skills.

Community/Economic Development and Business Development

Community development often refers to efforts to improve impoverished areas and fight poverty by bringing people in the neighborhood together to help themselves. These efforts can include local neighborhood or community groups organizing for a common goal, such as planting a community garden or starting a community watch program.

On a broader scale, community development corporations work to improve the economy of neighborhoods by doing the following:

- Fostering new business opportunities by encouraging investments in the community and bringing jobs to the area
- Adding new amenities and facilities to improve the lives of residents, such as new housing, parks, or shopping centers
- Building a sense of community among residents

In order to accomplish these goals, community organizations interface with the economic development agencies of local and state government, foundations, banks that lend money for community development, and federal agencies. An estimated 400,000 people work in community development in some way.

On the federal level, the Department of Housing and Urban Development has the largest role in community development. Through subunits such as the Office of Community Planning and Development and the Government National Mortgage Association (Ginnie Mae), it invests in public and low-income housing; provides insurance on mortgages; offers Section 8 housing subsidies to low-income people; funds public housing projects for very low-income individuals; and ensures that landlords do not discriminate against their tenants on the basis of race, ethnicity, disability, and so on.

Other federal agencies are involved with community development as well:

- The Department of Health and Human Services' Community Service Block Grant Program supports community programs working to alleviate poverty.
- The Federal Home Loan Bank System provides low-cost loans for housing and economic development projects.
- The Economic Development Administration of the Department of Commerce offers grants for development.

Federal regulations such as the Community Reinvestment Act also require banks to offer loans in low-income areas.

State agencies involved with community and economic development include Housing Finance Organizations, Economic Development Agencies, and Social Service Agencies. State Housing Finance Agencies issue bonds to help build affordable housing and help first-time homebuyers buy homes. States also often have a Housing Finance Commission, a Housing Resources Corporation, a Housing Finance Agency, a Department of Housing and Community Affairs, or a Housing Development Authority. These agencies usually serve as a conduit for federal housing funds for community development and services and involve private investors in housing projects.

Local governments and cities typically have Economic Development Agencies, and some local governments also use tax dollars to provide neighborhood or community grants to fund new economic development and neighborhood improvement projects. Local city planners oversee zoning, which can have a big impact on where development projects are located (see Chapter 5 for details on urban planning). Larger cities usually have a housing authority that manages public housing projects in which the residents' rent is federally subsidized, assists residents with finding Section 8 housing, and so on.

Nonprofit organizations in the field range from small, neighborhood-based community groups to philanthropies that provide large grants for development. A number of organizations are considered Community Housing Development Organizations (CHDOs), authorized to receive government grants to provide low or moderate income housing. Some examples of economic development nonprofits include the New York City Economic Development Corporation, Self Help Ventures Fund (a community development lender), and Structured Employment Economic Development Corporation (Seedco). Land trusts (mentioned in Chapter 5) work to preserve open space or low-income housing for a community. In addition, technical help for community development corporations comes from organizations such as the Local Initiatives Support Corporation (LISC), the Enterprise Foundation, and NeighborWorks America. For-profit companies such as banks and local businesses partner significantly with community development organizations to help fund projects.

Business Development

In addition to encouraging the development of local communities, government and nonprofits also help foster new businesses in general. For example, the federal government's Small Business Administration (SBA) offers extensive free technical assistance to individuals who own or want to start a small business, including SBA-backed loans, training programs, and contract opportunities. These services are often offered through local Small Business Development Centers and SCORE (small business mentoring programs).

Other federal agencies assist businesses in different ways:

- The Department of Agriculture helps farmers by providing marketing assistance through the Agricultural Marketing Service and offering loans, disaster assistance, and other programs through the Farm Service Agency.
- The Department of Commerce grants funds to economically distressed areas in the United States through its Economic Development Administration. The purpose of these funds is to foster economic growth and increase employment. Through the Minority Business Development Agency, the Department of Commerce offers assistance to minority entrepreneurs who want to expand their businesses.
- The Patent and Trademark Office helps inventors protect their intellectual property.
- The U.S. Department of State includes the development of foreign trade among its foreign service positions (see Chapter 7).

Most states have an agency that focuses specifically on business development, such as a Department of Commerce or Economic Development. Many focus on bringing new businesses to their states and offer statistics on the economic indicators of the state, business development services, assistance to employers seeking employees, and business recruitment and marketing to attract investment. They may also oversee various industry councils, such as an Arts Council, Housing Development Commission, or Development Finance Board.

Local governments often have a Small Business Services Department or an Economic Development Department that works to increase business opportunities in their area. Public-private partnerships called *business improvement districts* help promote business in a particular area.

Nonprofit organizations that help improve business and trade include organizations such as boards of trade, industry associations, small business development organizations, and industry-related chambers of commerce (such as the National Restaurant Association Educational Foundation, U.S. Green Building Council, or Society of Manufacturing Engineers), local chambers of commerce, and business professional societies such as the American Management Association and the Conference Board.

PROFILE: JOHN "JACK" BIENKO

Deputy Director for Entrepreneurship Education,
U.S. Small Business Administration

What is your brief career history?

I began working in professional settings associated with my educational background during college. Internships evolved into fellowships and part-time, project-based positions, which in turn evolved into full-time positions. I have worked with the City of Buffalo (mayor's office), U.S. Department of Housing and Urban Development (Buffalo, New York, district office), and the United Way of Western New York prior to accepting a Presidential Management Fellowship with SBA headquarters in Washington, DC. I also worked on special events management, and this experience provided a great opportunity to develop my project management skills and make lifelong business contacts (and friends). I have worked with the World University Games, Olympics, Special Olympics, Super Bowl, NBA, and Kennedy Center Honors throughout the years.

How did you enter this profession?

I have an interest in community development and public service. My graduate degree allowed me to take courses in four different graduate schools at the university, so I was able to pursue specialized training that helped as I developed my career goals. When I got the Presidential Management Fellowship, SBA was a perfect fit for me as it plays an important role in community development through entrepreneurial and economic support products/services. I have worked with SBA for about a decade and been provided a series of positions with increased responsibilities.

What are some of the things you do on a typical day?

My current position as deputy for entrepreneurship development includes staff management, policy development, partnership recruitment and oversight, and special projects. On a typical day, I work with our staff project leads on their portfolios to assure milestones are being met and progress made, spend time with executive managers to align their efforts with the agency's goals, complete administrative tasks associated with budget and reporting, and interface with the agency's national partners on their efforts to support entrepreneurs. On a weekly basis, this equates to a series of internal meetings, conference calls, off-site special events, and closed-door time to work on administrative duties.

(continued)

(continued)

What do you like the most about this career?

I truly appreciate the opportunity to work with my team members to further develop their personal and professional goals. I have always enjoyed working with partner organizations (grantees, contractors, etc.). My proudest accomplishment is the fact that one of my team members just graduated from a highly regarded leadership development program. This accomplishment brings a bigger smile to my face because I know the personal impact it will have on this person's career. I have also worked on national initiatives for the federal government and partnered with many leading private sector companies to help entrepreneurs.

What are some of the challenges about this career?

Public service challenges me to do my best in meeting the needs of the American public, staying innovative, developing partnerships to get the work done, representing the federal government in a professional and responsive manner, and developing expertise in a number of different issue areas. These challenges keep me engaged as a public servant and provide me with ongoing learning opportunities to improve myself and the work of my team.

What skills, education/training, abilities, values, or personality are needed to succeed in this field?

Dedication, focus, determination, lifelong learning, commitment, and attention to customer service. I believe that public service is a "higher calling" and that people need to be committed to the cause of serving the American public (the "customer").

Any other advice for people who want to enter this field?

The interdisciplinary background of my education has served me well in different positions. I encourage people to take training or seek out diverse opportunities that will expose them to different areas of organizations and management. Expertise and experience can be gained in any role, whether it is as a community volunteer, intern, or entrepreneur. Strive to become a lifelong learner because the U.S. government needs people who are well-rounded and determined to find innovative solutions to current and future needs.

Personal Finance and Credit

Another way that individuals with an interest in both finance and public service can become involved is through helping people with their personal finances. Typically, lending and finance are for-profit enterprises, but some sources of financing are not for profit. Credit unions, for example, are member-owned cooperative organizations in which members pool their money to provide loans and financial services to other members. These organizations provide many of the same services as banks, but often can often offer lower fees and higher savings rates. Credit unions are regulated by an independent federal agency, the National Credit Union Administration (NCUA).

Various government-sponsored efforts focus on protecting citizens from predatory lending. One such effort is the Seattle/King County Coalition for Responsible Lending, which joins numerous nonprofit organizations and state agencies to educate the public and help people who have committed themselves to unfair loans. Also, various regulatory agencies prevent financial exploitation of vulnerable populations. These agencies are covered in more detail under regulation of business activities later on in this chapter.

Certain nonprofit organizations help individuals who have found themselves in financial difficulty or are facing bankruptcy. Examples include Money Management International, GreenPath, and ClearPoint Financial Solutions. By providing credit counseling, these organizations help individuals to avoid bankruptcy, manage their credit, pay back their debts, and build their financial awareness.

Economic Development Jobs

Jobs in community development, business development, and personal finance and credit include many of the common positions in government or nonprofit agencies, such as policy analysis, legislative affairs, case work, volunteer coordination, program management, and fundraising. In particular, community organizers fall into the broad category of advocacy work. Chapter 2 has more information on these types of jobs.

Some of the positions listed in Chapter 3, such as case workers or social workers, work in community development as employment specialists or residence managers. Urban planners often work in the community development arena as well. Check Chapter 5 for more details on planning as a profession.

Positions in community lending and finance include finance specialists, loan officers, and asset managers. A background in business, economics, finance, or accounting is useful for these positions, along with a desire to help people, strong sales abilities, and facility with numbers and details.

Housing- and real estate–related positions include property management and management of housing development programs. Such individuals work to ensure that housing facilities are properly maintained, bills are paid, rents are collected, and all building codes are met. An undergraduate degree in business, public administration, accounting, finance, or real estate will be helpful for this career. Property managers who manage public housing must be certified by the federal government. Median earnings for property managers who work for local governments were about $59,481 in 2008, and employment is expected to be as fast as average.

Commerce and Trade Regulations

On the flip side of the coin of fostering new business is regulating business. Like individuals, businesses are unfortunately capable of being selfish. They may sometimes take advantage of their customers, misrepresent their products or services, or produce negative impacts on the environment or on the communities in which they work. Many regulations and laws have been created specifically to prevent such problems, and many people work to produce new regulations and enforce the ones that are already on the books.

One of the more heavily regulated fields is that of finance and monetary policy. Numerous federal agencies are involved in this arena:

- The Federal Reserve System focuses on monetary policy and availability of credit.
- The Federal Trade Commission (FTC) is involved with consumer protection and antitrust cases and helps consumers avoid scams and rip-offs when buying cars, shopping online, taking out loans, or starting a business.
- The Securities and Exchange Commission (SEC) protects investors, investigates insider trading, and oversees inspections of brokers, securities firms, investment advisors, and ratings agencies.
- The Commodity Futures Trading Commission regulates commodity futures and options markets.
- The Federal Housing Finance Agency oversees Fannie Mae, Freddie Mac, and the Federal Home Loan Banks, all of which help to provide funding for home loans through the secondary mortgage market.

In addition, the following parts of the Department of the Treasury are involved with regulation:

- The Office of the Comptroller of the Currency oversees all national banks.
- The Office of Thrift Supervision (OTS) also regulates banks.
- The Alcohol and Tobacco Tax and Trade Bureau enforces laws concerning the marketing of alcohol, tobacco, firearms, and ammunition and collects excise taxes on these products.

Other federal agencies provide insurance for, and oversight of, investments, loans, and retirement funds, including the Federal Deposit Insurance Corporation (FDIC), National Credit Union Administration (NCUA), Pension Benefit Guaranty Corporation, and the Employee Benefits Security Administration (formerly Pension and Welfare Benefits Administration) of the Department of Labor.

Federal agencies help enforce laws and regulations that impact businesses in every field. For instance, the Department of Labor administers numerous labor regulations such as the federal minimum wage, worker safety, and child labor laws. The Environmental Protection Agency regulates various toxic chemicals, which impacts businesses producing those chemicals. The Consumer Product Safety Commission works to protect people from being injured as a result of using a product. (Agencies that focus on international trade regulation are described in Chapter 7.)

States typically have their own regulations related to businesses. For instance, a state may have a Public Service or Public Utility Commission that regulates the utilities industry, a Division of Finance that regulates and licenses financial institutions, and numerous other boards or departments that license other types of businesses. (For instance, to be a barber in Ohio, you must be licensed with the Ohio State Barber Board!) The state's Department of Labor also may enforce its own statewide minimum wage and other wage laws.

Local municipalities may also create regulations on businesses. For example, a city might pass a regulation that certain kinds of businesses cannot exist in its jurisdiction, or it may pass zoning regulations that specify where some businesses can exist. Cities also have their own business licenses and taxes.

Nonprofit organizations in the field include consumer protection organizations such as the Consumers Union of the United States (publishers of *Consumer Reports*), Underwriters Laboratories (focusing on product compliance), and the National Safe Skies Alliance (focusing on aviation safety).

Jobs in business regulation and compliance include positions such as wage and hour investigators, licensing analysts, financial examiners, and legal positions. There are also more technical positions, such as the statisticians who are hired by the Consumer Product Safety Commission to assess the risk of various products.

People in these positions may visit regulated businesses to ensure their compliance with regulations and must have a strong understanding of the various rules and regulations in their field as well as good interpersonal and communication skills. A total of 242,270 people worked as compliance officers in the United States in 2008, though many of this number worked for business. Median salaries were about $48,890. Projected job growth is slower than average.

Auditing, Accountability, and Evaluation

In addition to regulating business, government must also regulate itself. Throughout government, there are checks and balances to ensure that work is being done correctly and that the taxpayer dollar is being used most efficiently. As a local government recruiter once told me, "With every decision we make, I need to be able to look my neighbors in the eye when we ride the bus to work together in the morning and be able to say I used their money properly."

At the federal level, the Government Accountability Office (GAO), which reports directly to Congress, provides research into policy questions, testifies on issues, and produces policy reports. Other audit-related positions also exist throughout the federal government as oversight or review functions within different agencies or as part of an agency's Inspector General's Office. The Office of Government Ethics, a small agency in the executive branch, looks out for conflicts of interest among federal employees.

Most states and local governments also include an Auditor's Office or a Comptroller's Office, which handles investigations into finances of government agencies and contractors to ensure their most efficient performance and financial accountability and to prevent waste or fraud. Some of these agencies also conduct performance audits, whereby they seek to find measurements of the quality of service provided by other agencies. Other audit functions exist within specific government agencies to provide quality control on their work.

Many of the qualifications for government auditors are similar to those required by tax-related positions or other regulatory compliance positions. Specifically, a background in accounting with knowledge of relevant regulations, the ability to understand and analyze complex information, facility with numbers, and strong communication skills are all important for these types of positions.

Various independent nonprofit organizations also focus on ensuring responsive government. Some of the many think tanks, which produce in-depth reports on policy issues, fit into this area. Other nonprofits also focus on promoting better governmental effectiveness, such as the Center for Responsive Politics and Center for American Progress (a think tank).

Nonprofits also must evaluate their own achievements and report them to donors and the public. The people who work in outcomes measurement or program evaluation help agencies prove the benefits of their work. Program evaluation in the nonprofit sector can be its own job, or it can be incorporated into other jobs such as program management. Job tasks can entail conducting surveys and writing reports for distribution to donors.

PROFILE: CATHLEEN BERRICK

Managing Director, Homeland Security and Justice,
U.S. Government Accountability Office

What is your brief career history?

I started my career as a GS-7 (entry-level) auditor with the Department of Defense Inspector General Office and rose to the position of a GS-13 audit team leader. In this capacity, I led audits of Department of Defense programs and operations, in particular major defense acquisitions and logistics issues.

I next moved to the U.S. Postal Service, Office of Inspector General, where I started as a senior evaluator and rose to the position of director for oversight. As the director for oversight, I led senior evaluators and criminal investigators in conducting audits and investigations of the operations of the Postal Inspection Service, a law enforcement organization of more than 4,000 criminal investigators.

I then moved to the Government Accountability Office, where I was elected to participate in their Senior Executive Service candidate program, a one-year developmental program, after which I became a senior executive. Initially, I was a director of tax administration and justice issues, and then moved to be a director of transportation security and Department of Homeland Security management issues. In this position, I led program evaluations, issuing reports to the federal agencies my team was reviewing and testifying before Congress as an expert witness. I also represented GAO in the media (TV and print). In my current position, I lead all of GAO's work at the Department of Homeland Security and Department of Justice.

I graduated from Heidelberg College with a BS in Accounting and became a Certified Public Accountant. I received the William A. Jump Award in 2005, which is awarded to one federal employee annually under the age of 37 for outstanding achievement in public administration. In 2009, I was a finalist for the Service to America Medal for Homeland Security.

How did you enter this profession?

My accounting degree led me into the auditing profession. As I advanced in my career, I ultimately moved to the U.S. Government Accountability Office (GAO), the leading accountability organization in the United States, who sets auditing standards for the country.

(continued)

(continued)

What are some of the things you do on a typical day?

I lead a team of about 200 professionals, including senior executives, managers, and analysts, who conduct audits of Department of Homeland Security and Department of Justice programs and operations. I review all reports and Congressional testimony my division issues, provide input on and lead organization-wide efforts (for example, I'm the senior GAO executive on the management team negotiating a final contract with GAO's union), chair key engagement stakeholder meetings, have "town hall" meetings with my staff, and interface with senior leadership at the Department of Homeland Security and the Department of Justice.

What do you like the most about this career?

GAO is a very influential organization—its reports get extensive media coverage and influence public opinion on a wide range of issues, Congress uses GAO's work to make decisions about what federal programs to fund and legislation to pass, and the federal agencies GAO reviews use its work to make improvements in their programs and operations. As a result, the most gratifying aspect of my work is seeing the significant impact that it has. Although federal agencies aren't usually happy to see GAO employees (since we are auditing them), building respect and showing these agencies that GAO is there to help and to improve government and getting agency officials to work constructively with GAO are very gratifying.

What are some of the challenges about this career?

I have to work with the federal agencies GAO audits and make sure I am getting the full story and all relevant information, while also making sure GAO meets its clients' (Congressional committees of jurisdiction who request or mandate GAO reviews) needs. Sometimes this may involve getting one week's notice that someone from GAO has to testify during a Congressional hearing on a topic.

What skills, education/training, abilities, values, or personality are needed to succeed in this field?

Education-wise, GAO hires people out of graduate school with a range of degrees, including public policy but also including degrees in just about every area. (GAO reviews any program or operation that receives federal funding, so its work covers essentially every area—health care, defense, financial markets, the environment, etc.). Because GAO is a very attractive place to work given its influence (GAO was just voted by the Partnership for Public Service as the second best place to work in the federal government), it attracts people from the top schools. Skills that are important are the ability to communicate effectively (oral and written), achieve results, think critically, and work in teams.

A graduate degree with good grades is necessary, as is being a well-rounded student. The other key aspect is wanting to have a positive influence on government and affect public policy.

Government Finance

> *"Taxes are what we pay for civilized society." —Oliver Wendell Holmes, Jr.*

One topic that is inevitable in any discussion of government is taxes. Federal, state, and local governments all have their ways of levying taxes, and all must provide staff for the calculation, collection, enforcement, and customer service related to taxes. The Internal Revenue Service (part of the Treasury Department) employs more than 111,570 people. This number includes not only the quintessential tax collector, but also a large legal staff to pursue claims against nonpayers and a variety of positions in between.

Every state also has a tax-collecting department, often called a Department of Revenue or Finance. Local governments have similar departments to collect property taxes, business taxes, and so on.

The opportunities for tax collectors or revenue officers, tax examiners, auditors, and policy specialists in taxation are numerous. Individuals who work in the field may provide assistance and guidance to taxpayers, handle accounting and processing of tax revenues, disburse tax dollars to agencies and local governments, handle appeals, and conduct research on tax policy. Some states even have auditors who travel or live out of state to ensure interstate taxes are paid. On the enforcement side, the IRS has a criminal investigation unit whose special agents handle investigations into tax law violations.

For most positions, a strong background in accounting is usually required, along with strong attention to detail, analytical skills, and interpersonal or political awareness. Some individuals in the field may possess a CPA (Certified Public Accountant) credential, which usually requires 150 semester hours of college coursework. Others may pursue the Certified Government Auditing Professional (CGAP) from the Institute of Internal Auditors. People who focus on fraud examination may pursue the Certified Fraud Examiner (CFE) credential.

According to the latest data (2008), about 72,700 earn their living as tax examiners, collectors, and revenue agents, and their median salary is $48,100. Job growth is expected to remain constant.

Corporate Social Responsibility, Fair Trade

Corporations are increasingly becoming more aware of their impact upon society and the environment. What once might have started as a desire by companies to follow government regulations and make a good public impression has expanded significantly beyond good corporate ethics into improving the quality of life of the company's workers (in the United States and overseas), minimizing environmental impact, and having a positive impact on the community in general. Companies also have started to measure their impacts not just by the "bottom line" of profit, but by the "triple bottom line" of people (for example, fair labor practices and impact on the community), planet (the ecological footprint of the company), and profit.

The result of this shift in thinking is more opportunity for careers in corporate compliance, philanthropy, and corporate social responsibility. Many companies don't have a specific corporate social responsibility department, but they may have opportunities in their community affairs, environment, or operational areas that could fall into this category.

People entering this field typically start in corporations in other areas, such as public relations, marketing, legal compliance, and so on. Some of the many tasks include ensuring that factories comply with the company's labor regulations, measuring environmental impacts, communicating with the community about the company's work, and conducting audits of the suppliers for the company's products.

Philanthropy/Foundations

> *"Pity the poor millionaire, for the way of the philanthropist is hard."*
> *—Andrew Carnegie*

Philanthropies make up only a tiny percentage of nonprofit sector employment—0.3 percent—but they can have a major impact on other nonprofits by determining funding priorities and providing significant financial support. Private philanthropies and foundations gave away $45.6 billion in 2008, according to the Foundation Center.

Various kinds of philanthropies exist:

- Corporate foundations are funded by one company (and/or employees of one company) such as the Avon Foundation or the Safeway Foundation.
- Community foundations receive donations from members of a certain geographic region, such as the Oregon Community Foundation or San Francisco Foundation.
- Federated giving programs are organized fundraising efforts administered by a nonprofit organization that raises and distributes funds, such as the United Way.
- Organizations such as the National Philanthropic Trust or Rockefeller Philanthropy Advisors work with individual donors or foundations to advise them on giving.

- Private independent or family foundations, such as the Ford Foundation, are funded by one wealthy person or family. The Foundation Center determined that 72 percent of foundation giving in 2008 came from independent foundations.
- Operating foundations such as the Kaiser Family Foundation both operate programs and give money away.

Jobs in philanthropy vary by the size and type of foundation. Small foundations may employ just one person to help look through the numerous applications for grant funding that a foundation may receive and provide recommendations on funding to the board of directors or trustees. Large foundations, such as the Ford Foundation, may employ individuals as program officers, who develop, monitor, and coordinate grant-making efforts, serve as liaisons to grant recipients, and serve as experts in a particular area (such as how to build successful development projects in sub-Saharan Africa or how to deliver health programs to teenagers). There are also positions for asset managers or investment analysts who manage funds and for information technology staff and other support roles. Positions in federated giving programs tend to focus on fundraising, community outreach, and education to the various donor groups targeted by a campaign (see Chapter 2 for details on fundraising positions).

Although serving as a program officer in a foundation is different in some ways from being a program manager in a nonprofit organization, there are some similarities. The focus of a foundation program officer is on determining the best use of a donor's funds and ensuring that funds have been properly used, while program managers in nonprofit groups execute programs directly. Both positions require excellent interpersonal skills, the ability to communicate to internal and external groups, and a facility at executing projects. Read the program manager position description in Chapter 2 for more detail.

References and Resources

For more information on the topics presented in this chapter, refer to the following sources.

Community/Economic Development and Business Development

Brophy, Paul C., and Shabecoff, Alice; *A Guide to Careers in Community Development* (Island Press, 2001)
Coalition of Community Development Financial Institutions, www.cdfi.org
Council of State Community Development Agencies, www.coscda.org
International Economic Development Council, www.iedconline.org
National Congress for Community Economic Development, www.ncced.org

Business Development

America's Small Business Development Center Network, www.asbdc-us.org
National Association of Housing and Redevelopment Officials, www.nahro.org
Public Housing Authorities Directors Association, www.phada.org
SCORE, small business mentoring programs, www.score.org
U.S. Small Business Administration, www.sba.gov

Personal Finance and Credit

America's Credit Unions, www.creditunion.coop
The Association of Independent Consumer Credit Counseling Agencies (AICCCA), www.aiccca.org
National Foundation for Credit Counseling (NFCC), www.nfcc.org

Government Finance

Association of Local Government Auditors, www.governmentauditors.org
International Association of Assessing Officers, www.iaao.org
National Association of State Auditors, Comptrollers, and Treasurers, www.nasact.org
National Association of State Budget Officers, http://nasbo.org
U.S. Office of Personnel Management, Federal Civilian Workforce Statistics—Employment and Trends, www.opm.gov/feddata

Corporate Social Responsibility, Fair Trade

Business Ethics magazine, www.business-ethics.com
Business for Social Responsibility, www.bsr.org
CSRWire, www.csrwire.com
Ethical Performance, www.ethicalperformance.com
Justmeans, www.justmeans.com
Net Impact, www.netimpact.org

Philanthropy

The Chronicle of Philanthropy, www.philanthropy.com
Council on Foundations, www.cof.org
Foundation Center, www.fdncenter.org

CHAPTER 7

Helping the World: International Development, Relief, Relations, and Trade

"In the field of world policy, I would dedicate this nation to the policy of the good neighbor." —Franklin D. Roosevelt

The world is an increasingly interconnected place. We are tied together through more international trade, much faster worldwide communications, and far easier international travel than ever before. Many people are drawn to an international career because of a desire to immerse themselves in another culture, to represent their country to people of other nations in a positive manner, to alleviate poverty and suffering in countries that have far fewer resources than those in more developed countries, or to travel the world.

Many other sections of this book cover public service careers which, when translated into the international setting, become international careers. For example, health (Chapter 3), education (Chapter 4), environmental protection (Chapter 5), and disaster management and relief (Chapter 8) are all issues that can be pursued in the international arena.

Certain public service fields, however, have a definite international focus. International relief—the immediate intervention into war-torn or famine-stricken areas—is one of the more well-known fields, especially in the nonprofit area. International development, which focuses on longer-term economic development, education, and health programs to help countries fight poverty, is a closely related field. In fact, many organizations focus on both of these fields. International relations focuses on diplomatic affairs, maintaining embassies and consulates, interfacing with foreign governments, assisting Americans overseas, and working with visitors from other nations. International educational exchanges deal with scholars and students visiting the U.S. from other countries and vice versa. Finally, international trade focuses on encouraging and regulating commerce between countries. This chapter highlights opportunities available in all of these fields. (International security and peacekeeping are covered in more detail in Chapter 8, "Keeping People Safe.")

The majority of this international work is accomplished at the federal, intergovernmental, and nonprofit levels. Through various federal agencies, the U.S government gives billions of dollars in foreign grants and credits to other countries ($31.2 billion in 2007). Public multinationals, international governmental organizations, or intergovernmental organizations work on peacekeeping, development and relief, and international relations. These organizations are comprised of various member nations and include the United Nations and its affiliates as well as other non-UN organizations. (The end of the chapter has special tips on the hiring process for some of these organizations.) In addition, much international work is performed by nonprofit organizations (known in this context as *nongovernmental organizations* or *NGOs*), networks of NGOs such as Caritas or the International Council of Voluntary Agencies, and corporate contractors. This chapter describes how these types of organizations work in the different international public service fields.

International Relief and Development

Many people envision international relief and development when thinking about international public service careers. International relief efforts focus on immediate responses to humanitarian disasters, and development efforts focus on building a country's long-term economic, health, educational, governance, infrastructure, and environmental capacity.

The federal government provides significant funding for international aid and relief. For example, in 2006, the U.S. Agency for International Development (USAID) distributed $9.8 billion, U.S. Department of Agriculture $2 billion, State Department $5.3 billion, and other agencies $8.3 billion. Federal agencies conducting international development work include the following:

- The United States Agency for International Development (USAID) employs 2,575 people, of whom 953 work abroad, and provides money, materials, and other aid to countries around the world.

- The Peace Corps employs 821 people, and currently has 7,876 trained volunteers working in 76 countries.
- The Millennium Challenge Corporation employs 280 people to bolster economic growth in developing countries in order to decrease the amount of poverty worldwide.

Significant humanitarian aid and disaster relief are provided by the military as well.

Intergovernmental agencies involved in relief and development efforts include many affiliated with the United Nations, such as the United Nations Office for the Coordination of Humanitarian Affairs (OCHA), World Food Program, High Commissioner for Refugees (UNHCR), United Nations Children's Fund (UNICEF), UN Development Programme (UNDP), and UN Development Group. Non-UN intergovernmental organizations conducting this work include the International Organization for Migration (IOM), the Asian Development Bank, and ECHO (European Commission Humanitarian Aid).

Many nonprofit organizations provide humanitarian relief and also often work in international development, including the following:

Catholic Relief Services	Doctors Without Borders
Feed the Children	Food for the Poor
Red Cross	Mercy Corps
Save the Children	Samaritan's Purse
World Vision	U.S. Fund for UNICEF
Direct Relief International	Habitat for Humanity International
American Jewish Joint Distribution Committee	International Relief and Development, Inc.

Many, though not all, such organizations are funded by churches and other religious groups.

Organizations focused on economic development, including many offering very small loans to entrepreneurs in developing countries, include ACCION, FINCA, Global Impact, the Grameen Foundation, and Kiva. Some organizations work on agriculture and rural development, such as Heifer International.

NOTE

There are many tiny, all-volunteer (or nearly all volunteer) organizations providing international aid. These organizations can be good places to find internships or volunteer work to build your resume.

Also, a number of private contractors/corporations conduct international development work. For example, Chemonics is one of the largest contractors for USAID and implements much of its development work worldwide. Other examples include DAI, Management Systems International (MSI), International Resources Group (IRG), Abt Associates, and Futures Group International. Although these organizations may be quite similar to NGOs in the work they do, their mission, vision, and goals are different because they must make a profit.

PROFILE: VICKI AKEN

Head of Programmes, GOAL Sudan (formerly Program Development Officer, United Methodist Committee on Relief, Sudan)

What is your brief career history?

My current position is head of programmes, GOAL Sudan. Prior to that, I was a program development coordinator for United Methodist Committee on Relief, Sudan. My career history is long and varied, but primarily spent in the university/nonprofit/government sectors as a writer, trainer, evaluator, manager, and consultant. I have a Master of Public Administration from the Evans School of Public Affairs at the University of Washington.

How did you enter this profession?

As a Peace Corps volunteer in Tonga, I worked on community development and education projects. I realized that I wanted to continue doing this type of work, and I knew I needed additional skills to pursue development professionally, so I selected an MPA program that had a focus on international development. I wanted a program that focused more on skills development than policy analysis. As I manage multimillion-dollar projects, financial management, monitoring and evaluation, and project management are particularly valuable skills I picked up, in part, in graduate school. Because experience is key to getting a job in international development, I pursued any and all opportunities to stay involved even while in school—internships, volunteering, consulting, etc.

What are some of the things you do on a typical day?

There is no such thing as a typical day, which is one of the reasons I love this job. On any given day, I could be writing proposals, meeting with donors, coordinating with other NGOs and government agencies, devising communication strategies, interviewing beneficiaries, monitoring and evaluating projects in the field, analyzing budgets, dealing with staff management issues, or handling a security crisis.

What do you like the most about this career?

The job is always a challenge. I feel like I learn something new nearly every day. I visited a rural village the other day where my organization is the only form of support for the local population. Before we restored the water source and rebuilt the school, both of which had been destroyed in a conflict, the residents had fled to other areas, living the life of internal refugees. Today, the village thrives. I'm most proud of whatever support I can provide to field staff to ensure that they continue the great work they are doing.

What are some of the challenges about this career?

Dealing with stress is the greatest challenge. Stress stems from, among other things, being isolated, living in an insecure environment, and witnessing the devastating impact of poverty and conflict.

What skills, education/training, abilities, values, or personality are needed to succeed in this field?

My organization gets numerous applications for each open position. On average, I spend about 30 seconds looking at each resume during the first pass, during which I eliminate at least 70 percent of the candidates. During this phase, I look at experience in the relevant sector, experience in the region, and education credentials.

The specific skills depend on what kind of position you are applying for, but there are definitely abilities, personality traits, and values that I believe are essential. These include high tolerance for stress, cultural sensitivity, initiative, independence, and willingness to put in long hours.

Any other advice for people who want to enter this field?

Make sure that any agency you work for has a solid security plan and provides a supportive environment, particularly if you are doing deep field work.

If you want to work in the humanitarian field, read up on the Sphere Project, as Sphere standards are commonly used as reference points.

Experience is essential. Much of what relief and development workers do is not taught in any college course. If you don't have experience, volunteer. Although humanitarian work and development have common elements, they can be very different. Take time to learn about the differences and figure out which would be the best fit for you.

International Relations and Educational Exchanges

International relations careers focus on the promotion of international understanding through diplomatic and educational efforts.

On the federal level, the State Department is the largest agency involved. It employs Foreign Service officers, otherwise known as diplomats, who typically work in U.S. embassies and consulates globally in consular, economic, political, public diplomacy, or management areas. Foreign service specialists provide specific assistance internationally, such as medical, administrative, or technical help to U.S. citizens abroad and others. Civil service positions, which are usually based in Washington, DC, range from engineering to international policy. The State Department manages several international exchange programs, such as the Fulbright Program and Exchange Visitor Program. The Broadcasting Board of Governors (BBG) also produces international communications through operations such as the Voice of America radio and Radio Free Europe.

Nonprofit organizations are prominent in international exchange programs, including study or work abroad programs. Some examples include People to People International, Youth for Understanding USA, Cross-Cultural Solutions, Global Volunteers, American Youth Hostels, AIESEC, Friendship Ambassadors Foundation, Institute of International Education, and American Councils for International Education.

International Trade

Like other forms of commerce (see Chapter 6), international trade is mainly a private sector endeavor. However, both government and nonprofit organizations are involved in encouraging international trade, and government is involved with trade regulation. Some organizations focus on building the economic capacity of developing countries by bringing investors to these countries or by helping people in these countries build businesses. Other organizations focus on improving the U.S. economy by promoting good trade relations and encouraging business development in the international arena.

On the federal level, numerous agencies are involved with international trade. The following organizations are involved with the finance and encouragement of international trade to help build American businesses:

- The International Trade Administration of the Department of Commerce promotes trade and investment, ensures fair trade, and strengthens industry competitiveness.
- The Export-Import Bank of the United States extends credit to U.S businesses to help them sell their goods and services in other countries.

- The Overseas Private Investment Corporation offers insurance and financing to help U.S. companies invest in developing nations.
- The U.S. Trade and Development Agency makes economic development grants to other countries for infrastructure improvements that make it easier for U.S. exporters to conduct business in these markets.
- The Foreign Agricultural Service (part of the Department of Agriculture) provides food aid to other countries and works to promote U.S. agriculture products internationally.
- The Bureau of Economic, Business, and Agricultural Affairs in the State Department has seven subunits that work to stabilize worldwide communication and transportation infrastructure, handle sanctions, and assist U.S. businesses in their dealings with other countries.
- The Office of the U.S. Trade Representative advises the President on trade policy and handles international trade negotiations.

Entities that regulate international trade include the following:

- The United States International Trade Commission is an independent federal agency that investigates importers to determine if they infringe on U.S. intellectual property rights or use unfair trade practices and to assess the effect of their products on U.S. economic competitiveness.
- The Bureau of Industry and Security in the Department of Commerce enforces export rules and regulations, especially as they concern matters of U.S. security.
- The Foreign Claims Settlement Commission adjudicates international claims.

Some agencies both encourage and regulate trade, such as the International Trade Administration of the Department of Commerce. This organization both encourages trade and enforces existing trade agreements and laws.

Other federal agencies are involved with international trade regulation in different ways. For example, the Department of the Treasury has a Financial Crimes Enforcement Network with international programs. The Department of Labor's Bureau of International Labor Affairs focuses on U.S. foreign labor policy objectives and works to prevent international child labor, forced labor, and human trafficking.

Intergovernmental organizations related to trade include the following:

- The World Trade Organization regulates trade between its member countries and helps with negotiations.

- The International Monetary Fund provides advice, technical assistance, and funds to its 186 member countries in order to reduce poverty and stabilize national economies.
- The World Bank Group makes leveraged loans to developing countries.
- The United Nations Conference on Trade and Development (UNCTAD) is the UN General Assembly's trade, development, and investment organization.
- The International Fund for Agricultural Development (IFAD) focuses on hunger relief by providing loans and grants to programs that help people in rural areas overcome poverty.
- The United Nations Industrial Development Organization works to increase sustainable business in developing nations.
- The International Labor Organization is a United Nations agency that maintains a list of international standards for working and promotes decent work for employees around the world.

Nonprofit organizations encourage fair and equitable trade internationally. Many organizations advocate for fair trade, such as Fairtrade Labeling Organizations International, World Fair Trade Organization, Fair Trade Federation, and United Students for Fair Trade. In addition, some nonprofits promote international trade, such as TradeRoots, a grassroots division of the U.S. Chamber of Commerce's International Division.

International Environmental Issues

Nations have borders, but the natural world does not. Many agencies work to protect the environment on the international level.

Federal agencies include the Environmental Protection Agency, the State Department's Bureau of Oceans and International Environmental and Scientific Affairs, and the USDA Forest Service's International Forestry Program and invasive species research. Intergovernmental agencies include the United Nations Environment Program (UNEP). In addition, there are international associations such as ICLEI—Local Governments for Sustainability.

Numerous environmental NGOs work on the international level. Many focus on preventing environmental degradation in endangered habitats in countries with large areas of rainforest, such as the Rainforest Alliance. Others advocate for other international environmental issues, such as World Wildlife Fund, Rare Conservation, Conservation International, the National Coalition for Marine Conservation, or Greenpeace.

International Law and Human Rights

According to the United Nations' Universal Declaration of Human Rights,

> *"everyone has the right to life, liberty, and security of person, no one shall be held in slavery or servitude; no one shall be subjected to torture or to cruel, inhuman, or degrading treatment."*

Human rights also includes equal protection under the law; prevention of discrimination; and rights to privacy, freedom of movement, property, thought, conscience, religion, opinion, and peaceful assembly.

Unfortunately, violations of basic human rights happen every day in all corners of the world. Many organizations focus on investigating offenses, bringing international attention to violations, pressuring perpetrators to stop their behavior, and changing laws to better protect people. Federal entities that deal with human rights issues include the Department of Labor's Bureau of International Labor Affairs, which fights child labor and human trafficking. The United Nations Human Rights Council works to promote human rights worldwide, and various other UN-related organizations, such as the International Labour Organization, focus on specific areas of human rights.

Nonprofit human rights organizations include international NGOs such as Amnesty International, Human Rights Watch, the International Justice Mission, the Committee to Protect Journalists, GlobalRights.org, and the Elie Wiesel Foundation. Most work in partnership with local organizations in various countries to effect change. Career opportunities in this area include many that exist in all nonprofits, such as fundraising and development, communications, and finance. Other opportunities include program management, investigation and documentation of human rights violations, advocacy, coalition building, and legal work.

International Jobs

Many positions in the international realm are quite competitive, due to the large numbers of people interested in the field. Some years of in-country experience (through programs such as the Peace Corps) as well as fluency in the in-demand languages (such as French, Spanish, Chinese, or Arabic) are typically necessary, but they are not sufficient by themselves to launch a career. Willingness to gain additional experience (volunteer or otherwise) and education, to relocate to cities such as New York or Washington, DC, or to developing countries, and to be persistent with job searching and networking can take job seekers to the level needed to land an entry-level position.

Also, consider the fact that it is risky and expensive for international organizations to hire expatriates, because their salaries and the hiring costs (visas, transport, and so on) are higher than those of in-country staff. Also, some of the less experienced individuals who want an international career are not prepared for the tremendous differences in lifestyle they will encounter in developing countries and may quit early in an assignment. In addition, the focus of modern development efforts is to empower people within a country to improve their own lives, rather than having people from developed countries come in and dictate what needs to be done. Lastly, most international NGOs would rather spend donor dollars on direct services rather than headquarters staff in the United States. Therefore, much of the actual development and relief work that is done is conducted by in-country staff and funded by external organizations, with some coordination, training, or oversight offered by expatriate staff.

That said, there are many international careers available for individuals who are focused and willing to take the necessary steps to achieve their goals. This section highlights the kinds of jobs that are available.

Foreign Affairs Officers

The classic example of an international position with the federal government is that of a State Department foreign affairs officer, otherwise known as a diplomat. These individuals often work with U.S. embassies overseas, managing visa applications, interacting with the local government, protecting U.S. citizens abroad, handling public relations, developing international trade partnerships, and responding to international emergencies.

The State Department has a special hiring process for individuals wishing to work in the Foreign Service (as diplomats or other official representatives of the United States in other countries). The process includes the following steps:

1. Set up an application online.
2. Take the Foreign Service Officer Test (a written test).
3. Complete an oral, in-person test, which is a day-long group interview process in which a small group of candidates are asked to role-play various scenarios that could occur in a U.S. embassy or consulate in an invented country.
4. If you pass both tests, you move on to in-depth background checks and clearances.

NOTE

Preference in Foreign Service jobs is given to individuals who speak *critical needs languages.* These include Arabic, Mandarin Chinese, Dari, Farsi, Hindi, and Urdu.

If accepted, you will be assigned to a country and given additional in-depth training. Most new Foreign Service officers must be willing to accept a "hardship post" in the beginning, in a country experiencing conflict or with fewer resources. However, the

State Department treats its Foreign Service officers well and provides for relocation, medical benefits in-country, and various other protections.

The State Department also offers (mainly unpaid) student internships, as well as civil service positions which are typically filled via USAJOBS or through programs such as the Presidential Management Fellowship (see Chapter 11 for more information). Additional positions in the Washington, DC, headquarters of the State Department include working on issues ranging from helping refugees to reducing international nuclear proliferation. About 11,700 people worked for the State Department in 2009.

The U.S. Agency for International Development (USAID) also offers opportunities for people in international development. Positions such as crisis, stabilization, and governance officers; program analysts; agriculture officers; economists; health and nutrition officers; and education officers are available. This agency is very competitive to enter, and often seeks those with advanced degrees and experience in international development. Two of the best means of entry are through the Presidential Management Fellows Program (PMF) or the highly competitive Junior Officer Program (JOP).

Other federal agencies also have foreign affairs officers. For example, the Department of Commerce has foreign commerce officers, the USDA has foreign agricultural officers, and the Departments of Energy, Homeland Security, and Defense all have foreign affairs specialist positions. Note, however, that the hiring process for these agencies differs from the State Department's.

Program or Project Managers and Officers

Many international organizations have positions for project managers or program officers. There are two types of program officers: those who typically work in the headquarters office rather than in a foreign country and those who work in-country. The role of headquarters staff is to manage the administrative details of international development grants, to provide advice and feedback to in-country program officers, and to ensure that the requirements of grants are met. In-country program officers plan and implement programs and projects in the field and manage logistics, budgets, and staff.

Duties of program managers vary by the type of program they are involved with. For example, those who focus on international educational exchanges should have experience working with youth in international settings. See Chapter 2 for more details on program management as a career.

Technical Experts and Specialists

Positions in technical fields, such as international/global health, international environmental protection, water and sanitation, food security, education, or disaster management usually have qualifications similar to their counterparts in the domestic realm, but they also require foreign language proficiency or in-country experience. More entry-level opportunities to work in technical areas seem to exist in NGOs rather than government agencies. The Peace Corps or similar program is an excellent place to pick up a technical specialization.

The requirements for technical staff can vary a great deal, with some positions having more advanced requirements than others. For example, a global health position often requires a Master of Public Health, an MD, or even a PhD, and expertise in working in rural or resource-limited environments or with people from different cultures.

Many of the donor agencies that fund international work, such as the World Bank, USAID, or the United Kingdom's Department for International Development (DFID), have advanced requirements for technical experts, including numerous years of experience, advanced degrees, and foreign language fluency.

International Trade Specialists

Trade specialists investigate international trade violations and situations in which a domestic industry is harmed by international trade, review international trade agreements, provide technical assistance on trade policy to foreign and domestic agencies, or conduct audits of international trade transactions. Federal agencies hiring such specialists include the Departments of Agriculture, Homeland Security, and Commerce; the International Trade Administration (which employs about 1,300 people); and the IRS.

The great majority of international trade positions are in the private sector. Those that relate most closely to public service are in corporate social responsibility or compliance (discussed in Chapter 6). Hiring managers for these positions look for experience in business, logistics, international trade law, and international relations.

Other Opportunities

A variety of other opportunities exist in international organizations that are similar to opportunities found in domestic public service, such as human resources, social services, teaching, information technology, and emergency management or security. In particular, international organizations need the following:

- **Fundraising and development or grant-writing staff:** A very large proportion of the U.S. office staff in many international nonprofit organizations works as fundraisers. These professionals ensure that the organizations have productive relationships with their donors. Check Chapter 2 for more on fundraising and contract management positions.
- **Monitoring and evaluation (or M&E) specialists:** These professionals typically work in international nongovernmental organizations or donor agencies, ensuring that grants and contracts are properly used to deliver effective

development programs. They research program outcomes, coordinate with in-country staff to gather information, and write reports for donor agencies.

Tips for Getting a United Nations Job

Many people consider the United Nations the epitome of an international career. Because of its relatively high pay and excellent benefits, the United Nations is extremely competitive, and hiring can sometimes be limited for U.S. citizens. However, there are a few ways to get a job with the United Nations, including taking the National Competitive Recruitment Exam or other exams, applying online for posted opportunities, or finding a contract position.

The United Nations itself has a quota system in which it hires professionals in numbers that reflect a country's donations and representation within the UN and other factors. For many years, and up until 2008, there was no hiring of U.S. citizens at all via the National Competitive Recruitment Exam (NCRE), which is the way the UN usually fills P2 level (Junior Professional) positions. In 2008, the UN opened this examination process to U.S. citizens because a large number of U.S. employees retired. The examination process itself is extremely competitive and rigorous, including a written test, a series of panel interviews, and more. You can be no older than 32 years old to take the NCRE. Agencies affiliated with the UN, such as UNICEF, have a different hiring process and are not always bound by national hiring quotas.

NOTE

> Individuals who apply for positions with the UN also must be fluent in English or French, and additional languages (especially Arabic, Chinese, Russian, and Spanish) are looked upon favorably.

The UN has various employment scales:

- P1–2 level requires a master's degree and two to three years of relevant (paid) work experience.
- P3 level requires a master's degree and five years of experience.
- P4 level requires a master's degree and eight years of experience.

Most applicants for UN positions requiring at least five years of experience will have much more experience than that, often combined with a PhD. Also, positions at the P3 level and higher are usually filled through an online application process instead of through an exam such as the NCRE.

Online applications have to be extremely thorough and use the keywords from the job announcement. You need to go into much more detail than you would for a typical American job application or resume. A UNICEF recruiter told me that the online resume or CV should be at least 5 pages for a P2 position or 12 pages for a P4 position. Don't leave anything to chance—if you don't spell out your specific relevant experience, the hiring manager will not make any assumptions or inferences from other parts of your resume that you have the required experience. If your application is accepted, you will likely go through an assessment, including a written test and a panel interview with competency-based questions (such as "Describe a time when you were an effective change agent in an environment resistant to change").

Other ways to get UN experience include internships (which in the UN are only for graduate students and are always unpaid). You also can sometimes find contract or temporary opportunities by inquiring directly with a particular office. It's not a bad idea to "follow the money." For example, with organizations such as UNICEF, donations tend to rise in response to emergencies, so if you are willing to work in a disaster area, you may have a better chance of finding a position.

PROFILE: MATTHEW PERKINS

United Nations Economic and Social Commission for Western Asia (ESCWA), Beirut, IT for Development, Information, and Communication Technology Division

What is your career history?

I have worked in a broad range of occupational fields, including health care and higher education. Outside my UN experience, I have worked as a software engineer, IT specialist, and data warehouse architect. I have been fortunate to be able to work in the U.S. and internationally before my current position with the UN.

How did you enter this profession?

I have always had a strong affinity for IT. I enjoy using computers to solve problems. I obtained a bachelor's in computer science to have a firm grounding in technical applications and a master's in project management to facilitate implementation. As I progressed through my career, I searched for a way to more directly utilize my technical skills in helping to make the world a better place. The UN is an ideal mechanism to achieve that goal.

What are some of the things you do on a typical day?

My day is a blend between research, IT development, and project evaluation. Tasks can range from facilitating expert group meetings to catalyze change to development of statistical systems to foster insight and better decision making. My work requires versatility and a willingness to learn.

What do you like the most about this career?

As part of the UN's efforts to rebuild Iraq, I had the opportunity to train civil servants in modern project management techniques. Being able to have an impact on the success of these projects was very meaningful to me.

What are some of the challenges about this career?

Although working with developing nations requires adaptability and resilience, it also offers unique opportunities. Logistic challenges, infrastructure issues, and cultural gaps can sometimes be daunting. It takes vision and patience to address these challenges and create solutions.

What skills, education/training, abilities, values, or personality are needed to succeed in this field?

The United Nations uses a system of central core competencies to drive hiring decisions. These include values such as integrity, respect for diversity, communication, and teamwork. I have also found that having a sense of humor and a commitment to making the world a better place will serve you very well in the UN.

Any other advice for people who want to enter this field?

Employment with the UN is very competitive. The hiring process can sometimes be long and difficult, but ultimately rewarding. For individuals starting their career, I recommend pursuing the National Competitive Recruitment process. This annual process facilitates bringing in the best and brightest professionals from under-represented nations into the UN system. In addition, applying through the online portal jobs.un.org is a great way for mid-career and senior staff to find an opportunity. The UN system is more than just the iconic general assembly building in New York. There are many career paths open in the diverse funds and programs such as UNESCO, UNDP, and UNICEF to name a few.

References and Resources

For more information on the topics presented in this chapter, refer to the following sources.

International Relief and Development

American Council for Voluntary International Action, www.interaction.org
Association of Professional Schools of International Affairs (APSIA), www.apsia.org
Brinkerhoff, Derick, and Brinkerhoff, Jennifer; *Working for Change—Making a Career in International Public Service* (Kumarian Press, 2005)
Development Executives, www.devex.com
Foreign Policy Association, www.fpa.org
Global Health Council, Global Health Career Network, http://careers.globalhealth.org

International Career Employment Weekly, www.internationaljobs.org
International Development Jobs, www.devnetjobs.org
ReliefWeb, www.reliefweb.int
Society for International Development, www.sidw.org

International Relations and Educational Exchanges

Council on Foreign Relations, *Foreign Affairs* Job Board, jobs.foreignaffairs.org
NAFSA: Association of International Educators, www.nafsa.org
Society for Intercultural Education, Training and Research (SIETAR), www.sietar.org
Young Professionals in Foreign Policy, www.ypfp.org

International Trade

Federation of International Trade Associations, www.fita.org/useful
Foreign Trade Association, www.fta-eu.org

International Law and Human Rights

Human Rights Tools, http://jobs.humanrightstools.org

International Jobs

American Foreign Service Association, Shawn Dorman, editor; *Inside a U.S. Embassy: How the Foreign Service Works for America,* Second Edition (Potomac Books, 2009)
Foreign Service Officer Test, www.act.org/fsot
United Nations Conditions of Service, Salaries and Post Adjustment, www.un.org/Depts/OHRM/salaries_allowances/salary.htm
United Nations Exam Programme, Examinations and Tests Section, www.un.org/Depts/OHRM/examin/exam.htm
United Nations Office of Human Resources Management, Current openings in other UN organizations, www.un.org/Depts/OHRM/indexpo.htm
United Nations Online Volunteering Service, www.onlinevolunteering.org
United Nations System Employment Opportunities, www.unsystem.org/jobs/job_opportunities.htm
U.S. Department of State Careers, http://careers.state.gov/

CHAPTER 8

Keeping People Safe

"There is no security on this earth; there is only opportunity."
—General Douglas MacArthur

Keeping individuals safe from criminals, disasters, emergencies, and terrorists; enforcing laws and ensuring that the rights of the accused are maintained; and protecting the nation through international security and national defense efforts are all essential aspects of public service. Law enforcement, national security, and defense are provided by government, while disaster relief and legal defense are provided by both government and nonprofits. If you are concerned with protecting people or your country, these careers will be rewarding for you.

Intelligence and National/International Security

National security is a broad term that can include diplomacy, armed forces, civil defense, and intelligence efforts to pre-empt possible terrorist or international threats. The federal government is most heavily involved with national security issues.

The Office of the Director of National Intelligence is the head of the U.S. intelligence community, but numerous agencies engage in intelligence gathering. They accomplish their mission by intercepting communication, decrypting encoded data, tracking potential espionage, and analyzing collected data. Key federal agencies in this process include the Central Intelligence Agency (CIA). The CIA gathers data about plots against U.S. interests and assesses the capabilities of U.S. enemies. It then acts on the President's orders to mitigate possible threats against the United States.

The Department of Defense also has various intelligence units:

- The National Security Agency (NSA) uses and decodes cryptologic information.
- The National Reconnaissance Office builds national signals and imagery satellites.
- The National Geospatial Intelligence Agency provides maps and other imagery for use by the military and other security organizations.

Others are the Defense Intelligence Agency and the intelligence units of the Army, Marine Corps, Navy, and Air Force.

The Department of Homeland Security was established in 2003 in response to the September 11, 2001, terrorist attacks. With the FBI, the department ensures that state and local law enforcement officials have timely information on possible terrorist threats. The many agencies within Homeland Security work together to safeguard the United States:

- Customs and Border Protection, Immigration and Customs Enforcement, and Citizenship and Immigration Services patrol borders and set immigration policies.
- The Coast Guard secures American ports, coastlines, and waterways.
- The Transportation Security Administration protects travelers.
- The Office of Intelligence and Analysis, Directorate for Science and Technology, and Office of Cybersecurity and Communications conduct research.
- The Secret Service protects elected officials, candidates for office, and visiting diplomats and investigates financial crimes such as counterfeiting.

Other related units include the following:

- The State Department's Arms Control and International Security and Bureau of Intelligence and Research
- The Department of Energy's National Nuclear Security Administration, which works against nuclear proliferation
- The Department of Treasury's Office of Terrorism and Financial Intelligence

- The Drug Enforcement Administration
- The U.S. National Central Bureau of Interpol, which focuses on apprehension of international criminals

Some nonprofit groups also produce research on security and conflict issues. These include the World Security Institute and Arms Control Association. Other organizations focus on international conflict resolution, peace-building, and arms control. These include organizations such as the Ploughshares Fund, Physicians for Social Responsibility, Peaceworks, Peace Brigades, International Crisis Group, and the Global Security Institute.

Intelligence Jobs

Security specialists, international trade specialists, asylum and immigration officers, translators, cybersecurity analysts, foreign forensic financial researchers, investigative operations analysts, statisticians, criminal investigators, and counterterrorism analysts are just some of the numerous positions available in international intelligence and security. Most require an advanced security clearance involving in-depth background checks. Chapter 11 has more information about security clearances.

Although various support positions within the intelligence community are hired using the typical civil service process (see Chapter 11), for many jobs there is a special hiring process. The CIA, for example, has a specific hiring process that includes an online application followed by an in-depth background check and security clearance process.

PROFILE: JEFF ABRAMSON

Deputy Director, Arms Control Association

How did you enter this field?

I was leading a coalition of after-school providers and had a career in education and community development, but international issues were intellectually appealing to me. So I went back to school to do a master's in public policy at the Goldman School of the University of California at Berkeley. I found myself studying arms control, which was a specialization of the dean of the school.

My wife got a job in Washington, DC, that facilitated our move here, and it seemed like a likely location for me to

(continued)

(continued)

do something internationally related. When I got to Washington, DC, I did a ton of informational interviews. It was tough to do a mid-career transition. It took me a long time to find full-time work.

I landed with the Arms Control Association, originally taking a job as managing editor of their publication, *Arms Control Today.* This publication is well-known and well-respected in its niche. This experience was great because I got to do a lot of writing and develop my expertise. My current position is more fulfilling because I have a role in outreach with other organizations and growing the organization.

What was the actual process of finding this particular job?

I did a couple of things that I'd recommend to anyone looking for a position in the field: I networked whenever I could and found active professional associations that had events. When I moved to Washington, DC, I took advantage of the alumni network of my graduate school. I probably had, over the course of six months, 50 different informational interviews, some of whom were people from graduate school and the people they would recommend. I volunteered for events held by an organization called the Society for International Development. I went to a career fair they had, which got me some part-time work.

A number of people I had informational interviews with said the Arms Control Association was a great place to get experience in the field, which encouraged me to apply for the job. I think the organization was interested in me because I had worked at a major foundation, I was a little bit older, I had some leadership skills, and I had directed projects in the past. I think I was hired as managing editor for the magazine based on the fact I could do some other things, like help raise funds for the association.

What are some things you do on a typical day?

I have two major sets of work I do, administrative and policy-oriented. On the administrative side, I hire people, work on proposals, and monitor the budget. I reach out to raise funds or connect with other organizations. My policy-oriented work has both a learning component, which involves understanding and researching the issues, and an advocacy component. The problems I work on are related to conventional weapons. I might be doing some reading, tracking legislation, calling people on the Hill, and networking with people who are interested in these issues.

What do you like the most about your job and what is your proudest accomplishment?

The highlights are when we host events and ideas from those events come out in the media or are picked up by legislators or State Department leaders. I also have enjoyed seeing my writing published as part of the magazine. I also get to work with the interns, and they get very excited about having the chance to write for the magazine. It's fun to see other people feel they are accomplishing things, succeeding, and making a difference.

What are some of the challenges of this career?

The challenge is that a lot of the ultimate outcome of these issues is out of your hands.

What skills, education, training, and values are needed for this field?

It depends on what you want to do. If you want to work at a think tank, a PhD is valuable; a master's is a prerequisite. My boss is one of the few that heads an organization with just an undergraduate degree. Some master's programs, particularly those in DC, have great connections with the State Department.

Leaders in the nonprofit sector have often worked in government or in Congress. Even having experience as an intern or one or two years on the Hill makes a big difference in eventually being a leader in the nonprofit community.

You also have to be smart. You have to do your homework, understand the issues, and articulate them well. If you work in a nonprofit, you should be friendly and get along with people. Once you get into government, you need to be circumspect, because you are speaking for someone else. I know a number of people who have worked in government who enjoy working in the nonprofit sector because they can be a little bit freer in their expression.

Defense and Military

"I only regret that I have but one life to lose for my country."
—Nathan Hale

With a federal budget of nearly $700 billion in 2008 (not counting about $73 billion in veteran's benefits), the Department of Defense is one of the largest components of the federal government. This department includes the Army, Marine Corps, Navy, and Air Force, as well as various other agencies. With such a vast presence, the Department of Defense can offer careers to anyone, both military and civilian. About 1.4 million people are on active duty in the military, and another approximately 840,000 are in the reserves. The Department of Defense also employs more than 700,000 civilians.

Individuals who enlist in the military go through basic training, as well as additional training in their specialty fields. They can then achieve various ranks, starting with junior enlisted ranks and moving up into noncommissioned officers, up to the highest ranks of enlisted officers, such as Sergeant Major of the Army or Chief

Master Sergeant of the Air Force. Individuals can also become commissioned officers through programs such as the Reserve Officers' Training Corps (ROTC), Office Candidate School, or military academies such as West Point or the U.S. Naval Academy.

> **NOTE**
>
> In addition to classic military operations, the military is also involved with humanitarian projects, delivering emergency food supplies and serving as some of the first responders to disaster-stricken areas.

Careers in the military are classified according to Military Occupational Specialties (MOS). For enlisted personnel, the military uses aptitude exams (such as the Armed Services Vocational Aptitude Battery) to determine what kinds of programs to place people in. According to Today's Military (a Department of Defense website), opportunities are available in the following fields:

- Accounting, budget, and finance
- Arts, communications, media, and design, ranging from music directors to graphic designers to public information specialists
- Aviation, including positions such as air traffic control managers, pilots, and engineers
- Business administration and management
- Combat operations, including working in armored assault vehicles, combat support, special forces, and infantry
- Communications technology, such as operating sonar and radar
- Construction and building
- Counseling, social work, and human services
- Education and training
- Engineering and scientific research
- Environmental health and safety
- Food service and recreation
- Health care and medical technology
- Human resources
- Intelligence
- Information technology, computer science, and mathematics

- International relations, linguistics, and translation
- Law enforcement and legal professions
- Mechanics and repair
- Naval and maritime operations
- Transportation, supply, and logistics

Most individuals in the military work on or near military bases and may have to move frequently for training. Individuals in the military must be physically fit and may be deployed for lengths of time in dangerous situations far from home. Some benefits of military service include eligibility for retirement after 20 years.

You can find out more about civilian positions by visiting a Civilian Personnel Advisory Center near you or going online to the Department of Defense's Civilian Personnel Management Service at www.cpms.osd.mil or the U.S. Army's Civilian Personnel Online system at http://acpol.army.mil. Careers in veterans' affairs are discussed in Chapter 3.

PROFILE: JOHN P. BURNS

Captain, U.S. Army

What is your brief career history?

I started my Army experience by attending the United States Military Academy at West Point for four years. Upon graduation, I was commissioned as an armor officer. I attended Basic Officer Leadership Course and Mounted Officer Basic Course. After finishing my schooling, I was assigned to the Second Battalion, 69th Armor Regiment. While with 2-69 AR, I served for 4 months as an assistant human resources officer, 8 months as an assistant effects coordinator, and 14 months as the battalion's scout platoon leader. Finally, I served as the human resources officer for the battalion, which required me to manage the human resources for 940 soldiers and be the principal advisor to the battalion commander. Currently I am attending the Maneuver Officers Career Course at Fort Benning, Georgia.

How did you enter this profession?

While in middle and high school, I decided that I wanted to become a U.S. Army officer. I applied to several ROTC programs around the Northeast and also applied

(continued)

(continued)

to the United States Military Academy. I was selected to attend USMA. The Army has many different fields for officers to work in, and it gives ample opportunity to move between fields at key times in an officer's career.

What are some of the things you do on a typical day?

My current assignment is at an Army school, so it is not typical of an average day in the Army. In my last job, my typical day was as follows. I attended physical training every weekday morning from 0600 until 0730. At 0900, I would go to my office where I would handle paperwork and soldier issues until lunch at 1130. At 1300, I would be back taking care of paperwork and soldier issues until around 1800. Every Army officer's day is going to vary depending on their assignment. When I was a scout platoon leader, I spent much more time in the field supervising the training of my soldiers.

What do you like the most about this career?

The thing that I like most about my career is that the Army provides many different opportunities to me that most careers do not. In just three years, I have served as an assistant staff officer, a scout platoon leader, and a battalion human resources officer. I have done those jobs both in the United States and while deployed to Iraq for 15 months. After some more schooling, I will be able to work in a completely different field providing humanitarian relief to people around the world. Five years from now, I could be working in a completely different field.

My proudest accomplishment was the work I was able to do both as a nonlethal effects coordinator and a scout platoon leader in Baghdad during the Surge in 2007 and 2008. It was very satisfying to see the work I was supporting take effect and transform the security situation in Baghdad. Most Americans will never have the opportunity to positively affect history in the way my fellow soldiers and I did.

What are some of the challenges about this career?

One of the biggest challenges of this career is learning new skills quickly. Many Army officers will work in jobs for which they don't have formal training. I was trained as an armor officer, who would normally be responsible for tactically employing a tank or scout platoon in combat. I did that job for 14 months, but I have also had three other jobs completely unrelated in fields as varied as managing human resources, providing humanitarian relief, and advising a local government in Iraq.

What skills, education/training, abilities, values, or personality are needed to succeed in this field?

The most important abilities needed are to be flexible and to persevere. The Army will teach an officer everything else if that person is willing to learn and work.

Any other advice for people who want to enter this field?

Evaluate yourself and your life in order to be sure that the Army is what you want to do. There is a lot of sacrifice, especially when you are deployed. It is not for everyone. However, if you do decide to make it your career, you will meet a lot of great people, make friends for life, and be part of events and experiences that future generations will only be able to read about in history books. It can be a very rewarding and fulfilling career.

Disaster Recovery and Emergency Preparedness

"He who sees the calamity of other people finds his own calamity light." —Arabic Proverb

Protecting the public from natural and man-made disasters is a major, and quickly growing, career field. In addition to nurses, emergency medical technicians, and public health professionals, there are opportunities for disaster management and recovery planners who help plan and coordinate responses to disasters. Within the federal government, the Federal Emergency Management Agency (FEMA) of the Department of Homeland Security is the largest agency dealing with disaster management, but other agencies also hire disaster management professionals as well. Every state has a unit related to emergency management, as do most cities and counties. Many private nonprofits, such as larger hospitals or universities, have individuals on staff to create plans for emergencies. Most large corporations also have individuals in charge of ensuring that operations could continue in the face of a disaster.

In the nonprofit world, probably the largest disaster relief organization is the American Red Cross. Offering relief to disaster victims both nationally and worldwide, this organization also provides services to military members and their families, runs blood drives, produces educational programs to teach public safety, and runs international development and relief programs. Some organizations focus on more general safety education or research, such as the National Safety Council or the Insurance Institute for Highway Safety. There are also relief funds that distribute money directly to victims of disasters, such as the Cantor Fitzgerald Relief Fund, which was founded in the wake of 9/11, and the Louisiana Family Recovery Corps, founded after Hurricane Katrina.

Emergency planners or managers determine policies and create programs to help plan and respond to emergencies. They review emergency plans to look for errors or problems and train people in how to respond to emergencies. They also conduct tests and exercises to ensure that recovery operations run smoothly and coordinate evacuations and set up relief efforts such as shelters or clinics in disaster-stricken areas. Communication with other agencies across the state, federal, and local government as well as community organizations is essential in this field. Disaster management professionals may need expertise in mapping, project management, and emergency alert notification systems. There were about 12,000 emergency management specialists in 2008, with median earnings of $50,460 per year. Numerous other positions exist in the field, including emergency first responders, such as medical professionals and emergency medical technicians and communications officers.

PROFILE: CAROL DUNN

Disaster Management Professional, City of Bellevue, Washington

What is your career history?

My original career path was to work in opening up Russia to the West. I got a degree in Russian language and political science from the University of Washington. After working to set up joint ventures in Moscow in the early '90s, I got a master's in management in London, and then stayed and worked as an international management consultant for Ernst and Young.

During that period, I spent extensive time in Belarus, Ukraine, and Kazakhstan. I met my husband in Kazakhstan and, after having children, needed to find a career that wouldn't require as much traveling. While the children were very little, I increased the level of volunteer work I was doing. I began volunteering for the Red Cross as a Russian interpreter for its language bank. The people there asked me if I could help them by interpreting during the disaster education presentations—I figured if I could do it in Russian, I could do it in English, so I became a community disaster education presenter. This position led to my joining the Red Cross as a paid employee managing its Disaster Education Program, as well as multiple disaster response positions. I worked there for three years, and then moved to the Bellevue Fire Department's Emergency Preparedness Division where I also work in disaster education/risk communication.

How did you enter this profession?

My entry into disaster education, which is a subset of emergency management, came from learning skills through volunteering. When I joined the Red Cross as a volunteer interpreter, the people there explained that I would get email messages with interpreting opportunities that I could accept or decline at will. I proposed that I help them more than that, so they agreed to let me come in and work three days a week. In that period, I did a lot of day-to-day over-the-phone interpreting, but I also got a chance to use my computer skills to create various databases and try to show that I was useful. I was asked to interpret for the disaster education classes, and so I took the training to be a community disaster educator.

Once I came on as staff, the Red Cross provided me disaster response training. It helped that large storms kept crashing through our region, so I got a lot of hands-on experience very quickly. After a year, I joined the Disaster Services Human Resources (DSHR) system, which made me eligible to be sent to help with disaster responses around the country. The DSHR system is a great way to get real-world experience in disaster response. Even though I've moved to the Bellevue Fire Department, I am still a DSHR member and, therefore, still eligible to be sent around the country to help.

What are some of the things you do on a typical day?

When there is no situation taking place that might turn into a disaster, I work to devise programs that will encourage people to take actions to reduce their risks from disasters. Disasters impact some groups more than others. Some groups predictably end up the same or better than before the disaster, and some are pushed back—so a lot of the social schisms we see today are related to the cycle of disasters. Most harm from disasters is avoidable, so finding ways to reduce their impact has the potential for reducing the schisms. My job is finding ways to help people recognize that by identifying and reducing the bad things that can happen in their lives, it opens the way for more good things to happen. It's such a simple concept, and easily provable, but very difficult to make people see due to our subconscious optimism bias.

What do you like the most about this career?

During the aftermath of Hurricane Katrina, I kept thinking to myself, "I wish I was able to help." Since then, when something happens, I do help. The accomplishment I am most proud of has been working to find opportunities to empower individuals who face hurdle after hurdle during nondisaster times, and even more so during disasters, to find ways to increase their choices and options.

What are some of the challenges about this career?

It isn't a 9-to-5 job. Disaster education means meeting people when they have time to meet—that often means evenings and weekends. When there is a disaster, you have to be able to drop things on short notice, and then pick up where you leave off when it has passed. It can be exhausting, mentally and physically.

What skills, education/training, abilities, values, or personality are needed to succeed in this field?

The field depends on individuals who can effectively communicate and encourage changes in behaviors. I can see the future of the field being transformed by the entry of people who understand teaching, but also marketing and communications. There

(continued)

(continued)

is a great need for good designers: both people who understand how design can encourage specific behavior (user experience and interface design) and people who are experts in the visualization of data (infographics).

The Red Cross provides free training for their community disaster educators. Many communities also have Community Emergency Response Teams (CERT) that provide training. There are numerous AmeriCorps program opportunities in emergency management and risk communication.

Protective Services: Law Enforcement, Corrections, and Fire Protection

Law and order are the backbone of a civil society. People depend on police officers, corrections officers, and firefighters to protect their lives and property. The following sections highlight information about careers in this area.

Law Enforcement and Crime Prevention

Brave individuals willing to prevent, halt, and investigate crimes are in constant demand. There are opportunities at the federal, state, and local levels.

The federal government employs about 7 percent of law enforcement officers. The Federal Law Enforcement Training Center of the Department of Homeland Security trains these officers, who then may work in any number of federal agencies.

The Department of Justice includes a number of law enforcement agencies, such as the following:

- The Federal Bureau of Investigation combats terrorism, cybercrime, public corruption, organized crime, civil rights violations, and white-collar crime.
- The U.S. Marshals Service apprehends fugitives, protects federal judges and courts, and safeguards witnesses.
- Community Oriented Policing Services (COPS) provides grants and resources to state and local community policing initiatives.
- The Bureau of Alcohol, Tobacco, Firearms, and Explosives investigates arson, bombings, and illegal trafficking in weapons.
- The Drug Enforcement Administration works to prevent the manufacture, distribution, and sales of illegal controlled substances in the United States.
- The Office of Justice Programs collects information on crime and crime prevention and distributes funds to local programs for victim assistance, youth violence prevention, and more.

Many other federal agencies also have law enforcement units, including the USDA and USDA Forest Service, the Department of Commerce, the Department of Defense, the Department of Energy, the Food and Drug Administration, numerous agencies within the Department of Homeland Security, the Department of Treasury (including the IRS's Criminal Investigation Division and Financial Crimes Enforcement Network), the Department of State's Diplomatic Security Service, and the Department of the Interior (which includes the National Park Police and Fish and Wildlife Service law enforcement).

About 11 percent of police and detectives are employed at the state level to enforce state laws. The most visible positions are the State Highway Patrols, which conduct vehicle violation enforcement and intervene in highway accidents, but a state police force has many other aspects. Divisions of a state police force can include the following:

- A Commercial Vehicle Enforcement Division
- Criminal investigations, including investigating major crimes, working on drug enforcement, and handling criminal intelligence
- Specialty fields, such as explosives disposal, emergency response, drug trafficking interdiction, and hostage negotiators
- Support divisions, including human resources, data collection, and emergency and other communications
- Laboratories, including evidence tracking, photography, DNA exams, forensic document investigation, and fingerprint and firearms identification
- Records management

States also may have a Homeland Security Bureau.

Local governments employ about 79 percent of police and detectives. A large number of uniformed police officers work a "beat," or geographic area, while others focus on auto theft, drug trafficking, or child safety. Police departments collaborate with local agencies and community-based councils and organizations. Local counties also have sheriff's offices that provide law enforcement services for their jurisdictions and offer services for those areas that are not covered by a city police department. Universities and colleges, as well as school districts and transportation systems, often also employ their own police force or security service.

Nonprofit organizations are also involved in educating the public to help prevent crime. Organizations with this mission include the National Center for Missing and Exploited Children, National Child Safety Council, National Crime Prevention Council, Mothers Against Drunk Driving, and youth and domestic violence prevention programs. Other nonprofit organizations support law enforcement and justice professions, such as the International Association of Chiefs of Police and the New York City Police Foundation.

Corrections

At the federal level, agencies that handle federal offenders and prisoners include the Federal Bureau of Prisons and the U.S. Parole Commission. State Departments of Correction keep offenders from the public and reduce recidivism by providing re-entry programs to help ex-offenders reintegrate into society after their release. Some cities also have a Department of Corrections that houses sentenced inmates and detainees who are facing trial.

Many nonprofits work with the offender population as well. Halfway houses and rehabilitation programs, for example, support ex-offenders. Inmate support organizations, such as Prison Fellowship Ministries, work with those still in prison. Some organizations also seek to provide alternatives to incarceration for lower-risk individuals.

Fire Protection and Safety

About 90 percent of individuals who work in fire safety work for local governments. A large number of individuals also volunteer as firefighters (about 71 percent of fire companies were staffed entirely by volunteer firefighters in 2005). States may also have a fire marshal and a Fire Protection Bureau. To prevent accidents, state officials also help conduct public safety education programs and inspections of facilities to ensure fire and other safety measures are in place.

Protective Services Jobs

In addition to the jobs listed in the following sections, a large number of "civilian" professions are needed to support the important work of police, corrections, and fire departments. These range from communications workers who work in dispatch to support roles in human resources and information technology. There are also opportunities for counselors, caseworkers, psychiatric professionals, medical professionals, institutional teachers for youth and juvenile detention facilities, facilities managers, laboratory technicians, chaplains, and librarians.

Police Officers, Detectives, and Special Agents

Law enforcement positions require a high level of personal integrity, the ability to make quick decisions under pressure, and the ability to write meticulous and accurate reports to be used to investigate violations and as a basis for courtroom testimony. Many positions also require excellent physical fitness and agility. Police work can be dangerous, requiring confrontations with threatening individuals and involvement in life-threatening situations. Shift work, including nights or weekends, is common because crimes and accidents occur at any time of the day or night. Many law enforcement officers are also expected to be armed and ready to exercise their authority, whether they are on or off duty.

Hiring for these positions is often conducted through a formal civil service system requiring examinations. Most positions require a high school degree; many require one or two years of college or a college degree. Prior military service is looked upon very favorably. Most federal positions require a college degree, and some have additional requirements such as relevant experience, fluency in a foreign language, or a law degree. Extensive background checks are also usually conducted, which can include drug testing, polygraph examinations, personality tests, and psychological interviews. (For more information on the federal hiring process and security checks, refer to Chapter 11.)

Some federal law enforcement positions are particularly competitive and have a special, extremely rigorous, hiring process. For example, to apply to be a special agent with the FBI, you have to be between 23 and 36 years old and in excellent physical condition. You also need to have a college degree and three years of experience. If you meet these criteria, you can start the process:

1. Complete an online application.
2. Take the Phase I written, multiple-choice test that covers initiative, motivation, critical thinking, logical reasoning, and situational judgment.
3. Complete Phase II testing, which includes a structured interview and written exercise.

If you pass these tests, you will receive a conditional letter of appointment and must take a physical fitness test and pass an extremely in-depth background check, in which nearly everyone you have worked for or lived with may be interviewed about your character. The background check also includes a polygraph exam, credit check, arrest records, drug test, and verification of education.

Once hired, law enforcement candidates go through significant training programs in law, civil rights, investigation, first aid, self-defense, and emergency response. As in the military, police forces have specific ranks (corporal, sergeant, lieutenant, captain), which candidates can pursue after a certain amount of time with good on-the-job performance and success in written and other exams.

Uniformed officers are normally assigned to a regular patrol. Included in their activities are responding to calls for service, rendering first aid to injured citizens, assisting with problems that are not necessarily of a law enforcement nature, enforcing motor vehicle traffic rules, and pursuing criminal offenders. Community policing also requires officers to build relationships with community members to enlist their support in preventing crime. Some officers specialize in certain areas, such as forensic investigation or fingerprint identification, or are part of a special unit, such as a mounted or canine unit. There were 661,500 police officers in the United States in 2008. Median earnings for police officers were $51,410 in 2008; for supervisors, the median was $75,490. Job growth is average.

Detectives investigate major criminal offenses by gathering evidence, facts, and other information and interviewing witnesses, victims, and suspects to solve assigned cases. There were 112,200 detectives and investigators in the U.S. in 2008. Median earnings in 2008 were about $60,910. The job is expected to grow faster than average.

Many officers also receive additional pay due to the amount of overtime they work. Pension plans can be excellent, allowing officers to retire after 25 or 30 years of service.

PROFILE: RONALD S. NEUBAUER

Executive Director, Eastern Missouri Law Enforcement Training Center

What is your career background?

I am currently executive director of the Eastern Missouri Law Enforcement Training Center, where I manage a full-time law enforcement training center to include police recruit training, veteran police officer continuing education, and county licensing/training for security guards. Prior to my current role, I was a program manager for the U.S. Transportation Security Administration, where I assisted in the stand-up of a new federal agency and in the coordination of federalizing the airport screening workforce. I was also the chief of police for the city of St. Peters, Missouri.

How did you get into this career?

In college, I came into contact with a number of individuals in the Marine Corps, and I was convinced that it was the life I was looking for. I believed in personal discipline, commitment to the public, and service to others. It seemed a natural fit to become a Marine. I received my officer's commission right out of college. During my first tour in Vietnam, I was part of the military police units and that is where I was introduced to law enforcement, where I remained for 17 years. Most of my "training" was on the job.

When I retired from active military service, I became a chief of police in Palm Beach Gardens, Florida. Later I moved to St. Peters, Missouri to serve as the chief of police for 14 years. While there, I was elected to vice president of the International Association of Chiefs of Police. I also served as its president. I currently serve as the executive director of the Eastern Missouri Police Academy.

What is your typical day?

Typically, my day begins around 6 a.m. I clear out my email messages and attend to routine paper work. I coordinate with my assistant who is responsible for the basic training of the recruits. We discuss the day's activities for the recruit classes and any problems he may have encountered. Most every day I review continuing education classes we present to working police officers to ensure that they meet the state's training requirements. I also negotiate contracts with policing agencies to gain their membership to the academy. I teach classes to the recruits once each week. I am responsible for the financial and personnel matters relative to the academy, and each day presents challenges in each area.

What do you like best about your career?

I have various things that I liked about each of my careers. My Marine Corps time was punctuated by my successful tour in combat. Years afterward I was contacted by six of the Marines I had led during my first of two tours in Vietnam. They each told me that they were thankful that I had been their lieutenant in Vietnam because they knew that they returned home because of me. It was humbling to hear them tell me that.

One accomplishment when I was chief of police that stands out is becoming the president of the International Association of Chiefs of Police. This organization represents more than 80 countries, with a membership of 20,000 people.

The one thing that I love most about my present position is watching the positive changes in the lives of the recruits. I watch them grow from being fairly self-centered individuals into well-disciplined, selfless, giving people. The one thing that has followed me throughout my working career is the ability to help others whether I was charged with the responsibility of their well-being or not.

What are some of your career challenges?

As a civilian chief of police, the two areas of conflict were working with elected officials and responding to citizens' concerns and complaints. In each case, there had to be a balance between satisfying elected officials and citizens and remaining true to the calling of police service. I always took a neutral stance and gathered all the facts before passing judgment. In those cases where a police officer was wrong, I would either use the moment as a training situation (when the infraction was not severe) or institute discipline when indicated. In those cases where the officer was correct in his or her judgment, I would stand as a shield from others so that the officer could do his or her job without interference.

As an academy director, my challenge is to ensure that only those individuals who are truly qualified are allowed to enter the academy. I then must ensure that those who graduate to become police officers truly believe in the service aspect of the police service.

(continued)

(continued)

What skills and qualities are needed for this field?

Entry into police service has to be a calling, something that you want for yourself. Becoming a police officer is not something you do, it is who you are. You are required to possess a high sense of service to others, integrity that is above reproach, commitment to doing the right thing even when no one is looking, a desire to help others in their time of need, and both physical and mental courage to face the challenges of the profession. You must be "other" oriented and selfless.

You must have exceptional ability to communicate both orally and in writing. A minimum of a high school education is required; college work is preferred. Although criminal justice classes are nice, they are not needed to be successful in police work. You cannot have a criminal record, and a bad driving record is a quick eliminator to entry. Poor conduct will severely restrict your ability to obtain employment in law enforcement.

Youth can gain experience and knowledge of the field by joining law enforcement exploration programs. Others can attend a civilian police academy to gain insight into the profession.

Corrections Officers

Currently there are approximately 1.5 million inmates in state and federal prisons and 700,000 in local jails. Corrections officers maintain security in prisons and jails and are responsible for the care, control, custody, job training, and work performance of inmates. Corrections officers conduct searches to detect contraband, write reports, issue orders, and make recommendations for prisoners' psychiatric and medical treatments. Like police and firefighters, their work is highly physical and risky, and shift work is common.

About 518,200 corrections officers were employed in the United States, as of 2008. Most were employed in state and local facilities. Median earnings were $38,380; supervisors earned a median of $57,380. The projected job growth is average.

Probation and Parole Officers and Correctional Treatment Specialists

Probation and parole officers work with individuals who either have served a sentence in prison or jail or who have been sentenced to probation rather than incarceration. Their role is to monitor and supervise offenders to prevent them from committing further crimes and to help individuals receive job training or substance abuse treatment. Correctional treatment specialists serve as case workers to individuals in the community.

There were 103,400 probation and parole officers in 2008, with median earnings of $45,910. Job growth is projected to be faster than average.

Firefighters

To become a firefighter, a candidate typically must pass written and physical exams. Typically, a high school education is required, though additional training may be required for certain positions. For example, firefighters are usually required to be certified as emergency medical technicians. After being hired, firefighters receive extensive training. Many firefighters work long hours, and shift work is common in order to provide 24-hour protection.

About 365,600 people worked in firefighting occupations in 2008. Of these, most were firefighters; a smaller number were inspectors, investigators, or forest fire inspectors and prevention specialists. Median earnings were about $44,260, and supervisors earned about $67,440. Job growth in this field is faster than average, but competition for firefighting positions can be strong.

Judicial and Legal Professions

The administration of justice and interpretation of laws are essential components of civil society. Federal courts include those charged with interpreting the law, such as the Supreme Court, as well as those that deal with deciding whether individuals or organizations have violated laws (such as the U.S. Tax Court, U.S. Court of International Trade, and U.S. Bankruptcy Courts). States also have supreme courts, as well as trial courts, courts of appeals, and other divisions and commissions (such as commissions on children in foster care, gender and justice commissions, and sentencing guidelines commissions). Municipal courts in cities tend to focus on traffic tickets and misdemeanors. Municipal judges also officiate at marriage ceremonies.

Employment within the judicial system includes court administrators, court reporters, clerks, interpreters, and bailiffs or security providers. Positions exist at local, state, and federal courts.

Of course, lawyers are the most well-known profession in the judicial system. (There were about 759,200 lawyers in the United States as of 2008.) Although most lawyers work in private practice or for corporations, a significant number work for government or the nonprofit sector. The U.S. Department of Justice, under the Attorney General, employs thousands of lawyers to pursue federal cases. Many other parts of the federal government employ lawyers as well. For example, the IRS employs attorneys to prosecute people and companies who owe the government taxes.

Governments also provide public defenders to individuals who cannot pay for an attorney to defend them in a case. Many nonprofits, such as the Legal Aid Society and Legal Services Corporation, also provide legal services to those who cannot afford representation. Organizations such as the Northwest Justice Project, Southern

Poverty Law Center, and National Consumer Law Center work in public interest law. (Civil rights is another related area of the law, which is covered in Chapter 4. International human rights is discussed in Chapter 7.)

Of those lawyers employed by government, the majority worked for local governments. Median salaries ranged from $78,540 for those who worked for state government, $82,590 for local government, $116,550 for legal services, and $126,080 for federal government. A median salary for a recent law school graduate working for the government was about $50,000 (2007 data). Job growth is average in the legal profession, but there is a lot of competition.

References and Resources

For more information on the topics in this chapter, refer to the following sources.

Intelligence and National/International Security

U.S. Intelligence Community, www.intelligence.gov

Defense and Military

Department of Defense, www.defense.gov
Department of Defense's Civilian Personnel Management Service, www.cpms.osd.mil
Today's Military, www.todaysmilitary.com

Disaster Recovery and Emergency Preparedness

Coalition of Organizations for Disaster Education, www.redcross.org/disaster/disasterguide
Community Emergency Response Teams (CERT), www.citizencorps.gov/cert
Emergency Management Institute, http://training.fema.gov
International Association of Emergency Managers, www.iaem.com
National Emergency Management Association, www.nemaweb.org

Protective Services

American Correctional Association, www.aca.org
American Jail Association, www.corrections.com/aja
American Probation and Parole Association, www.appa-net.org
Commission on Accreditation of Law Enforcement Agencies, www.calea.org
Federal Bureau of Investigation, http://fbijobs.gov
International Association of Fire Fighters, www.iaff.org
Koletar, Joseph; *The FBI Career Guide: Inside Information on Getting Chosen for and Succeeding in One of the Toughest, Most Prestigious Jobs in the World* (AMACOM, 2006)
National Fire Academy, www.usfa.dhs.gov/nfa
National Sheriffs' Association, www.sheriffs.org

Judicial and Legal Professions

Equal Justice Works, www.equaljusticeworks.org
National Center for State Courts, www.ncsc.org

CHAPTER 9

Working with Arts, Culture, and Religion

"As soon as religion becomes prosaic or perfunctory, art appears somewhere else." —Susanne K. Langer

Arts and religion are two of the profound ways humanity expresses itself. What both have in common is that they are nearly entirely dominated by the nonprofit sector—government is slightly involved with both, but it does not conduct the work of either. If you are a creative or spiritual person, these fields may be the way you can nourish your own soul while inspiring others.

Arts and Culture

"Art is the soul of a people." —Romare Bearden

Music, drama, visual arts, and writing are what makes many communities great. Arts and culture include the performing arts (music, theater, opera, dance), visual arts (painting, photography), cultural institutions (museums, historical societies), and some recreation and leisure activities. Though government has some arts-related areas, the real action in the arts is in the nonprofit world.

In the United States, the predominant government role in the arts is funding. At the federal level, this task is handled through the National Endowment for the Arts (NEA), which provided over $111 million in 2007 to arts organizations in all 50 states, including rural areas, military bases, and inner cities, through partnerships with state arts agencies and regional arts organizations. It also provides educational services, such as teaching materials to help educators teach Shakespeare and institutes to teach journalists how to cover the arts, and bestows the nation's highest arts award, the National Medal of Arts. In addition, the Corporation for Public Broadcasting is a not-for-profit organization established by an act of Congress and primarily funded by the federal government. It provided more than $523 million to public radio and TV stations in 2007.

Other federal agencies in this area include the National Endowment for the Humanities, which focuses on improving the teaching of languages, literature, history, arts criticism, and more. The Smithsonian Institution includes 19 museums (and 156 affiliate museums), such as the American Indian Museum and African Art Museum. The President's Committee on the Arts and Humanities, Indian Arts and Crafts Board (part of the Department of the Interior), and the U.S. Commission of Fine Arts have missions related to arts and culture as well.

Each state also has a state arts agency, sometimes called an Arts Board or Arts Commission, that funds arts organizations, individual artists, and arts projects in schools. Cities also often have an Arts Commission or Arts and Cultural Affairs Department that provides funding to local arts organizations and individual artists, arts educational programs, and public art projects. The size of such departments varies tremendously. For example, Seattle's Office of Arts and Cultural Affairs had a budget of $8 million in 2008, while the budget for the City of New York's Department of Cultural Affairs was $152 million in 2009.

The actual production of arts and culture in the United States is accomplished by nonprofit groups and corporations. Opera companies, museums, community theatres, dance companies, symphonies, and arts festivals are nearly all nonprofit organizations. There are also nonprofit film companies and radio stations, choral groups, bands and ensembles, schools of performing arts, literary magazines and small publishers, artists' retreats, and arts appreciation societies. In addition to arts organizations, public radio and television provide music, news, educational, and cultural programs.

There is a broad array and diversity of arts organizations. For example, the United States has more than 1,890 professional theatres and 110 opera companies (as of 2006). Major arts nonprofits manage budgets in the hundreds of millions—the Metropolitan Museum of Art's budget was more than $310 million in 2008, and the Metropolitan Opera's budget was $250 million in 2007. However, many arts organizations, such as small acting troupes and community music venues, are entirely volunteer-run or even unincorporated.

Of course, certain art forms easily make a profit, such as rock and hip-hop concerts or even major Broadway productions and movies, but for many others, private donations and grants cover much of the cost of production. Although some funding for the arts does come from government, a larger percentage comes from private donations (from patrons of the arts) and ticket sales.

Arts and Culture Jobs

Nearly every arts organization, as a nonprofit, has positions that are typical to nonprofits, such as fundraising and donor relations, communications, finance, human resources, IT, and administration. Larger ones might have two high-level individuals who lead the organization: an artistic administrator or director, who makes some of the decisions about what kinds of performances or collections to produce, and an administrative director, who focuses on keeping the organization running.

Artists or performers themselves are usually freelancers who audition or are represented by agents who negotiate contracts for them and are often paid only for their performances. Of all the careers in the arts, the actual performing artists are in the most competitive position. Years of artistic training are required, as well as top-level talent and tremendous persistence.

Most artists are not considered staff of the organization, though musicians in professional symphonies are usually members of unions who are paid a set wage for each rehearsal or performance. Yet many working musicians (who totaled 186,400 as of 2008) also hold other jobs to supplement their music income. Music directors (of which there were 53,600 in 2008) earn a median of $41,270 per year.

Unique jobs in the arts include artist management, program management, production (stage management, production assistants, stage design and construction, makeup, costume design and production, lighting, and even pyrotechnicians!), or music library work. For example, there were 7,940 set designers in 2008, earning a median of $48,660 per year, with employment expected to grow faster than average; and there were 5,120 costume attendants. Other positions include arts education and outreach, ticket sales, security, ushering, and house management.

Visual arts collections also have some of the typical structure of a nonprofit, with a development or membership department and education programs. They also have curatorial staff as well as libraries and archives. There were 11,100 museum technicians and conservators in 2008, earning a median of $36,660 and with much faster than average job growth. About 11,700 people worked as curators, earning a median of $47,220, with job growth much faster than average.

A strong passion for, and appreciation of, the arts, as well as an arts education related to the field you are pursuing are highly valued in most arts positions. Some positions, especially related to more technical fields such as set or lighting design, require more hands-on apprenticeships. Those individuals who are more interested in the administration of arts organizations might pursue a master's degree in arts administration, theatre administration, music business, museum studies, or cultural production. Such degrees focus on building skills to strengthen arts organizations. Their curriculum may cover areas such as law and the arts, arts education, financial management of arts organizations, fundraising and development, and art theory.

PROFILE: JONATHAN DEAN

Author of English Captions and Director of Public Programs and Media, Seattle Opera (Photo by Alan Alabastro)

What is your brief career history?

I always found opera interesting—I loved listening to the singing and following a story told through music, and I loved learning about the cultures and the languages and the source literature and the history. In high school, I also figured out that I was pretty good at foreign languages: I studied French in school and German on the side. I went to college without any real career plan, hoping I could figure out what I found interesting and what I was good at and praying those subjects would intersect.

In college, I got lots of experience acting (badly), playing music (subprofessionally), and writing (reviews and criticism and original fiction and drama). One summer, when my friends were all auditioning for summer-stock theater, I applied for an internship at an opera house instead. I spent that summer in the box office, selling tickets, talking opera with high-maintenance patrons, going to every performance, and hanging out backstage as much as possible.

Once I had my foot in the door and saw how the company functioned, I knew exactly what I wanted to do: I belonged in a supertitles booth, translating opera librettos so patrons could read along during performances. I talked my way into the booth at the company where I was an intern and asked the man in charge for career guidance. He gave me a reality check and said it was hard to make a living doing titles, but that I might go far in opera education. So upon graduating college, I applied to the education departments of all the leading opera companies in America.

I came to Seattle for an unpaid internship, because it sounded like it would be a fun summer for a 21-year-old. Honestly, I never expected to be here now, almost 15 years later. When I got to Seattle, I noticed right away that the guy who had the job I wanted (calling titles in the supertitles booth) was unlikely to stay for very long. I found a way to apprentice with him while interning in another department. I had no idea, at the time, how tricky it was to pull this maneuver off, diplomatically.

Anyways, he quit. I was hired, with extremely minor responsibilities and compensation, and immediately set out to go above and beyond, to bring everything I had to the job. I studied Italian in night school (by now I was fluent in French and German). I took an unpaid break to wander around Europe learning more, firsthand, about opera and the cultures that produced them; and I got loads of experience talking about opera to groups of students and adult opera patrons.

My employers knew my goal was to write my own translations. At the time, they were renting them from one of the two companies who supplied most of the opera houses in America. I took over when there was an upgrade in technology: I showed my employer how new technology made it much more cost- and time-effective to write the translations in house, thus maintaining closer control over our artistic product. Within a year, the company was hiring me to write original translations of every opera produced in Italian, German, or French.

My current position evolved out of that position. My work has always been about teaching and writing, two strengths that I've continued to develop.

What are some of the things you do on a typical day?

It's all over the map. I've been a truck driver, a photographer, and a game show host. I've given lectures for hundreds of elite patrons, which have to stand up to academic scrutiny, and used opera in prison therapy programs to get convicts talking about their feelings. A typical day for me includes both introvert time (sitting alone with an opera score; translating; reading; studying; writing; or editing text, audio, video, or PowerPoint shows on the computer) and extrovert time (working on projects with colleagues, teaching or lecturing, attending auditions and performances).

What do you like the most about this career?

Opera is still what I like most about my career. If I didn't feel the way I do about opera, I couldn't possibly do my job. The work is predicated on opera's value, and my need to break down the barriers that prevent people from enjoying this wonderful art form. My proudest accomplishment is a program I devised, over the course of about 10 years, that involves elementary school students as performers and audience in productions of (my adaptations of) Wagner's *Ring*.

What are some of the challenges about this career?

The arts are subjective, so there's no consensus possible on whether a given work of art is any good or whether people should understand and/or appreciate it. You better have confidence in your own taste.

There's no money in arts education and very little in the arts in general, so you must be motivated by something else. Most of the people I know who do this kind of work are motivated by enthusiasm and love for the arts, by the desire to belong and be part of a team, and by simple ego. Sometimes this mixed bag of complicated motivations causes problems when you are trying to assemble a successful team.

(continued)

(continued)

Also, the onwards rush of technology makes it harder to reach the audience: They have shorter attention spans and more competing options for what to do with their spare time. They're used to constant interaction, instead of the sustained, high-energy reception called for by the arts.

What skills, values, or personality are needed to succeed in this field?

As for the specifics of my particular job, I have studied French, German, Italian, and, most thoroughly, English (complete with Old English and Middle English). I've played music for 20 years and have studied music history, music theory, analysis, and aesthetics. I've studied plenty of history, enough to understand the basics of the time and place that created each of the works of art I teach. Although I'm hardly a computer expert, I'm not shy around computers and have learned basic music, photo, audio, and video engineering skills and have taught several online classes and kept several blogs. And don't underestimate the cumulative effect of on-the-job training. The quirks of my personality that play into my job include being slightly obsessive, wanting to know everything, being high-energy, brimming with contagious enthusiasm for my subject, and being both pedantic and flamboyant.

Any other advice for people who want to enter this field or arts in general?

Go to arts events, good, bad, and mediocre. Go to everything! Hear concerts, see plays, watch ballets, check out galleries and art museums, and pay attention, because everything is connected.

Religion

"Religion in its humility restores man to his only dignity, the courage to live by grace." —George Santayana

Religious and faith-based organizations are a huge part of American society. According to the National Council of Churches USA's *2009 Yearbook of American and Canadian Churches*, there were more than 326,762 different churches in the United States—and this number does not include the thousands of synagogues, temples, mosques, and other religious institutions. Religious organizations account for about 20 percent of all nonprofits in the United States.

In addition to religious institutions such as churches or temples, thousands of nonprofit organizations are "faith-based." For example, the Salvation Army, which provides numerous social services, describes itself as "an international movement and an evangelical part of the universal Christian Church." Similarly, many of the largest international relief and development organizations, such as World Vision and Catholic Relief Services, are faith-based. Some faith-based nonprofits require all employees to sign a faith agreement stating their religious affiliation; others have no such requirement.

> **NOTE**
> Due to the separation of church and state in the United States, by definition a religious organization is nongovernmental. However, government may contract with "faith-based" organizations to provide social and human services.

For the most part, individuals who work in faith-based organizations fill a host of roles that are similar to those found in other nonprofit organizations. These include fundraising, membership support, education, administration, and facilities management.

One job, however, is unique to the religious field, and that is the clergy. Clergy and ministry workers perform spiritual functions for religious organizations, ranging from providing moral guidance to members, leading religious services, visiting people in hospitals or prisons, and administering religious ceremonies. Advanced training, such as a master's-level degree, is usually needed. There were about 42,040 clergy in 2008, with median salaries of about $45,440. This career is expected to grow faster than average.

> **NOTE**
> Many people with a background in religious studies go on to work in other fields, such as social services, community affairs, and many of the other "jobs that matter" listed in this book.

PROFILE: HOPE JOHNSON

Minister, Unitarian Universalist Congregation of Central Nassau, New York

What is your brief career history?

My sister and I had a travel agency and special event planning business. We also were both involved in our congregation, Community Church of New York. At some point, we realized our volunteer work was more interesting and exciting—we were more passionate about it—than our business.

When I was called to ministry, it was a little bit out of my control, but I felt I had to do it. I went into the field

(continued)

(continued)

kicking and screaming. The last thing I wanted to admit was that I was involved in organized religion. But I realized that my gifts and talents were in helping and caring for people so that they can realize their dreams. It was much like the travel and special event planning industry in that you pay attention to people and what their hopes and dreams are and help them to get there.

To become a minister in the Unitarian Universalist Church, I had to get a Master of Divinity. I also completed practical training as an intern minister and clinical pastoral education (CPE). I did my CPE training in the Mt. Sinai organ transplantation unit—it was an amazing experience. I learned how to minister to people who needed me, to give up my control. It was hard, but I did it, and it took me four or five years.

It is such an incredible privilege to be involved in people's lives. Unitarian Universalists have a breadth and diversity of individual beliefs, guided by principles and shared values. When I am sitting at the bedside of someone who has different beliefs than I do, I have to let the spirit work through me so I can give comfort to that person.

What is your typical day like?

I might be visiting the sick in a hospital, stopping at the home of someone who's dying, doing a baby dedication, or officiating a wedding. Or I might be doing what I do most, which is listening to people as they talk about what's going on, what's troubling them. More than half of my job is listening. When I was a newer minister, it was, "Oh, I can fix this, I know what to do." As the years go by, you learn that the job is to listen and to let people uncover their own answers.

I'm one of the few ministers where every member of the congregation can find me 24/7. They all have my cell number, and they can find me when they need me. They have never abused the situation, and this is my third congregation. I'm there any time people need me. Day or night, I'm there.

What are some of the challenges of this field?

A congregational setting is a microcosm of regular life. For example, the Sunday service has a part called Joys and Sorrows. It's not my favorite part, but the congregation loves it. One of the challenges I face, I know it sounds like pity, but some people have something to share every Sunday. Some of the stuff is trite; sometimes it's political. My challenge is to make space for people with real sorrow they need to share.

Another challenge is that in this tradition, I am employed as a member of staff. I am the spiritual leader, but the board is my boss. Usually, we see eye-to-eye, but if we don't see eye-to-eye, how do I as a spiritual leader interfere with the day-to-day workings of the congregation? The way I deal with it is that I'm a team player. The president and board and I work well together. Sometimes we agree to disagree, but this is rare.

What personality or qualities are needed for this profession?

You have to love the people you serve. You have to want to serve and be able to focus on the people you're serving. You can't be busy doing your nails or reading a book; you have to drop everything and be present to the need.

The skills needed include having a deep faith in the people you serve and your ability to bring out the best in people. You must love people inherently. Not just some people, but all people. You must have very clear values, but know that there are other values that are as valuable as yours.

Your personality must be upbeat. You can't be a walking dirge. You have to give people hope and faith, empower them, and have a little fun. You have to have the ability to laugh and move on.

If you want to enter this field, you have to know that you are responding to a call. You can't do it as theatre or performance—you will burn out. It has to come from deep within.

What is your favorite accomplishment?

As a minister of color, a black minister, I remember saying to the credentialing body that I hope they see in me a wonderful minister who happens to be of color. The reason I say that is that my denomination is overwhelming white. But this denomination is my plane, so I belong here, and I'm not moving.

One of the proudest accomplishments is encouraging my little town on Long Island to see beyond the neighborhood. So the congregation and I have reached out—we had a youth march for Darfur. When I got there, the town had never heard of Darfur or fair trade anything. It was wonderful to me that my congregation could bring this awareness. This past June, we celebrated Juneteenth, and this year we're doing Día de los Muertos. So the congregation and I are bringing into Garden City a recognition that we all are part of a pluralistic and multicultural world.

References and Resources

For more information on the topics presented in this chapter, refer to the following sources.

Arts and Culture

American Association of Museums, www.aam-us.org
Association of Arts Administration Educators, www.artsadministration.org
International Society for the Performing Arts, www.ispa.org
National Endowment for the Arts, State and Regional Partners, www.arts.gov/partner/state/SAA_RAO_list.html
State and Local Government on the Net, State Art Sites, www.statelocalgov.net/50states-arts.cfm

Religion

American Association of Pastoral Counselors, https://aapc.org
Association of Professional Chaplains, www.professionalchaplains.org

CHAPTER 10

Preparing for a Public Service Job Search: Resumes and Cover Letters

"The first duty of a human being is to assume the right functional relationship to society—more briefly, to find your real job, and do it."
—Charlotte Perkins Gilman

When you are job searching or switching careers, you need to perform certain tasks. Here is an overview of the steps involved:

1. Assess yourself. Look at your skills, interests, and values. Write out accomplishment stories.
2. Research the field.
3. Create a resume and cover letter.
4. Get organized for the search.
5. Identify and apply for opportunities.
6. Interview.
7. Evaluate and negotiate offers.

Although these steps take you through the tasks one after the other, the job search process—or career transformation process—is really a circular one. You will want to revisit each step from time to time. The rest of this chapter deals with the first three steps. Chapter 11 deals with steps four and five. The last two steps are handled in Chapter 12.

Assess Yourself

Finding a job is much easier when you know what you are looking for and where to look. Revisit the exercises in Chapter 1 from time to time as you proceed with your job search to help identify whether your values or interests have changed and to use feedback from your search to determine whether you need to develop a new skill.

What is especially important at this stage is to come up with at least five or six "problem-action-result" stories (see Chapter 1) that illustrate your skills and strengths and identify what you have to offer. It is also important to have a target job description and/or list of your target organizations in mind so that you can research the field.

Research the Field

Especially if you are entering a new career field, you will need to absorb the language, culture, and context you are getting into. Reading Chapters 3 to 9, and then following up with a library or online search to learn more about the organizations mentioned, is a good first step. Other suggestions for research are mentioned in Chapter 1.

While researching the field, you will likely begin to identify actionable job leads. In fact, one of the main research techniques for learning about a new career field, informational interviewing, counts as both a research technique and a job search technique (informational interviewing is covered in Chapter 11).

Develop a Resume

In order to act on the job leads you will be identifying, you will need to have a good resume ready. A resume is a prerequisite for nearly all job applications. However, you should not expect your resume to get you a job—it only will help you get an interview. To have the best chance at getting you an interview, your resume should be letter-perfect, easy to read, logically and consistently formatted, and tailored for your new career (you can use feedback from people in your network to best tailor it). Keep in mind, however, that just because a resume is well written doesn't mean that it will be read. You may improve your resume's chances of being read by making connections within organizations you are targeting and sending it to those people.

In the following sections, I outline the main parts of a resume and the type of information you should include. I also explain how to write good resume content and format your resume in order to make it appealing. Answers to frequently asked questions about resumes, resume tips for new graduates and for career changers, and several resume examples are provided as well. This information is based on my years of experience reviewing resumes, but there are always exceptions to the rules I present. Getting feedback on your resume from many people in the field will help you decide what will work best for you.

Resume Sections

The following sections describe the essential components of the resume. These sections do not have to go in exactly the order presented here, though contact information should go first, followed by a profile, summary, or objective, if you use one. The order in which you arrange the other sections will depend on your specific situation.

NOTE

> Although the most common type of resume is the reverse chronological version discussed in this section, there are several exceptions. Federal resumes, international resumes, and some state government resumes often require more detail, can be much longer, and can be written in a paragraph or narrative style rather than with bullet points. International resumes also vary by the country you are going to work in. The academic curriculum vita can also be much lengthier than a standard resume, going on for as many pages as you have publications. Chapter 11 provides more detail on the federal resume format and state hiring, and Chapter 7 touches on international job search tips.

Name and Contact Information

This section is the most important part of your whole resume. If employers cannot get in touch with you—quickly—they will not interview you. Make sure you are easily reachable by phone and email and that you return all calls and email messages promptly. Also, don't have a silly voice mail greeting or an inappropriate or cutesy email address. Lastly, check your email spam folder regularly during the job search process.

Profile or Summary

This optional section of the resume comes right after contact information. I suggest using a profile when there are particular skills, education, or experience that might end up being listed toward the end of the resume (perhaps because that is where they fit chronologically), but would be very important to highlight from the employer's perspective. Also, if you have quite a bit of experience, a summary gives you a concise, compelling way to showcase that fact.

The profile is one of the hardest parts of the resume to write, so I typically write it last. It should be highly customized for the particular job you are applying for. Don't use it to make vague claims (see "Quantify, Quantify, Quantify; Then Prove Outcomes," later in the chapter).

A profile usually has the following format:

> *[Adjective] [noun] with [number] years of experience in [special skill], a proven ability to [relevant, measurable skills], and a strong background in [relevant contexts in which you have worked] seeks a position as [relevant objective].*

Here is a completed example:

> *Highly motivated nonprofit professional with three years of experience in program management, service delivery, and fundraising; a proven ability to lead groups of up to 50 volunteers, organize events with up to 500 participants, effectively raise over $100,000 in grants yearly, and streamline processes to maximize efficiency; and a strong background in youth services programs with underserved populations seeks a position as a leader in a human services nonprofit.*

There are many other styles of profiles, summaries, and objectives. For example, a highly technical person (for example, in information technology) might have a bulleted list of software, programming languages, and hardware he or she knows. Someone with little relevant experience might list only an Objective statement (for example, "Seeking program assistant position in an environmental nonprofit organization").

Experience

For individuals with years of work experience or who finished their education more than a year or two ago, the experience section should usually follow the contact information (or the profile, if there is one). In the most common, *chronological* resume format, experience should be listed in reverse chronological order, with the most recent or current experience listed first. Note that internships can also be listed under experience.

Each job listing needs to include the following information:

- **Job title and employer's name and location:** Whether you list the employer's name first or your job title first is a decision you can make based on whether you think the job title or employer name is more impressive—but whatever you choose, be consistent throughout the resume. For the employer location, just list the city and state (or country).
- **Dates of employment:** Usually you need to just list the month and year of employment. If you are returning to work after a long absence or otherwise have gaps of employment, you might just list the years of employment, but this is not recommended for most people.
- **Bulleted list of accomplishments:** These bullet points describe what you did at each job (see the Resume Content section for more information).

In cases of a more significant career transition, or when returning to the workplace after a long absence, it may be better to list experience in a *functional*, rather than *chronological* format. Because the functional format is less commonly used, and therefore may make recruiters a little suspicious, I typically steer clear of it. However, it is especially helpful for individuals making a major career change who want to highlight relevant skills that were developed in a different career context or for individuals with gaps in their employment history.

In the functional format, bullet points for your work accomplishments are not listed according to the specific job where you accomplished them, but rather under major skills headings (such as *Program Management, Communication,* or *Financial Management*). For example, I once worked with a professional actor (and bartender) who wanted to move into management or sales. He was able to list his acting and directing experience under "Public Speaking" and "Leadership/Supervision" headings, and his handling of cash, ordering of inventory, and supervision of staff under "Financial Management." If you use a functional format, you still need to list your work history, with dates, but you can do this toward the end of the resume, which de-emphasizes the specific titles and dates of employment. Samuel Franklin's resume shows what this format looks like.

Samuel Franklin

123 W. 56th Street, Lansing, MI 48823 • (517) 987-6543 • samfranklin@yahoo.com

Summary

Experienced manager with extensive skills in training and project planning within both nonprofit and corporate environments seeks to use technical and managerial skills as project manager in local government agency. Experience includes providing support for up to 2,000+ clients nationwide; designing, planning, and implementing large-scale technical installations, upgrades, and related projects; and evaluating and decision making with respect to asset management and procurement of hardware and software.

Experience

Leadership

- Effectively managed up to 5 staff who provided second- and third-level companywide support and training to more than 2,000 end users.
- Supervised hiring of numerous new support technicians and engineers.
- Provided for support technician development with training programs, including both technical and interpersonal skills, measurably increasing technicians' productivity.

Process Improvement

- Built knowledge base of common and uncommon problems and their resolutions, greatly reducing the time it took to resolve most calls.
- Created and maintained extensive library of latest software upgrades, patches, and drivers and ensured deployment to everyone who required them.
- Evaluated call and status reports from help desk tracking software and made recommendations that improved workflow and led to effective problem resolution.
- Instituted and enforced policies with regard to asset management, resulting in nearly 100% accuracy with respect to tracking hardware and software.
- Analyzed trends in order to identify companywide or network issues.

Project Management

- Coordinated large-scale projects, such as departmental installations and upgrades consisting of hundreds of workstations, assessing needs from the ground up and following through to completion.
- Responded to numerous on-the-spot demands to immediately shift work priorities and reassign projects in order to accommodate urgent needs and ensure smooth workflow.
- Performed in-depth research and investigation with respect to complex problems, using technical support on the Internet and other resources.
- Inventoried all hardware and software with provisions for tracking license agreements.

Client Support/Interpersonal Communication

- Assigned and supervised up to 250 technical support calls per week in conjunction with the help desk, following through on each and every call until completion.
- Individually supported as many as 50 end users per week in order to resolve complex issues.
- Prioritized special support and training for VIPs, celebrities, and high-profile individuals.
- Effectively communicated with anxious clients who had urgent needs.
- Trained numerous users in network and PC literacy.

continued

This functional resume works for a candidate who's transitioning from a technical to a managerial position.

SAMUEL FRANKLIN, SAMFRANKLIN@YAHOO.COM PAGE 2

TECHNICAL SUPPORT

- Ensured compatibility for an extensive library of software and hardware products and maintained workstations with the latest patches and updates.
- Provided installation and support for large base of computing devices, such as Blackberries, PDAs, and other PIM devices.
- Installed and maintained Novell NetWare hardware and software, such as file servers, PC clients, and peripheral devices.
- Performed local area network (LAN) administration, such as setting up users, configuring network printing devices, and setting up and maintaining clients for email.
- Controlled user and network logic through the use of cleverly designed login scripts and deployment methods.
- Troubleshot hardware and software problems and replaced components as necessary.
- Performed site surveys and recommended upgrades when necessary.
- Set up and configured multimedia components for company presentations.
- Troubleshot and resolved telecommunications problems.
- Performed LAN cleanups to make room for new software products and upgrades.
- Backed up, catalogued, and archived network data and recovered lost or corrupted data.
- Supported all areas of the association with regard to computer hardware, software, and network operations.
- Maintained LAN inventory database with provisions for tracking all hardware and software on the LAN both at the server and workstation levels.

WORK HISTORY

BALLARD ENVIRONMENTAL ORGANIZATION, Detroit, Michigan
Technical Services Manager, January [year]–October [year]

ABC SHIPPING MANAGEMENT, INC., New York City, New York
LAN Administrator, October [year]–December [year]

AMERICAN SERVICES GROUP, New York City, New York
LAN Administrator, October [year]–October [year]

TOPHILL BANK, Cranford, New Jersey
Network Administration Officer, January [year]–September [year]

Education

If you are a recent college or graduate school graduate or current student, the Education section should go near the top of the resume, right after address (and profile, if you are using one). If you graduated more than a year ago, usually the Education section goes at the end of the resume (a few other sections, such as a Skills section, might go after the Education section).

Like experience, education is usually listed in reverse chronological order, with more recent degrees listed first. In most cases, it is important to list all degrees you have completed, except for a high school diploma (high school may be listed in a federal resume or when a high school diploma is listed as a requirement of the job). List the month and year you graduated from each school (you do not need to list the date you started a certain program, just when you finished). If you are still in school, list your expected graduation date—employers need to know this information to determine when you would be available to work full-time. If you graduated many years ago and are concerned about age discrimination, you might decide not to list your graduation date.

If you have transferred between multiple colleges, it might not be worth listing each one of them, especially if the Education section would then take up too much room in the resume or would give a negative impression that you have trouble making up your mind about what school to attend. Other things to list in the Education section might include a major thesis project or research work, study abroad, and relevant courses or class projects. I suggest listing courses when they reflect skills that are not listed elsewhere in the resume or when you have little relevant experience but highly relevant education.

If you were (or are) an honor student or received merit-based scholarships, this should be listed in the Education section (you can have an "Honors" subsection). Also, if you worked your way through school, you might list this as the last point in the Education section to show you are able to balance work and school. List grade point averages only if they are above average or required by the employer.

Skills, Volunteer Leadership, and Other Optional Sections

A Skills section, at the very end of the resume, is a good place to list technical skills (such as specific computer programs) and foreign languages you speak. When you list languages, make sure you indicate your proficiency level, such as "fluent," "conversational," "advanced beginner," or "some knowledge of."

List volunteer experiences in a Volunteer Leadership or Community Service section. Describe your volunteering experiences the same way you would describe work experiences—with quantifiers and explanations of what you accomplished. If you have substantial volunteer experience at a leadership or commitment level approaching that of a job and are making a career transition in which your other work experience is less relevant, you might put the Volunteer Leadership section before your other work experience. In general, though, a Volunteer Leadership section goes toward the end of the resume.

Professional training that does not lead to a degree can be listed under a "Professional Training" or "Licenses and Certifications" section near the end of the resume. You may also want to list professional publications, presentations, or affiliations. Publications and professional presentations can be quite impressive, especially when you are moving into a research-oriented or academic field.

Some people have an interests or hobbies section. Like the rest of the resume, this section needs to be specific. Don't list that you enjoy "Reading and cooking." Something like "Reading international-relations nonfiction and cooking Thai and Malaysian food" is much more interesting. However, such details are worth listing only if they help illustrate your interest in a field or show a side of your personality that is not shown elsewhere in the resume.

Resume Content

If you think of your job search as a sales campaign, in which you are selling your skills and abilities to an employer, the resume is equivalent to a printed advertisement. Like an ad, the focus should be on how the product (you) will benefit the consumer (the employer), never the other way around. An ad would never say, "Please buy my product, because I need the money to pay for my mortgage," and your resume and cover letter should not focus on how the job would benefit you by saying things like, "Seeking an opportunity with a prestigious organization where I can learn and grow."

Similarly, a good advertisement never asks the reader to try to guess why the product will be beneficial or what the product's purpose is. It is always written in a way that the reader can easily understand and is highly focused on presenting benefits targeted to the consumer's needs. The following sections explain how to write your resume to capture an employer's attention.

Use Keywords

To understand the employer's needs, scrutinize the job description of the position you are targeting. Pinpoint the daily tasks you will encounter as well as the required skills and technical knowledge. Then ensure that you have covered this information as best you can throughout your resume. Knowing as much as possible about the culture of the profession will also help you write it in the profession's lingo (this is why the step of researching the field comes *before* writing the resume).

In certain cases, especially within large agencies such as the federal government and the United Nations, recruiters will use a computerized keyword search to determine whether candidates meet their required skills. Including the keywords exactly as they appear in the description is important, even if that means rewriting some of the resume content. For example, if the job description asks for you to know a specific statistical computer program (such as SPSS), the recruiter may be searching for the term *SPSS.* If you wrote "knowledge of statistical software" in your resume, it might be overlooked. (Chapter 11 has more information on finding and using keywords in your application materials.)

Quantify, Quantify, Quantify; Then Prove Outcomes

Nearly every resume I have reviewed in the last 11 years could be greatly improved by listing numbers and results. A reader has no idea how much work you did, what the scale of a project was, or what you really accomplished until you quantify points on your resume.

For example, "Handled cash" is a decent starting place for a resume bullet point, but "Handled up to $3,000 in cash per day" is far better. Suddenly, the reader can visualize you with a large sum of cash. Inferences follow: You must be highly responsible and accurate. You can emphasize that you were good at your job by adding a few adverbs: "Accurately handled up to $3,000 in cash per day."

What if you were better at this task than your coworkers? Perhaps you improved the cash-handling process or were faster or more accurate. If this is true, list something like, "Handled up to $3,000 in cash per day in a fast-paced environment, with an accuracy rate 5% higher than average." Or, "Created new cash-handling system that reduced payment errors by 5%, saving more than $5,000 per year." Don't just list numbers, but try to include your end results.

Similarly, don't waste space in your resume with vague claims. "Excellent interpersonal and communication skills" is a vague claim. These alternatives are better:

> *Proven ability to communicate with individuals of diverse backgrounds, ranging from teenagers to volunteers to elected officials.*

> *Three years of experience in public speaking and leading teams of up to 50 people. Ability to produce focused memos and reports that successfully lead to policy change.*

Another little quantifying tip: Use the phrases "up to" or "more than" when listing numbers. Suppose you had a job processing applications for scholarships, and the day before the deadline, you received 100 applications. Every prior week, you received an average of 20 applications. You can still say "Accurately processed up to 100 scholarship applications per day" on your resume without bending the truth. After all, you have the ability to process that many applications.

To get a better idea of how to best highlight your accomplishments in bullet points, take a look at the Anatomy of a Bullet Point worksheet. Mark Moore's resume (which comes after the worksheet) is a good example of how to highlight accomplishments by incorporating numbers whenever possible.

Anatomy of a Bullet Point

To write better bullet points for your resume, use this simple formula to help you quantify your accomplishments:

Adverb + Verb + Number + Object+ Measure/Tool = Result/Goal

This example shows this formula in action:

Accurately entered more than 200 records into an Access database to more efficiently track client outcomes.

When you dissect this phrase, you can see how it answers the questions an employer has about your qualifications.

Sample word or phrase	**Description/Purpose**
Accurately	Adverbs are optional, but they are helpful in explaining *how* you performed your verb.
entered	The verb explains *what* you did.
more than 200	The number states *how many.*
records	The object states *what* your verb acted upon.
into an Access database	The tool or measure clarifies *what* you used to do your verb or *how much* or *how often* you did it. This item is optional, but good to mention if the tool or measure is used in your field.
to more efficiently track client outcomes.	The result or goal explains *why* you did this and *what* the end result was. It clarifies *how* you measure your success.

This diagram identifies these parts in another bullet point:

Effectively tutored up to 20 students per month, greatly improving their test scores.

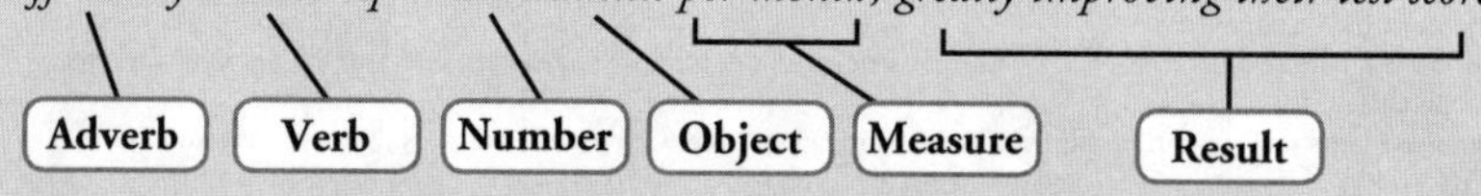

Now that you have mastered bullet point anatomy, write one for your resume:

______________ ______________ ______________

Adverb **Verb** **Number**

______________ ______________, ______________.

Object **Measure/Tool** **Result/Goal**

MARK MOORE

123 NW 45th Street, Apartment #123 • Seattle, Washington 98106 • (206) 123-4567• mark.moore@gmail.com

SUMMARY

Master of Public Administration candidate and Returned Peace Corps Volunteer with excellent management, research, and analytical skills nurtured by graduate education and employment in the public, private, and nonprofit sectors. Proven ability to effectively manage multiple projects and reporting requirements in a deadline-driven environment. Fast learner with proficiency in MS Office Suite, Adobe, database entry and management, web tools, as well as Russian language. Seeks opportunities related to international business, trade, and development, and corporate social responsibility.

EDUCATION AND TRAINING

EVANS SCHOOL OF PUBLIC AFFAIRS, UNIVERSITY OF WASHINGTON, Seattle, WA — June [year]
Master of Public Administration (M.P.A.) in International Affairs
International Development Certificate Program
Relevant coursework: Development Economics, Global Policy Management, Development Ethics, Public Policy Analysis, Program Evaluation, Public Management, Microeconomics, Quantitative Analysis, Public Budgeting, Project Management
Degree project: Can Voluntary Codes of Conduct Reduce Human Rights Abuses?

UNIVERSITY OF MICHIGAN, Ann Arbor, MI — May [year]
Bachelor of Arts in Political Science, Journalism minor
International Relations and Polish and Central European Studies Certificates

CHARLES UNIVERSITY, Prague, Czech Republic — Spring [year]
Semester-long study exchange program with emphasis on the Czech Republic's socioeconomic and political transition

WORK EXPERIENCE

FANCYFASHION WORLDWIDE, Seattle, WA — Winter [year]–present
Corporate Social Responsibility Intern

- Researched and supported the communications effort behind an internationally known fashion designer's first major corporate social responsibility initiative
- Developed effective interview protocol for a stakeholder outreach campaign to gather insight on education policy from leaders of Washington state's diverse ethnic communities and conducted interviews with 25 community leaders, resulting in greatly improved community relations
- Monitored media and provided pitch material to journalists across the country, resulting in 15 published articles

GLOBAL HEALTH INC., Seattle, WA — Summer [year]
Program Assistant (Temporary Employee), Reproductive Health Global Program

- Managed material development, technical, and editorial review processes for 2 World Health Organization workshops with 50 participants each, focusing on supply chain management and compliance issues in global contraceptive procurement
- Formatted, edited, and researched 30 journal articles, donor reports, fact sheets, and internal communications documents
- Provided logistical support, organization, and correspondence with outside partners for an organization with 20 staff

continued

This candidate uses quantified bullet points to make his skills stand out.

Mark Moore mark.moore@gmail.com page 2

OKLAHOMA CITY PUBLIC UTILITIES (OCPU), Oklahoma City, OK November [year]–May [year]
Graduate Intern, Historically Underutilized Business (HUB) Initiative

- Supported the program coordinator in the Citywide Equity Initiative to eliminate barriers to contracting within Oklahoma City Public Utilities for women- and minority-owned businesses
- Initiated efforts that increased initiative utilization by 10% within the 20 branches of OCPU
- Created outreach campaigns to effectively engage new firms and increase access to information
- Developed accurate monthly utilization reports for each OCPU branch for review by director

MANAGEMENT SOCIETIES INTERNATIONAL (MSI), Washington, DC June [year]–May [year]
Project Manager, Democracy and Governance Analytical Support and Implementation Services

- Managed MSI's U.S. Agency for International Development (USAID) Democracy and Governance Analytical Implementation and Support Services Indefinite Quantity Contract (IQC), totaling $5.2 million over 5 years
- Successfully executed more than 45 global task orders, valued at over $800,000
- Performed financial management and reporting, proposal and budget preparation, long- and short-term budget tracking, contract negotiation, quality control of deliverables, activity reporting, recruitment and consultant preparation for assignments, research and logistical coordination
- Developed and maintained cordial relationships with IQC client and MSI subcontractors; enhanced transparent communications by developing and maintaining MSI Infogate website to inform partners of upcoming task orders
- Organized workshops in both Washington, DC and Bangkok, Thailand with 30–70 participants from USAID, Department of State, Washington-area think tanks, implementing partners, and academia. Topics included the democratic breakthroughs in Georgia, Ukraine, and Serbia; and anticorruption in the Asia/Near East region
- Trained and mentored new project managers on effectively managing various client relationships and best practices for contract and project management; supervised 3 interns per semester

INTERNATIONAL INSTITUTE OF BUFFALO, Buffalo, NY Summer [year]
Volunteer Teacher Assistant, Legal Department Researcher

- Supported 15 refugee children from Liberia and Burma in their preparation for public school by instructing them in English as Second Language (ESL) and culture norms and familiarizing them with a structured classroom setting
- Accurately compiled refugee legal documents to ensure smooth processing

UNITED STATES PEACE CORPS, Vapniarka, Ukraine February [year]–April [year]
Business/NGO Facilitator (Volunteer)

- Assisted 15 local NGO clients in grant writing, budget preparation, publicity campaigns, and partner searches as a staff member at a provincial NGO resource center, measurably improving effectiveness
- Streamlined and oversaw the Student Consulting Center, which provided career and study abroad information, consultation, and seminars to 40 students and professionals per year
- Produced 2 annual editions of *Scholarship Opportunities,* a 200-page booklet listing legitimate study and work exchange opportunities available to Ukrainian students and professionals; distributed more than 1,000 copies of the booklet throughout Ukraine annually
- Taught weekly English language and literature courses to university-level students
- Member of the HIV/AIDS working group, which provided fellow Peace Corps volunteers with programming and classroom materials to promote HIV/AIDS awareness
- Developed and facilitated numerous community projects, including a weekly English-speaking club, HIV/AIDS and sexual health trainings, a film club, and monthly concerts for local amateur musicians

TRANSPARENCY INTERNATIONAL, Prague, Czech Republic May–August [year]
Intern

- Assisted with the logistics and coordination of the eighth annual International Anti-Corruption Conference (IACC), held in Prague, with 800 participants from 20 countries

COUNTRY EXPERIENCE: Azerbaijan, Canada, Czech Republic, France, Georgia, Germany, Hungary, Ireland, Italy, Pakistan, Poland, Russia, Slovakia, Spain, Thailand, Turkey, Ukraine, United Kingdom, Uzbekistan

Prioritize

Take a step back from your resume and ask how much room each section or experience occupies. The amount of space something occupies gives a subconscious message to the reader—longer equals more important. Consciously emphasize what is most relevant or important. Ask yourself, for *each word* on the resume, "What benefit does this provide, which is not listed elsewhere in the resume, to my target audience? What skills or accomplishments, which are of value to my target employer, are illustrated by this point?" Delete anything extraneous. You can always keep a "kitchen sink" version of your resume stored somewhere that has everything in it, especially if you are going to apply for federal positions with background checks.

> **NOTE**
>
> You *must* proofread your resume. After you read through it, go back and read it backwards, word by word. This method will help you catch spelling and grammar errors. Get a professional career counselor and five friends to proofread it as well. Then proofread it again. This advice goes double for your cover letter. Recruiters who are confronted by stacks of resumes use quick grammar or spelling checks to determine which resumes can go directly into the recycling bin.

Resume Format and Design

Designing your resume so that it is attractive, easy to read, and emphasizes the points that are most relevant to the employer is important. Keep in mind that the reader's eye goes from the top down, left to right. Therefore, the more important something is, the closer it must go to the top and the further to the left it should go. When in doubt, scrutinize the job description (if you have one to go on). List those accomplishments that illustrate the skills requested by the job posting first.

Following these tips will help you make your resume simple and attractive and emphasize the most important information:

- Move dates to the right-hand side of the page, rather than the left, and do *not* bold them. The dates of employment are not the most important item on a resume, and thus should not be overly emphasized.
- Judiciously use white space. Not enough white space (for example, no blank lines between sections) is hard to read. On the other hand, large swaths of white space can make the reader think you have no experience. If you have trouble keeping your resume to one page, get creative: Use slightly smaller margins or use a five-point font as your blank line between job listings or sections.
- Do not use more than two fonts, maximum (one is probably better), and use them consistently.

- Stick to businesslike fonts, such as Times New Roman and Arial. Funny, curly fonts are hard to read and distract from the content, and some fonts do not transfer between different computer platforms.
- Use appropriate font sizes and use them consistently. When one bullet point is a font size bigger than the rest of the bullet points in the resume, it looks sloppy. Also, the font size needs to be readable—I would never go any smaller than a 10-point font, keeping in mind that 10-point Times New Roman is much harder to read than 10-point Arial.
- Be consistent in your use of bold, italics, or underlining. Think about which words should be in bold—for instance, if the names of your former employers are more impressive than your job titles, consider bolding all the employer names.
- Unless you are a graphic designer, avoid adding anything unusual to the resume in terms of fonts, colors, graphics, or pictures—let the resume content speak for itself. Note that photographs are not used in resumes in the United States (except for models or actors).
- Take out a ruler and make sure your margins (including internal margins and indents) are not wavy. One way to prevent uneven margins is to use tabs to indent material instead of using spaces.
- Avoid splitting a job across two pages wherever possible. If you do have to split a job description between two pages, say something such as "XYZ Agency, X Position, continued" to warn the reader.

If you are in doubt about your resume's readability, try the 15-second test: Give your resume to a friend to read, and give him or her 15 seconds to read it. At 15 seconds, grab the resume back and ask what he or she saw. Then you will know what jumps out from the resume, whether it was readable, and what you might be visually emphasizing without realizing it.

NOTE

Some employers use online application systems that remove all the formatting from your resume. In this case, you should copy your formatted resume into a text editor such as Notepad and edit it to ensure that it is still readable. Note that you can still format in plain text. Rather than bold, use all capital letters; rather than bullets, use asterisks.

Frequently Asked Questions About Resumes

The following are commonly asked questions about resumes. Most do not have a yes or no answer, and opinions may vary depending on whom you talk to and the field you are going into.

One Page or Two?

For recent graduates or those with less experience, I lean toward a one-page resume. If you have enough relevant experience and education to justify two pages, use it. If, however, you have a half page of relevant experience and another page and a half of unrelated experience, lower-level experience, or school activities, make it one page. Again, some resumes, such as federal or international resumes, allow four or more pages.

How Far Back Do I Go?

Some people recommend listing only the last 10 years of experience to prevent possible age discrimination. Following this guideline might be advisable if your earlier experience is redundant with your current experience or is at a lower level. However, always following the 10-year rule not only encourages age discrimination, it also devalues the benefits of having years of experience and may encourage people to leave off important information. If you prioritize information according to the job you are targeting, you can best determine which experience to include.

How Do I Handle Employment Gaps or Frequent Employment Changes?

Gaps of employment raise the attention of hiring managers, who may make negative assumptions about where you were during the gap years. Frequent job changes also can raise employer concerns about your loyalty or ability to keep a job.

You can minimize employment gaps to an extent by using a functional resume format. However, some hiring managers might prefer that the gaps be discussed briefly at the end of a cover letter. For example, you might state something like, "If you have any concerns regarding the period from 2003–2005, note that at that time I had an illness from which I have fully recovered;" or "I spent 2000–2004 raising a family."

In some cases, frequent job changes are not necessarily an issue of concern. For example, a recent college graduate with many different internship experiences is generally seen in a positive light. Individuals who have worked as freelancers or consultants and now seek permanent employment also may be expected to have a variety of work experience on their resumes, though they may need to explain why they are leaving freelance work.

Creating a smooth narrative that helps explain frequent employment changes is an art form. A good way to do this is to address this issue in a cover letter—or, even better, to build networking connections before applying to jobs so that the hiring manager knows your story beforehand (see Chapter 11 for networking tips). Keep the story positive as much as you can. Either leave out the negative stories in your history, or, if you must bring them up for the sake of honesty, talk about the positive side of what you've learned from the changes you have made.

Resume Tips for First-Time Job Seekers

If you are a recent college graduate or otherwise are seeking a job for the first time, the same advice for all job seekers applies to you, too. You have to do research, build up skills and experience as much as possible before graduating, and network.

A large majority of employers will consider recent graduates only if they have had at least one internship or other relevant work experience, and probably half will consider only those applicants with two or more internship or work experiences. Prior to graduating or embarking on your search, make the most of your school's career center and try to build up as many internship or relevant part-time job experiences as possible. Student leadership and volunteer experiences, especially ones showing initiative (such as serving in student government or creating a new student organization) are also excellent, especially when complemented with work experience. Just try to avoid creating an "attack of the student activities" resume that's full of student leadership, study abroad, or research projects and empty of work experience.

Don't underestimate yourself. Even seemingly low-level work experience can demonstrate your skills:

- Camp counseling, for example, requires great responsibility.
- Restaurant and retail sales jobs use customer service skills that are highly valued by many employers.
- Basic office duties illustrate attention to detail.

Holding down any job shows some level of interpersonal skills and dependability.

Resume Tips for Career Changers

Making a career change—whether switching sectors or industries or returning to civilian work after a military career—requires transforming your communication style. You have been working in a certain field, in a particular culture with its own language, acronyms, assumptions, and standards. But company-specific, or even industry-specific, acronyms will be unintelligible to your future employer. Inspect your resume and make sure that every acronym and unusual term is spelled out, unless you can be absolutely sure your future employer will know (and appreciate) what it stands for. Matching an employer's language and describing your accomplishments in terms that employer can understand are important.

Experience can be split into two categories: what you did (skills) and where you did it (context). Look at your skills (Chapter 1 will help identify them) and find those that match your future employer's needs; de-emphasize the irrelevant context in which you used those skills. Also look at the contexts you worked in and try to find any of relevance to your future employer.

For example, I counseled an engineer who had worked for a large international aeronautics company for 30 years. He wanted to switch to international development and relief work and was pursuing a degree in the field along with doing significant volunteer work. What he did not realize is that one of his work projects, which involved partnering with the national airlines of and building airports in various developing countries, showed his experience in working with people in developing countries and building large-scale projects abroad. He could also emphasize his relevant engineering, management, and budgeting skills, even though they were used for a private sector employer, because they could be useful in international technical projects. The Cindy Chen resume provides another example of how to emphasize relevant experience.

NOTE

As a career changer, you may have to explain in a cover letter or during an interview why you want to make the shift from your former to your future career. Explain this in a positive way—focus on what inspires you about the new field, not what's making you leave the old field.

When you are changing from the private to the nonprofit or government sector, you need to take the difference in culture between these sectors into account. In general, nonprofit organizations tend to emphasize communications among various levels of an organization and many bring their clients into discussions. For example, a youth service organization may have some teenagers on an advisory board. This may be quite different from how a corporate board would be structured! And although many nonprofit or government organizations appreciate a business background, you can never make an assumption that business is better or that your role is to make a nonprofit or government agency "run like a business." To say this would probably be an immediate turn-off to many nonprofit or government agencies. By doing research, you will be best positioned to make the cultural leap to a new sector.

Cindy Chen

1234 Development Drive • Chicago, IL 88888 • (987) 654-3210 • cchen@ngo.org

PROFILE: Highly motivated professional with proven ability to organize fundraising events that raise up to $300,000 each and to solicit donations of up to $100,000, 8 years of technical sales experience, significant customer service and project management background, and strong marketing and writing skills seeks position in individual giving or development for a nonprofit health services organization.

FUNDRAISING/VOLUNTEER LEADERSHIP

Executive Chair, Board of Advisors, May [year]–present
Cancer Alliance, Detroit, MI

- Executive Chairperson for *Celebration of Life* benefit, which has raised more than $1.6 million for cancer research
- Individually raised gifts of up to $100,000 to benefit Cancer Alliance, breaking all past volunteer records
- Ongoing volunteer efforts for Cancer Alliance include serving on advisory board, mentoring 3 cancer patients per month, and creating a long-term fundraising plan

PROFESSIONAL EXPERIENCE

Specialty Application Account Manager, March [year]–present
NewBook Corporation, Chicago, IL

- Manage 25 pressure-sensitive accounts located in Illinois, Indiana, Iowa, Michigan, North Carolina, Ohio, and Wisconsin, generating estimated revenue of $12 million
- Facilitate communication and maintain relationships between the paper mills, marketing, sales, customer service, and technical support to effectively service customers
- Introduce new products for specialty applications and work with customers to test products for highly specialized uses; effectively communicate complex information to clients
- Ensure the overall service to the customer, including quality, pricing, distribution, inventory, account receivables, and claims; received Account Manager of the month award 3 times

Marketing Representative, September [year]–March [year]
Westfalia Corporation, Detroit, MI

- Introduced the Platinum Ultra grade line of paper stock to over 400 advertising agencies, graphic designers, and corporate users in Michigan and Ohio for annual reports, corporate brochures, direct mail, publications, magazines, catalogs, and marketing collateral projects, successfully reaching and exceeding monthly sales goals
- Presented Platinum Ultra to over 150 prospects during a 2-month period
- Researched "nontraditional" customers, building over 100 new leads
- Developed strong relationships with prospective customers, leading to 20% sales increase

Marketing Manager, March [year]-August [year]
Compusoft Corporation, Peoria, IL

- Developed effective marketing programs to generate prospective leads
- Created marketing collateral and presentations to improve sales effectiveness
- Generated market awareness through press relations, promotional activities, and web campaigns

EDUCATION

Saint Joseph's College, Notre Dame, IN
Bachelor of Arts, Marketing, Cum Laude, May [year]
Minors: Business Administration and Spanish

This career changer lists her nonprofit experience first and highlights accomplishments in marketing and customer service to make the transition from corporate sales to nonprofit fundraising.

Create Cover Letters

Cover letters are an essential bridge between a job posting and your resume, helping to point out exactly why you fit the job's requirements. They also serve as a writing sample and, to some extent, a way for the employer to try to "read in" to your personality.

The tone of the cover letter is very important. To strike the right tone, you must be confident, yet humble. The idea is that you believe you could do a great job if given the chance and are willing to prove you have the skills required for the position, but you also understand that it is the employer's decision whether or not to interview you. As with a resume, it is also essential to prove your points rather than make vague claims.

Here are some examples of what **not** to write:

- "I look forward to working with you." This statement is aggressive instead of confident. You don't even know if the employer will be interviewing you, so how can you look forward to working with him or her?
- "I possess vast skills in the field of…" Applying overly strong words such as *vast, tremendous,* or *incredible* to yourself seems conceited instead of confident. Try using words such as *extensive, strong,* or *well-developed* to describe your skills instead.
- "While I lack direct experience in the area of …" This phrase is too insecure. Rather than highlight a deficiency, highlight strengths such as your ability to learn quickly and work hard (and prove it with examples).
- "I look forward to learning more about this field with your organization." This statement could be interpreted as both too insecure (why point out that you need to learn so much more about the field?) and possibly too selfish (unless this is an internship or very entry-level position, the organization is not altruistically hiring you in order to teach you).

The cover letter consists of three main parts, the introduction, the body, and the conclusion. The introduction is a somewhat standard first paragraph stating why you are applying for the position and giving a brief overview of why you would be the best candidate.

The body of the cover letter is the most challenging part to write. Here, it is vital to target specific points from the job description and try to make it abundantly obvious that you have each and every requirement listed. (Chapter 11 explains how to find the keywords in a job description so you can then incorporate them into your cover letter.)

For example, if the employer is asking for project management experience, make sure you have a sentence like "I possess a strong project management background; for example, in my last role, I ensured that a development project with a $250,000 budget was finished on time and under budget while meeting all of the required outcomes milestones." Give examples for each requirement, focusing most heavily on those that are emphasized in the job description.

The conclusion is a brief statement saying that you look forward to hearing from the employer and can be contacted at his or her convenience and listing your phone number and email address. The Marissa Montez and Greta Greene cover letters show how these three parts work together.

Marissa Montez
36-97 Top Street
Apt. 2M
Brooklyn, NY 11215

February 17, [year]

Mr. Maxwell Hammer
Director of Personnel
Sierra Club
234 Madison Avenue
New York, NY 10010

Dear Mr. Hammer:

I was referred to you by Dr. George Daily, my Journalism professor at Best City College, who suggested that your organization might have an opening for an Editorial Assistant in the Publications Division. I am a recent graduate of Best City College with a degree in English and a minor in Journalism, and I have a strong interest in the mission of the Sierra Club.

My background includes training and experience in various aspects of writing, editing, research, and public speaking, which would fit what your organization is seeking in an Editorial Assistant. The following accomplishments are noteworthy:

- Serving as Opinions Editor of *The Daily* (Best City College student newspaper), with a circulation of 5,000, and directing a staff of 3 people (clips are available)
- Winning the 2010 Best City Award for Creative Writing after competing against 225 other college students
- Representing Best City College for the past 2 years as a member of the debate team, which ranked second regionally each of these years
- Maintaining a high GPA while working up to 30 hours per week throughout college
- Volunteering for numerous environmental clean-up projects and Earth Day activities

I am very interested in learning more about opportunities in the Publications Division at the Sierra Club and would like the opportunity to elaborate on how my communication and research skills could benefit your publication. Please feel free to contact me at (718) 000-0000 or mm12345@bestcity.edu. Thank you for your time and consideration.

Sincerely,

Marissa Montez

This recent college graduate wants an entry-level nonprofit communications position.

Greta Greene
999 44th Ave.
Minneapolis, MN 55199

October 31, [year]

Alexander Jones and Selection Committee
City of Minneapolis Personnel Department
Minneapolis Municipal Tower
PO Box 100
Minneapolis, MN 55199

To Mr. Jones and the Selection Committee:

I am writing to apply for the Parks Strategy Analyst position within the Department of Finance (announcement #123). I believe my interdisciplinary education, strong research skills, and diverse experiences writing grant and business proposals would make me a strong candidate for this position.

I am currently a second-year graduate student in Environmental Health (Master of Science) and Public Affairs (Master of Public Administration) and expect to graduate with both degrees this December. A large part of my interdisciplinary education has been focused on business management and environmental science. I have relevant coursework in accounting, economics, and environmental sustainability that will be valuable when assessing short- and long-term feasibility of business decisions affecting parks in the Minneapolis area.

In addition to my education, I have experience as an environmental consultant, analyzing data from online federal databases, interviewing clients, researching cases at the EPA's library, and then synthesizing this information into an Environmental Site Assessment. When I was a research assistant, I studied the demographics of indigenous groups across six states, their land use, and proximity to industrial contamination using GIS. I believe these experiences will be helpful when researching local and national park usage as well as demographics.

In addition, I have experience finding and winning alternative funding through writing effective grant and business proposals. In 2009, I wrote a research proposal for the Native American Health Fund that won $150,000 from the U.S. Indian Health Service. Last year, I was a finalist at the Global Social Entrepreneurship Competition, having written a business proposal that was selected as one of the top 5 from over 100 proposals. My skills in writing business proposals were honed throughout my experiences founding, funding, and leading large volunteer organizations, such as the Organic Food Cooperative at Ball State University.

This position is a wonderful opportunity for me to continue towards my career goal of working at the intersection of environmental health and policy at the government level. I am confident I would be an asset to your project and I hope to speak with you about this opportunity at your convenience. You can always reach me at 612-987-6543 or at greta.greene@gmail.com.

Sincerely,

Greta Greene

This graduate student seeks a position in city government after graduation.

References and Resources

For more information on the topics presented in this chapter, refer to the following sources:

Berkshire, Jennifer; *The Chronicle of Philanthropy,* "Résumés Matter: What Nonprofit Employers Want to Know about Job Seekers" (August 6, 2009, http://philanthropy.com/article/R-sum-s-Matter-What/57414/)

Enelow, Wendy S., and Kursmark, Louise M.; *Cover Letter Magic,* Fourth Edition (JIST Publishing, 2010)

Whitcomb, Susan Britton; *Résumé Magic,* Fourth Edition (JIST Publishing, 2010)

CHAPTER 11

Identifying Public Service Opportunities: Networking and Navigating the Application Process

"Success consists in the climb." —*Elbert Hubbard*

The standard job search advice is to look for posted job descriptions and apply to them. For certain positions, such as those posted by government agencies that require a civil service test, this method is the best way to be considered for opportunities. However, a common mistake of job seekers is to rely solely on applying for posted job opportunities. You can boost your odds of success by trying the job opportunity sourcing techniques described in this chapter, which have worked for thousands of job seekers.

Once you find opportunities, the next step is to apply for them. This chapter gives a thorough overview of the somewhat complicated federal hiring process, including information on hiring levels, required essays, and special hiring authorities. In addition, this chapter includes hints on scoring a state or local government job, suggestions about running for office yourself, and tips on applying to nonprofits.

Getting Organized and Motivated

Conducting a good job search takes organizational skill. Before you apply for jobs, you must prepare a resume (see Chapter 10) and collect any materials you might need in the search, such as transcripts, identification, or contact information. Next, you need to establish a method of keeping track of your networking appointments, follow-up calls, outreach visits, job applications, target organizations/agencies, and thank-you notes. You can use contact manager software, calendars, planners, Excel files, notebooks, or online organizational tools such as JibberJobber.com—whatever tools work best for you. With a good system in place, you won't miss any follow-up appointments, calls, or interviews.

A key item to track is where you have applied and what positions you have applied for. A good idea is to copy and paste the text of the job descriptions you have applied for into an email message and send it to yourself. These job descriptions have a nasty tendency to vanish from the Internet just when you get a call from the employer for an interview. In particular, save any detailed information (such as a job announcement number) and contact information for postings in case you have questions later.

Staying focused and motivated in the job search is also important. Setting aside a specific amount of time each week to go on informational interviews, conduct self-assessment, get your resume ready, research opportunities, and apply for jobs will make a big difference in your search. Tracking your job search time and activities will give you a reality check on how much work you are actually doing to find a job. Once you have decided which job search strategies you want to focus on (the next section describes several you can try) and what percentage of time you need to spend on them, create a simple to-do list, along with some measurable, achievable goals for each week. Use the following worksheet as a guideline.

Job Search Task Exercise

Use this worksheet to help you set job search goals for yourself, such as applying for a certain number of jobs per week, networking with a certain number of people per month, or researching certain organizations.

Job search task: ______________________________

What is the very first step needed for this task?

____

When or how often will you do this task?

____

How will you hold yourself accountable for this task? How will you remind yourself to accomplish it?

___

What are the barriers preventing you from accomplishing this task?

___

What support or resources do you have (or can you enlist) to help you accomplish this task? What is your time frame for enlisting this help?

___

What result do you expect from accomplishing this task? How will you know when it's accomplished?

___

___

Finding a job takes time, energy, persistence, and optimism. Rejection is common in the job search, and it is easy to fall into a trap of overanalyzing why you didn't get a particular job or, worse, getting discouraged. The key is to look forward to new opportunities, stay focused, and get support.

NOTE

One way to stay motivated is to find a job search group or partner you check in with every week or two, to make sure you both stay on track with your search process. Because job searching is a self-motivated activity (like dieting or exercise), you will be more successful if you have someone else to be held accountable to.

Identifying Job Opportunities

Think for a moment of a time when you needed a referral for a trusted professional—a new dentist, doctor, or hairdresser/barber, for instance. Did you look through the Internet or Yellow Pages, post a "help wanted" ad and receive responses from strangers, or ask a friend for a referral? Most people start by asking their friends and family for a referral to someone they can recommend.

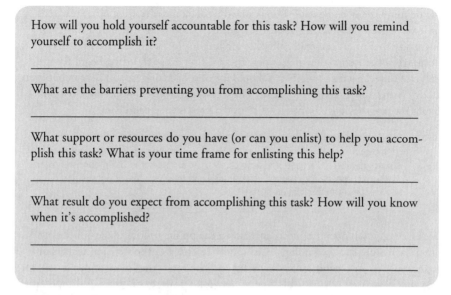

Employers are usually the same way. If they have a job opening, many times they start by asking their coworkers, colleagues, and friends for referrals. After that, they might post a position description to an email list or discussion group that targets professionals in the field they need. A next step, these days, could include searching through online profiles on Linkedin.com to see who has recommendations in the field (a little like choosing a book on Amazon.com by reading other readers' reviews). Employers also might post the position on the job board of a college or university that offers the major they are looking for (or is the one they graduated from). As a last resort, they might post the position on a job listing board for the universe to see, such as craigslist, Yahoo! HotJobs, or Monster, and they might even ask for help from a temporary agency or executive recruiter (also known as a *headhunter*) where they have to pay a fee to find a prescreened candidate.

> **NOTE** Even public sector employers with specific rules and regulations about how jobs must be advertised and how candidates are selected often consider referrals. Networking in the public sector also can help you better understand how to navigate the application process.

Because many job openings never make it to the public posting stage, job seekers often have more success finding a position by reaching out to decision makers or recommenders in organizations they want to work for, rather than applying only for jobs that have been posted. This type of networking strategy is especially important in a tough job market where employers are receiving hundreds of applications for a job.

Networking is an important technique to master, yet it is just one of many ways to find job opportunities. To uncover all possible job leads, you must use a mix of job search techniques. The following sections explain the best ones.

Networking

Networking is another word for relationship-building in a professional context. It refers to the process of reaching out to, connecting with, and creating reciprocal relationships in a field you are interested in. Professionals know that by helping others, they build an environment in which they can rely on future help from other professionals. Professionals continually build contacts in their network.

There are multiple reasons to network:

- To research the field you want to enter
- To gain valuable information about employers that you could not get otherwise
- To make yourself known—in a positive way—by the organizations and people you want to target
- To get feedback on your resume and job search skills
- To uncover new connections or gain introductions to new people in your field
- To have a mutually beneficial experience with the people you network with
- To gain referrals or recommendations for job leads

Networking is not a "hard sell" technique. Therefore, you should *not* directly ask for a job in a networking situation. However, the people you connect with while networking are likely to guess that you could use job search help.

Networking can help even when you are targeting positions that seem to be filled through a more impersonal hiring process (such as many public sector positions). You can gain many tips on the application process from your networking contacts, such as how to study for a hiring exam or how to maximize the keywords in your application. You also might get leads on positions that do not go through the formal testing process or ideas on how to find a position with a contractor or consultant.

Try to start networking *before* you are in the intense process of a job search, so that you already have established relationships in your field to reach out to once you are ready to start applying for positions. Once you land a job, you should continue networking in order to build reciprocal professional connections throughout your career.

The following sections describe the three phases of networking: sourcing contacts, cultivating a contact, and following up and nurturing a relationship with a contact.

Sourcing Networking Contacts

When you look for networking contacts, it's often best to aim your efforts at someone 3 to 10 years ahead of you in his or her career, who might have the power to recommend you for a job but is not so high up as to be inaccessible (though a high-level contact can be invaluable if you can get one). On the other hand, don't underestimate anyone you meet during your outreach efforts. Receptionists or office managers are often the most well connected and, in some cases, most powerful gatekeepers in an organization. Consider asking them for informational interviews as well—you will often learn more about the organization's culture that way, and possibly gain valuable introductions to hiring managers.

A common complaint of job seekers is: "You tell me to network, but I don't know anyone!" We'll soon fix that. The following sections describe three key sources for networking contacts: online tools, professional associations, and people you already know.

Online Tools

The Internet has made finding networking contacts much easier than it once was. Hundreds of online tools exist for finding connections, and more pop up daily. These include social networks such as Facebook and more traditional tools such as email lists or discussion groups.

With more than 50 million members worldwide as of this writing, LinkedIn is one of the largest professional networking sites. Its search capability enables you to easily find individuals who match criteria such as geographic location, company or organization, keywords, industries, and education. Other advantages of LinkedIn include the ability to search through the connections of the people you connect with—that is, to see whom a contact person is connected to—and to ask for and give recommendations of other people, which serve as a powerful addition to an online career presence or resume.

Twitter.com is another interesting site where you can see very short posts from people in your field. By searching this site for keywords related to your career, you can find and connect with numerous professionals and stay current on news in your field. There are also specialized networking sites, including the relatively new www.govloop.com, which is an excellent social/professional networking site for people who work for, or have an interest in, government. Others include Devex.com for international development and NetImpact for corporate social responsibility.

You can also use the Internet to stay abreast of important developments in your chosen career field, which can help you identify job leads and improve your interview performance. A simple way to do this is to create a Google Alert, which can send you a news feed of items relevant to a specific keyword. You also can connect to people by reading and commenting on their blogs as a way of showing your sincere interest in their career field.

The real purpose of all of this online connecting is still to meet people in person or by phone to conduct an informational interview. Just linking to someone online, without having a conversation, is not networking.

Professional Organizations

Professional organizations often host in-person conferences and events that can be fantastic networking opportunities (some conferences even have a formal recruiting component). You may meet more individuals at one professional conference or networking event than you might in weeks or months of other sourcing techniques. Sometimes professional association websites also maintain lists of their members, which can provide you with interesting leads on organizations you are targeting. (Note that the References and Resources sections at the end of Chapters 2–9 list websites for many different professional organizations.) Some professional organizations also have printed publications you can subscribe to, in which employers may post job opportunities.

Becoming a member of a professional organization has various benefits, such as members-only job boards, meetings, online networks, or newsletters. Most organizations have a student membership fee at a reduced rate. If they don't offer such a program, it couldn't hurt you to take the initiative and propose one to them if you are a student or new professional.

Likewise, if you can't afford to attend a conference, call the organizer and offer to volunteer at the conference to get a reduced rate. Volunteering is a great way to gain more visibility at what might be an otherwise impersonal event. If you have an area of expertise, it's even better to offer to present a workshop at a conference to gain additional visibility.

People You Already Know

Don't overlook the people you already know. Make a list of everyone you know, starting with those closest to you: family, friends, and contacts from your existing social circles. Include friends you have lost touch with, such as former roommates, classmates, teachers, professors, and neighbors. Think of your life as circles of experience—people you know from hobbies, activities, religious groups, previous jobs, volunteer work, classes, organizations and associations, and people you have met once and have a business card for. Start to get your contacts organized, and make notes about your relationship with each person. Think about what reasons you might have to connect with each person.

Cultivating Relationships

Once you have a list of contacts, get strategic about what you want from or can offer each person. Make a list of questions you need answered about your new career, based on the exercises in Chapter 1. For each contact, ask

- What information could this person provide?
- Who could this person introduce you to?
- Where might this person recommend you?
- What can you offer this person, now and in future—the nice feeling of having helped a new professional enter the field? A chance to talk about his or her career? An introduction to one of your own connections or possibly a good new hire? A chance for this person to do a favor for the person who introduced you?

One of the best ways to cultivate a relationship with a new contact you have found is through a request for an *informational interview* (a short meeting where you ask career-related questions). By asking career questions of people in the field, you will gain insight beyond what you can typically find in a book or website. You also might get "off the record" responses to delicate, insider questions about organizational culture.

Besides being a source of great insider career tips, informational interviews also provide you with an opportunity to make a good impression on people who may eventually become helpful in a future job search. If you make a good connection with a professional in your chosen field, that person may even become your "job search advocate," keeping an eye out for you as you pursue your career.

Once you have decided on the people you want to contact and why, take the plunge: Write them an email (see the following sample) or call them, and ask for a brief meeting. Start by explaining how you found their contact information (so they know they can trust you and have a reason to reply). Mentioning the name of a person who referred you, or an organization you have in common, can make a big difference. Compliments never hurt—explain that you think they are the perfect people to help you in your career research process because they are experts in their field. Let them know that you are interested in hearing about their careers and the organizations they work for. Introduce yourself briefly so they know who you are and why you are interested in talking to them. Then end by stating some specific dates or a time frame when you are available to meet and ask for a half-hour meeting at their convenience.

Dear Mr. Kent:

You might remember me from the Metropolis Chamber of Commerce meeting last week—we spoke briefly about your work with the City of Metropolis. After our conversation, I think you would be a perfect person for me to speak with about a career in public finance because of your expertise in the field.

In June, I received my bachelor's degree in finance. My goal is to apply this degree along with the experiences acquired through internships and class projects to obtain a position in public finance. I am hoping that you might allow me to speak with you either in person or over the phone for a half hour to hear about your professional career experience. I am particularly interested in hearing about what you do at the City of Metropolis Public Finance Agency, how you got there, and if you have any advice for someone looking to enter this field.

My schedule is flexible, and I am happy to work around your availability to meet in the next two weeks, if that would be convenient for you.

I can be reached at 212-998-0000 or jolsen@gmail.com. Thank you in advance for your time, and I look forward to speaking with you soon.

Sincerely,

James Olsen

A sample email to send.

Make sure you come on time to your meeting, and do some background research so you don't waste your valuable contact person's time with elementary questions (such as "what does your agency do?"). Send a reminder the day before if the meeting was scheduled a long time in advance. Dress professionally, and bring a thoughtful list of questions.

These are some sample questions:

- What is your typical day like? What are some of the types of projects you do, in general?
- What do you like the most about your job? What is your biggest challenge?
- How did you get this job?
- What is a typical career path in your organization?
- What advice do you have for someone like me who wants to enter this profession?
- Are there any books or journals I should be reading, websites I should check, or professional organizations I should join?
- What skills, abilities, training, or personality traits make someone successful in this career? What qualities are employers in this field seeking in a new hire?
- Is this a growing or shrinking field? Where is the field headed, and what trends might affect this field?
- Could you please take a look at my resume and give me any feedback on things I can improve or gaps in my skills I should try to fill?
- What other organizations work in this field?
- What are the salary ranges for entry-level positions in this field?
- Can you recommend anyone else for me to contact?

Take notes from your meetings and reflect on what you learn. Make sure to keep track of follow-up activities and referrals. Most importantly, show your gratitude for the meeting.

Maintaining Relationships

After you meet someone for an informational interview, *always, always, always* send a thank-you note! I recommend sending an email note, because it is quicker, but you should also send a written note or card (a courtesy that is becoming rarer and rarer). Especially if your networking contact is of a generation that didn't grow up glued to a computer, a written note will be greatly appreciated.

Dear Ms. Grable:

Thank you so much for taking time from your busy schedule to meet with me yesterday. It was a pleasure to meet you, and I found our conversation very helpful. In particular, I enjoyed hearing about your work at Acme International Development Agency, the path you took to obtain your position, and the suggestions you had for me as I aim to enter this field.

Based on our conversation, it became clear to me that my skills in program development, strategic management, and conflict management will be useful for me to highlight as I look for work in this area. It was helpful to hear that I need to gain more field experience in my region of interest in order to elevate my candidacy in the eyes of a potential employer and that grant proposal development is a major aspect of the work that I may be called upon to do.

I appreciate your encouragement of my career plans, and as you suggested, I will keep you posted on my progress. I will also follow up with the two professional contacts you recommended, Jane Doe and Robert Smith; I truly appreciate your willingness to refer me to them. In the meantime, should you wish to contact me, I can be reached at 206-998-0000 or at enriquejones@abc.com. Thank you again for your time and assistance.

Sincerely,

Enrique Jones

An example of a thank-you email message.

Remind yourself to contact the person again in the next few weeks or months. Think of an article you have come across that might be interesting to that person or someone you can introduce that person to. Consider writing a short "newsletter" about your career path or progress in school and sending it to your networking contacts. These updates can be very helpful in making sure your valued connections don't forget you. Perhaps some of your networking contacts will forward you job leads or recommend you for positions. When you get a job, be sure to thank all the people in your network and update them about your good news.

Researching Posted Positions

The big job boards, such as Monster, Yahoo! HotJobs, craigslist, and CareerBuilder.com, have thousands of job listings, but don't stop your search there. Websites of local newspapers sometimes have regional job postings. Notifications that are sent out through your networking contacts and the email lists that you subscribe to are another good place to find job leads. And every week, you should check the hiring web pages of the employers you are targeting for new available jobs.

Some of the best places to look for posted jobs are small, boutique websites and publications that are geared to your field, such as those run by the professional associations mentioned in the Networking section. There are also publications that have a broad appeal to people with certain educational backgrounds or interests, such as *The Economist.* Other specialty websites are hosted by printed publications, such as the *Chronicle of Philanthropy* and the *Chronicle of Higher Education.* Not only are these sites a good source of possible jobs, they also are a good way to keep current on information that's relevant to your field and the people in your network.

If you are an alumnus of a college (regardless of when you graduated), ask whether it offers job listing services or a database for alumni. Many of them do—and many offer free or low-cost career counseling and workshops for their alumni as well.

If you can, set up job search agents (automatic email alerts about new jobs) from databases, websites, and organizations you like so you will be notified of positions as soon as they are posted. This way, you will not have to remind yourself to log in and search for opportunities. In addition, you can set up search agents in meta-search sites such as Indeed.com or Simplyhired.com. You can also set up Google alerts for certain keywords to get listings sent to you—in particular, you might want to look at www.google.com/unclesam for government listings.

Attending Job Fairs and Employer Information Sessions

Job fairs and employer presentations and open houses can be a good way to connect with employers in person.

Job Fairs

Job fairs are an opportunity to meet a large number of employers at one time and are frequently hosted by colleges and universities or public organizations. On occasion, only members of a certain organization, or students from a particular college, are allowed to attend, so ask first before you show up at the fair. In addition, some employers will hold a job fair or open house just for their organization, where interested candidates can walk in with resumes and interview on the spot. Such opportunities are often listed through the organization's website, newsletters, or occasionally through newspapers or publications or a college's career center.

A job fair is a lot like an amusement park: At both, you wait in long lines, and then finally get a three-minute thrill ride. At a job fair, your thrill ride is a short conversation with an employer. Afterwards, you stand in line to meet another one.

Sound discouraging? It shouldn't be. Those three minutes can be the start of a relationship with a recruiter, alumnus from your school, or other contact at an organization you would really like to work for. A job fair might also open your eyes to employers you have never considered (or heard of!). And the opportunity to introduce yourself 50 different times in one day is great practice for future interviewing.

You have to make those three minutes count, though. Start by researching the organizations that will be attending the fair in advance. A list of attending employers will usually be available online before the fair. Nothing impresses a recruiter more than candidates who know what the organization does and can explain why they are interested in the organization.

In addition, prepare a "personal pitch": This 15-second "infomercial" includes your name (said clearly and slowly!) and some quick "headlines" of your top accomplishments or career background. It doesn't hurt to show off some knowledge of the organization, as in this example:

> *Hello, I'm Cathy Careerchanger. I am very interested in your organization because I have five years of experience in project management in the private sector and now I am excited to work in public service. I also have strong financial management skills. I know the city is starting a new initiative to improve school buildings, and my real estate experience could be helpful with that. Can you tell me more about the project manager position you have available?*

When you go to the job fair, bring several copies of a polished resume, printed on good resume paper (no bright colors, just nice white or off-white bond or linen paper). Also, wear business attire, keeping in mind that more formal attire is probably safer. (Chapter 12 has more information on how to dress for an interview.)

When you meet a recruiter, smile and give a strong handshake, offer your resume, introduce yourself, and have a conversation. Start by asking some questions and showing interest in the organization. When you are invited to say more about yourself, offer your personal pitch. Talk about your skills, your interests, and why you are interested in the organization, and especially, how you could benefit its mission. Show enthusiasm, make eye contact, and smile. Ask good questions to get a better sense of what the organization is looking for.

You might notice recruiters writing notes on your resume; they also often put resumes into three separate piles (for example, "definitely interview," "maybe interview," and "don't interview now"). If you are lucky, and you have prepared for the fair, you will be put in the "definitely interview" pile and will hear from the employer soon.

Don't be discouraged by recruiters who refer you to apply on the organization's website or go through some other application process. Many organizations have rules and regulations that require all candidates to apply via their web-based application process or take a civil service test. Make the most of the conversation you have and try to build a relationship with the recruiter so you can follow up. Ask detailed questions about the application or testing process so you are best equipped to be selected.

Remember that the recruiters are human beings, too. Why not ask them how they are or how the fair is going? You will probably be the only person who thought to do that, and they will remember you for it. If you have made a connection and are interested in the organization, ask for the recruiter's business card.

Treat those business cards like gold (don't lose them!). Use them to send a quick "thank you for coming to the job fair" email message. In this message, follow up on the brief conversation you had and remind the recruiter of any memorable points about yourself or your discussion. Attach your resume to the email "just in case" the recruiter might want to review it. Follow up again in a week or two and try to arrange an informational interview with the recruiter. Continue to express interest in the opportunity to work for the organization.

Employer Presentations and Open Houses

Employers also often have presentations, either at various colleges or conferences or sometimes at their organization's offices. Many presentations are open to the public; others are open only to students or alumni from a particular college or university. The purpose of a presentation is to provide information to candidates about the organization, the job opportunities available, and the different divisions within the organization. One common format for a presentation is a PowerPoint and/or video presentation, followed by speeches and question-answer sessions with representatives from the employer and ending with some networking time.

When you attend these events, try to meet employer representatives and impress them with your interest in, and knowledge of, the organization. Engage them in a conversation about their field, current events that might affect their work, the college they attended, the way they became successful in their chosen profession, advice they might have for you, and so on. Again, collect business cards from the people you talk to and treat them like gold. When you get a business card from someone at a big event, write some notes on the back as soon as the conversation is over so you remember what you talked about, who the person was, what he or she looked like, and what follow-up action you want to take.

Volunteering and Interning

Like networking, volunteering or interning for an organization does not come with an expectation that the organization will hire you. The main motivation for volunteering or interning is to help a cause you care about or to gain new skills that will help your career transition. Volunteering is also an excellent way to fill time and possible gaps in the resume during a period of unemployment. That said, volunteering or interning can also be one of the most powerful ways of finding a job. Of course, volunteering is time-consuming, so think through which opportunities you would find most rewarding and beneficial to you before you commit yourself.

Benefits can include making networking connections, building your references, and reality-testing whether you are really interested in a field. By making yourself known to an organization and showing the staff your abilities, you also become an obvious candidate should a job opening arise.

You can also use volunteering to build marketable skills. Nonprofit organizations, for instance, constantly need grant writers and fundraisers. Volunteering to write a grant proposal, especially if it turns out to be a successful one, can make your resume much stronger. Similarly, if you are interested in communications, start writing a blog or volunteering to write a newsletter, and get yourself known on Twitter.

One other special form of volunteering is board membership. Nonprofit organizations all have to have a volunteer board of directors, and although many larger organizations seek board members with specific expertise (such as legal or accounting experience) or wealthy individuals who can fundraise for the organization, many other nonprofits look for individuals who can commit their time and energy to help the nonprofit grow. As a board member, you can gain exposure to the inner workings of a nonprofit organization, learn how nonprofit governance works, gain many new connections (many board members are very well connected), and demonstrate your leadership skills. Similarly, it is sometimes possible for people to get involved in local government (especially in small cities) by joining various boards and commissions or even seeking a small elected post.

Making Cold Calls

I am an example of someone for whom cold calling led to a great internship. When I was a graduate student, I was seeking an internship in a very specific field, management consulting for nonprofit organizations. Only a handful of organizations in New York City (where I lived) provided this type of service. With a tiny bit of trepidation, I called one of the largest of these organizations and mentioned I was a graduate student studying nonprofit management and was wondering if the organization had an internship program. My future boss, who took my call, said, "Well, we don't have a program, but I've been thinking about getting an intern for a long time." It was the beginning of a beautiful internship. Some of my students also have made cold calls to recruiters—seemingly the toughest audience to talk to—and landed internships or even jobs as a result.

If you plan to do cold calling, make sure to research the organization in advance and consider preparing a script (make sure it sounds natural, though). Introduce yourself with your 15-second personal pitch over the phone and ask if you can speak to the internship coordinator, recruiter, or human resources department. Better yet, find out the name of the head of the department you want to work for and ask for that person. When you get a chance to speak to that person, briefly introduce yourself and ask if the person has a moment to talk. Convey the idea that you are providing an opportunity for the organization to benefit by your service as an employee or intern. Ask if you can email your resume to him or her, and follow up shortly thereafter to ask for a meeting.

Using Government Employment Agencies

Especially if you qualify for unemployment, have a disability, or receive public assistance, government agencies are a great, free resource to help you find employment. States usually offer a job database, links to employment services, job market information, career assessments, and job search tips. Community colleges and community-based organizations also often offer free workshops on resume writing or interviewing for the public to attend.

Consulting and Contracting

If you have significant professional experience, are entrepreneurial, and can obtain the proper credentials or business license, you may want to investigate the possibility of starting a consulting practice. Many consulting opportunities arise within established consulting firms, but you can also work on a freelance or contract basis. This option can be especially important to consider during an economic downturn in which an employer does not have the budget to bring on a full-time employee with benefits, but might have project funding to hire a contractor. Look for government agencies and nonprofits that put out calls for contractor bids, search for databases of contracting opportunities, and use your network to see what might be available on a short-term or contract basis. The application process can be more involved than a job application, and the constant work required to find new contracts isn't for everyone, but it is an attractive option for some.

Using Headhunters and Employment Agencies

Headhunters, employment agencies, or temp agencies are known as "third-party recruiters." They are typically hired by employers to help source candidates for certain positions. Normally, an employer pays a fee to the recruiter, either a percentage of the earnings of the candidate the organization eventually hires or a flat-rate fee. High-level executive positions in nonprofit organizations or city government might be filled through executive recruiters, and some temporary positions are hired via temp agencies.

Always remember that the recruiter's client is the employer, not you. It is not the recruiter's job to help you determine what kind of position you want. Rather, the recruiter wants to fill the job order offered by the client. Sometimes the individual recruiter receives a bonus or commission for placing someone in a position. For these reasons, I suggest looking at temp agencies and third-party recruiters as a useful addition to your job search techniques portfolio, but not one you should rely on to find you a job.

Getting Hired Through Special Fellowships

Both government and nonprofit organizations sometimes have special fellowship programs that are available mainly to recent graduates of certain graduate programs. If you are a recent graduate of a master's or PhD program, don't overlook these fellowship opportunities.

Typical postgraduate fellowship programs are designed as a one- or two-year, full-time, paid position with additional training, networking, and possibly rotational job assignments. In most cases, the organizations hosting the fellowship see the fellows as a natural candidate pool for hiring (having seen them perform in their jobs for a year or two) and seek to convert them to full-time, permanent hires. The fellowships themselves are also often quite well known and prestigious within the fields in which they exist, so just having been selected for one can be an honor that will help with future job searching.

Many fellowships are quite competitive, and many more are relatively obscure or hard to find without doing in-depth research on an organization's website. (A list of fellowships is at the end of this chapter.) If you are still in graduate school, start checking out these fellowship opportunities in the early part of your final year (no later than September of the school year in which you will be graduating). Ask your career services provider at your school for tips on making a good application.

Applying for Jobs

You have done thorough research, written your resume, gotten organized and motivated, made networking contacts, and identified job leads; now it's time to actually apply for jobs.

Some people take the scattershot approach and apply to everything, regardless of whether they are interested in or qualified for the opportunity. (Employers have sometimes complained to me that applicants didn't take the time to read the job description!) Hitting the Apply button on an online job posting database is sometimes just too easy. Don't waste your time, and the employer's time, by sending resumes to opportunities you don't really want.

On the other hand, some job seekers apply only for the handful of positions they are extremely interested in. These job seekers limit themselves to a small pool of opportunities and are sometimes aiming for jobs they are not yet qualified for. Candidates who are entering a new field or lack relevant experience need to cast a wider net just to get some related experience on their resume.

Keep in mind that just applying for a position does not obligate you to accept an interview, and going on an interview does not obligate you to accept a position if you are offered one. There is usually little harm in simply applying for jobs, so if you have the time to make a quality application, and are sincerely interested in a job and feel you meet the qualifications, you might as well apply.

I recommend applying for as many positions that you might be interested in as possible, and keep applying on a weekly basis until you get a job offer—even after you've had a few interviews. Many job seekers make the mistake of no longer applying to jobs when they get an interview with an organization they are excited about. Yet there is no guarantee that any interview will turn into a job offer. You may even be told that you are a good candidate, only to find out later that the organization has offered the position to someone else. If you have stopped sending out applications in the meantime, you will be set back in your job search by weeks or months. Keep on applying until you have an offer that you plan to accept.

Job seekers sometimes wonder if it might be considered "overkill" if they apply to the same organization through more than one venue (for example, applying directly through the organization's website, approaching someone you met at a presentation or job fair, and networking with someone at the organization). I have found, rather, that the opposite is true—employers are usually impressed by a job seeker who is so passionate about their organization that he or she attends every presentation, applies online, says hello at the job fair, and networks to meet people in the organization. However, this type of enthusiasm is not the same thing as pestering a hiring manager by calling or emailing repeatedly about the same job.

Following all the directions in an application process is vital—leaving out a form or a required document will usually land you in the "no" pile. The sections that follow take you through the steps involved in making a good application.

Analyzing the Job Description

Take a deep look at the job description before you apply. The job description in the following figure is adapted from one listed on Idealist.org. I have highlighted those points that illustrate the most important skills needed for this particular job. Points in *italics* highlight the type of people you would interact with in this job; underlined points are technical skills and training; and **bold** indicates special experience or general abilities.

Associate Director of Development

General Duties: Assist the Development Director in support of programs and activities.

Specific Responsibilities:

1. Foundation Development: Work with *development team and board of trustees* to develop and implement the annual fundraising plan, including preparing and keeping the annual calendar current. Participate in annual budget development process, recommending appropriate goals for the annual campaign.

2. Donor & Public Relations: Assist the *development team* with increasing visibility and support for the foundation. Collaborate with *development team* in **writing** and producing solicitations, an annual report to contributors, and other **marketing** materials. Work with *program staff* to identify and develop materials and publicity needed for their programs. Respond to telephone and email inquiries from *donors, trustees, and other volunteer* fundraisers, initiating **communication** as appropriate.

3. Grants & Prospect **Research:** Collaborate with *development team and board of trustees* in research on new fundraising and foundation grant opportunities. Prepare grant applications for submittal and prepare quarterly or annual reports as required by granting agencies.

4. Special Projects: Provide **leadership** on special projects. This may include program development, **recruitment** and support of *volunteers*, fundraising activities, budget oversight, monitoring, tracking and reporting, and evaluation.

5. Database Management: Assist the *development team* to develop and maintain the Raiser's Edge database, including generating periodic reports in relation to committee work, special events, and other development efforts.

6. Board & Committee Support: Participate actively in *board and committee* structure, attend meetings as requested, assist with meeting preparation, prepare meeting minutes/notes, and follow up as necessary.

7. Website: Assist in website development and maintenance. Help ensure updated information is on the website.

Qualifications:

- BA degree in social service, nonprofit, public relations, marketing, or related field plus 2 to 3 years of experience in event planning, fundraising, grant writing, public relations, or marketing.
- Proficient in MS Office and Raiser's Edge.
- Must possess **strong written, verbal, and interpersonal communication skills**.
- Ability to work varied hours, including nights and weekends as necessary.
- Knowledge of fundraising techniques, special events, grants, annual campaigns, working with a *board of trustees,* and some knowledge of public relations practices.

Sample job description.

An analysis of this job reveals the following requirements:

- **Technical skills and training:** MS Office and Raiser's Edge proficiency, website maintenance, budgeting, grant writing, fundraising plan development, setting goals for an annual campaign, annual report production, and BA degree
- **People you will need to be able to interact with:** Development team and board of trustees, committees, program staff, donors, and volunteers
- **"Soft" (nontechnical) skills:** Writing, communicating, leading, recruiting volunteers, doing research, and marketing

Another interesting way to analyze a job description is to add it to an online word cloud generator, such as www.tocloud.com, and see which words are larger. This tool will make repeated words look bigger. In the sample job description, the largest words are development, development team, fund, fundraising, assists, annual, board, public relations, raising, Raiser's Edge, special, support, trustees, work, foundation, collaborative, director, team, budget, events, grants, prepare, and writing. These words are the key requirements and skills needed in the job—and if you are applying for this job, these words should be emphasized in your cover letter and resume.

After you have analyzed the job description, determine whether you have all or at least most of the skills that the employer is looking for. If you do, the next step is to customize your resume (particularly the Profile section) and cover letter to fit the description and send them in. (If you don't have the required skills, refer to Chapter 1 for more information on handling skills gaps.)

Sending in Your Application

Preferably, you will be one of the first in line to apply for any position. Many organizations start reviewing applications as they are submitted rather than waiting until a deadline date to review them, meaning that earlier applications get more attention.

Carefully follow the instructions on how to apply. You may send resumes by applying online or by email, fax, or regular mail. If applying by mail, take the time to print your resume and cover letter on quality resume paper, send it in a large envelope so you don't have to fold it up, and type up an address label rather than handwriting the address (yes, these little things can matter). If sending your materials by email, note whether attachments are acceptable and in what format you should submit them. Some organizations may ask for specific additions to the typical resume or cover letter, such as copies of transcripts, writing samples, specific essays, or lists of references. Call or email the organization with any questions about the application process.

Following Up on Applications

In a tough job market, jobs may get hundreds of applications during a small time frame, and you are likely to be competing against people who have recently been laid off who have years of experience. But don't let that bother you! Instead, distinguish yourself by being the polite, bright, enthusiastic, and friendly candidate who follows up and is clearly excited about the job.

If at all possible (and unless the job posting says "no calls"), try to identify and call the hiring manager directly. Read the description and do research to try to find out whom the position reports to, and then research on the Web or call the receptionist to get the name of that person. Call the organization back later and ask for that person by name.

In your brief phone discussion, mention that you have recently applied for the open position and that you are very interested in it. Ask a few questions, such as what the person is looking for in the ideal candidate and when he or she might be conducting interviews. The tone of this call and what you ask reveal both your enthusiasm and your politeness. Avoid asking questions that cause the person on the other line to comb through piles of paper or start clicking the computer mouse, such as "Did you get my application?" Instead, try the following:

> *Jane Q. Employer: Hello, Jane Employer speaking.*
>
> *Bob Jobseeker: Good morning, Ms. Employer, my name is Bob Jobseeker, and I have a quick question about the public policy analyst position you have open. I'm sure you're busy—would you have just a minute to discuss it now, or should I call back later? (Respect the other person's time.)*
>
> *Jane: I have a moment now.*
>
> *Bob: Thank you so much for speaking with me. I think this positon would be a great fit for my background in policy work, and I'm excited about the opportunity. Your organization is also one I've admired for a long time.*
>
> *I was just wondering if there are any qualities not listed in the description that you think would make an ideal candidate? (Give the other person a chance to talk.)*
>
> *...I have some examples of prior policy memos I can send; would you be interested in that as part of the application?*
>
> *...Can you tell me if this is more of a quantitative or qualitative research role? (Be sure your question isn't answered by the job description.)*
>
> *...Do you have a sense of when interviews will be conducted?*
>
> *...I really appreciate your time.*

You could also ask if it's not too forward to connect over LinkedIn (if you have checked to see that the person has a LinkedIn profile) so that the person can see your recommendations.

Express enthusiasm and gratitude throughout your short conversation, and then follow up with the employer with a brief thank-you email. If you do this politely, you may lift your resume to the top of the pile.

All of the previous job search techniques apply to job searches in the corporate and nonprofit sectors and to many job applications in government. However, some of these techniques must be modified for certain government organizations where the hiring process can be quite different. The rest of this chapter offers specific tips and techniques to help you with these special job searches.

Understanding the Federal Job Search

The federal government is a huge employer with a hiring process that is very different from that of most other employers. With more than 30,600 open job listings as of this writing, and with excellent benefits, job security, and advancement opportunities, the federal government is an employer worth understanding.

The Competitive Examination Hiring Process Via USAJOBS

When most people ask about how to find a federal job, they are told to look at the postings on USAJOBS (the U.S. Office of Personnel Management's official federal jobs website). Most of these postings are referred to as positions where the hiring is by *competitive examination* (because you must "compete" for the positions and be considered best qualified to go forward with an interview). Yet a 2005 study conducted by the Merit Systems Protection Board found that only 28 percent of new hires came through the competitive examination process (many others went through special hiring authorities described later in this chapter). Certain organizations, such as the military and intelligence community, the U.S. Postal Service, and the State Department, have their own process in which some or all of their positions are not listed in USAJOBS. In addition, Congressional positions, such as legislative aides and positions with the Congressional Research Service, typically do not get listed on USAJOBS, though some Congressional agencies, such as the Government Accountability Office, do use USAJOBS. That being said, many federal jobs are filled through USAJOBS, so it's important to know how to best strategize to succeed in the system.

In the competitive examination process, the federal government uses certain preferences in hiring, which can sometimes make it difficult to get your first federal position (this is why the other, special hiring authorities detailed later on in this section are worth considering). For example, it is much easier for an agency to hire a current federal employee (called a *status candidate*) than a nonfederal one. In fact, many positions on USAJOBS are open *only* to status candidates. Even when a position is open to "all citizens," a federal agency can forward many more status candidates to be interviewed than it can nonstatus candidates.

Veterans also receive preference in federal hiring. Nonstatus candidates are ranked (usually on a 100-point scale) based on their applications, and veterans receive either a 5- or 10-point preference, meaning that if two applicants are equally qualified (both receiving 95 points, for example), the veteran will get 5 or 10 additional points and therefore must be interviewed. For these reasons, you should write a good federal application, consider those opportunities where multiple openings are listed (so you will have multiple chances to be considered), and look for alternative ways to be hired besides the competitive examination process. (Check www.opm.gov/hiringreform for updates about changes in the federal hiring process.)

The Federal Resume

USAJOBS requires several steps for setting up a profile, including a resume builder. Spend the time to make your profile as complete and accurate as possible. Federal agencies must evaluate you on how much relevant education and experience you have, down to the specific courses you have taken and the number of months of employment you have had. A functional resume format will not work here.

Required information includes the organization name, phone number, supervisor, salary, and dates of employment for all of your prior work experience. List as much information as you can and state that the supervisor can be contacted (if you don't, this can raise a red flag). If your supervisor is no longer at the place you worked, list at least a general phone number for the employer so your employment can be verified. If the company where you worked no longer exists, you may need to simply note that as well.

When describing your experience, make sure to list not only your accomplishments, but also your day-to-day functions. Note that you also can include unpaid and volunteer experience as work experience. Try to convey the level of knowledge or skills required for the position and the amount of independence you had. Quantify your work and accomplishments wherever possible. You can also list any awards, honors, or commendations you received. In addition, you can use the section for other qualifications and skills to describe any leadership positions, speaking engagements, publications, certifications, or licenses. It's also very important to customize your resume to include keywords from the job description you are applying for.

You can write in complete sentences or paragraphs and even write in the first person on a federal resume. You also can include much more detail about your education than you would in a regular resume, such as describing each of your relevant courses and thesis projects and listing your education as far back as high school. Pat M. Fellow's resume shows what a federal resume might look like.

Pat M. Fellow
111 Test Avenue
Lynwood, WA 98000
Mobile: 206.987.6543
Evening Phone: 206.876.5432
Day Phone: 206.765.4321
Email: pat.m.fellow@gmail.com

Country of citizenship: United States of America
Veterans' Preference: No
Contact Current Employer: Yes

AVAILABILITY **Job Type:** Permanent

Work Schedule: Full Time

DESIRED LOCATIONS US-CA-Los Angeles

US-WA-Seattle
US-DC

WORK EXPERIENCE **King County Department of Natural Resources and Parks**
Seattle, WA US

2/2004-Present

Salary: 50,000 USD Per Year
Hours per week: 40

WATER QUALITY PLANNER/PROJECT MANAGER II
POLICY ANALYSIS. Contributed to county Climate Plan and Shoreline Master Plan. Provided analysis of ESA listings, proposed state legislation, and salmon recovery plans.

STRATEGIC THINKING. Managed the strategic planning process for the county's Science Section with an emphasis on improvement of services provided, maintenance of client and customer focus, and achievement of results despite funding constraints.

PROGRAM EVALUATION AND ORGANIZATIONAL ANALYSIS. Analyzed current county practices of prioritizing and funding of environmental monitoring activities. Developed organizational structure options for consideration by management.

TEAM BUILDING. Motivated members of climate change adaptation team, section business planning team, and high-frequency monitoring team toward goal accomplishments.

ACCOUNTABILITY. Developed section performance measures and contributed to department annual performance measure report.

DATA COLLECTION. Reviewed documents and conducted interviews with management and customers to collect data to inform funding strategy development for county environmental science activities and programs. Developed data collection strategies for Puget Sound water and sediment quality data.

DATA ANALYSIS. Used statistics and other appropriate means to interpret scientific data collected by King County for annual performance measure report, and determined patterns and trends.

FINANCIAL MANAGEMENT. Assisted with developing, presenting, and defending section budget. Developed and proposed strategies for meeting funding shortfalls in the short- and long-term.

PROBLEM SOLVING. Identified and analyzed organizational issues adversely affecting section staff performance and made recommendations to management.

COLLABORATION. Member of county's Climate Change Adaptation Team and Puget Sound High-Frequency Monitoring Team.

This USAJOBS federal resume targets a GS-9 program analyst position with the EPA and uses federal resume expert Kathryn Troutman's Outline format, as explained in her book, Federal Resume Guidebook, *Fourth Edition (JIST Publishing, 2007).*

(continued)

(continued)

PARTNERING. Engaged in cross-functional activities with NOAA, Washington State Department of Ecology, City of Seattle, City of Olympia, USGS, and the University of Washington.

ORAL COMMUNICATION. Contributed to the effective delivery of information to staff, management, and clients through briefings, the use of visuals and graphics, and other appropriate means. Delivered several formal presentations. Assisted manager with briefings to director and county executive.

WRITTEN COMMUNICATION. Recorded information from interviews, summarized information from meetings in writing, and contributed to reports. Communicated technical data to the public and policy-makers. Contributed to 2007 King County Climate Plan and 2007 Puget Sound Update. Section strategic plan lead author.

ACCOMPLISHMENTS:
* Selected to lead the strategic planning effort for the county's Science Section.
* Selected to lead and organize the coastal zone breakout session at the 2005 King County Climate Change Conference.
* Selected to serve on county's climate change adaptation team and develop county climate change policy. (Contact Supervisor: Yes, Supervisor's Name: Jim Doe, Supervisor's Phone: 206.987.6543)

Earthside Geosciences **9/2003-2/2004**
Seattle, WA US

Salary: $20/hr
Hours per week: 60

PROJECT MANAGER
RESEARCH DESIGN. Designed and conducted original research on contaminated sediments and the effects of dredging.

DATA COLLECTION. Collected data in a variety of laboratory and field settings.

DATA ANALYSIS. Interpreted data using statistics and other appropriate means.

COLLABORATION. Worked in a team-based environment through effective communication and information sharing practices. Led and participated on project teams.

ORAL COMMUNICATION. Contributed to the effective delivery of information to internal staff and external clients and customers through briefings, the use of visuals and graphics, and other appropriate means.

WRITTEN COMMUNICATION. Recorded information and summarized information in writing in the form of client reports. Lead author and coauthor on professional journal publications and NSF grant application.

Long Beach Unified School District **9/2000- 6/2002**
Long Beach, CA US
Salary: $40,000/yr
Hours per week: 80

SCIENCE TEACHER
ORAL COMMUNICATION. Contributed to the effective delivery of information to students, parents, and administrators through lessons, demonstrations, laboratory experiments, the use of visual and graphics, and meetings.

WRITTEN COMMUNICATION. Provided written feedback and progress reports to students and parents.

MENTOR and MOTIVATE STUDENTS. Evaluated student performance and recommended strategies to increase individual and classroom performance. Coached and mentored students to resolve interpersonal issues. Facilitated problem solving and collaboration among students and colleagues.

EDUCATION

University of Washington, Evans School of Public Affairs
Seattle, WA US
Master's Degree - 6/2008
30 Quarter Hours
Major: Public Administration
GPA: 3.89 out of 4.0

Relevant Coursework, Licensures, and Certifications:

PUBLIC MANAGEMENT
Analyzes the institutional and political context of modern public management. Cases, readings, and discussion provide an integrated introduction to the major skills needed to successfully lead and manage government and nonprofit organizations.

PUBLIC BUDGETING AND FINANCIAL MANAGEMENT
Budgeting as a management process. Study of formulation and administration of government budgets, including role of budgeting in policy processes, approaches to budget formulation and analysis, and aspects of budget administration, such as revenue estimating, allotment control, cost accounting.

FINANCIAL MANAGEMENT IN THE PUBLIC SECTOR
Exploration of the managerial uses of accounting and other processes of financial management in the public sector. Topics covered include: financial planning and control, fund accounting, cost accounting, asset accounting, internal controls, auditing, financial analysis, and financial reporting.

MEDIATION AND NEGOTIATION AS INSTRUMENTS OF PUBLIC MANAGEMENT AND POLICY MAKING
Use of negotiation and mediation techniques to resolve disputes and disagreements over public-policy issues.

MICROECONOMIC POLICY ANALYSIS
Ways in which microeconomic analysis can contribute to the analysis of public sector issues. Policy applications of theory.

QUANTITATIVE ANALYSIS
Two-quarter sequence explores how to formulate research questions, gain experience with conducting research, and learn how to assess which statistical tools or research methods are appropriate to answer different types of policy or management questions. Covers probability, descriptive statistics, hypothesis testing, and confidence intervals.

PUBLIC LEADERSHIP
Focus on the societal context of managerial life.

ETHICS AND PUBLIC POLICY
Special focus on the integration of moral concerns into public discussion in a manner that contributes to good policy and does not polarize issues.

University of Michigan, Dept. of Chemistry
Ann Arbor, MI, US
Master's Degree- 12/1992
62 Semester Hours
Major: Chemistry
GPA: 3.85 out of 4.0
Relevant Coursework, Licensures, and Certifications:
Advisor: Dr. Sandy Chem, Thesis: "Selective transcription of genes encoding telomerase RNA, other proteins during telomere synthesis and other stages of macronuclear development."

Graduate Research Assistantship. Graduate Teaching Assistantship. Coursework in advanced topics in the fields of chemistry, biochemistry, and molecular biology.

California State University Long Beach, Dept. of Chemistry and Biochemistry
Long Beach, CA US
Bachelor's Degree- 6/1989
146.67 Semester Hours
Major: Biochemistry
GPA: 3.264 out of 4.0

University of Hawaii at Manoa, Dept. of Oceanography
Honolulu, HI US
Some College Coursework Completed - 5/1999
81 Semester Hours
Major: Oceanography
GPA: 3.92 out of 4.0
Relevant Coursework, Licensures and Certifications:
Advisor:Fred Fishbone, Ph.D. Candidacy Achieved

Graduate Research Assistantship. Graduate Teaching Assistantship. Coursework in advanced topics in the fields of oceanography, geology, and geochemistry.

(continued)

(continued)

California State University Long Beach, Dept. of Science Education
Long Beach, CA US
Certification- 12/2000
41 Semester Hours
GPA: 3.739 out of 4.0
Relevant Coursework, Licensures, and Certifications:
Single-Subject Teaching Credential, Chemistry

JOB RELATED TRAINING

PROJECT MANAGEMENT, March, 2004
STRATEGIC MARKETING IN THE PUBLIC SECTOR, March 2008
MAPPING, PLANNING, AND ACTION: A FRAMEWORK FOR STRATEGY, April, 2008
EFFECTIVE MANAGEMENT IN A POLITICAL ENVIRONMENT, May, 2008
ACCOUNTABILITY FOR RESULTS: PERFORMANCE MEASUREMENT, May, 2008
MANAGING PEOPLE TO IMPROVE PROGRAMS, June, 2008

LANGUAGES

English

Spoken:	Advanced
Written:	Advanced
Read:	Advanced

PROFESSIONAL PUBLICATIONS

Please note that Smith is my maiden name.

JOURNAL ARTICLES - PEER REVIEWED
Fellow, P.M., Doe, J., and Grant, U., 2005. Development and complete validation of a method for the determination of dimethyl mercury in air and other media. Analytica Chimica 123:45-66
Fellow, P.M., and Bloom, F., 2003. Muddying the waters of debate: Is dredging a significant sources of trace metals to the estuarine environment? Geochimica 55:A-6.
Fish, A., Waters, K., Chaulk, B., and Smith, P.M., 1999.
Biologically mediated dissolution of calcium carbonate above the chemical lysocline. Deep Sea Journals. 55:1653-1669.

REPORTS and THESES
Fellow, P.M., and Fishbone, K., 2007. Seattle Aquarium high-frequency marine monitoring pilot project report. King County Department of Natural Resources and Parks, Seattle, WA.
Able, B., Fellow, P.M., and Bean, C., 2006. Water quality status report for marine waters, 2004. King County Department of Natural Resources and Parks, Seattle, WA. 165 pp.
Taylor, A., Green, R., and Fellow, P.M., 2005. Water quality status report for marine waters, 2002 and 2003. King County Department of Natural Resources and Parks, Seattle, WA, 140 pp.

REFERENCES

Jim Smith	King County Department of Natural Resources and Parks	Supervisor, Water Quality and Quantity Unit
Phone Number:	(206)987-6574	
Email Address:	jim.smith@kingcounty.gov	
Reference Type:	Professional	
Dr. Bill Brain	King County Department of Natural Resources and Parks	Manager, Science Section
Phone Number:	(206)321-6547	
Email Address:	bill.brain@kingcounty.gov	
Reference Type:	Professional	
Mark Greenleaf	King County Department of Natural Resources and Parks	Director, Water and Land Resources Division
Phone Number:	(206)765-4321	
Email Address:	mark.greenleaf@kingcounty.gov	

	Reference Type:	Professional	
	Elizabeth Cloud	King County Executive Office	Climate Change Coordinator
	Phone Number:	(206)999-9999	
	Email Address:	elizabeth.cloud@kingcounty.gov	
	Reference Type:	Professional	
	Kate Waters	King County Department of Natural Resources and Parks	Supervisor, Watershed and Ecological Assessment Team
	Phone Number:	(206)888-8888	
	Email Address:	kate.waters@kingcounty.gov	
	Reference Type:	Professional	
ADDITIONAL INFORMATION	Highly proficient in Microsoft Word, Excel, PowerPoint, Outlook, and Visio. Highly proficient in SigmaPlot. Proficient in the statistical software packages SPSS and R.		

Federal Vacancy Announcements and Applications

A USAJOBS job description has five sections:

- **Overview:** This section lists the deadline to apply (don't wait until the deadline, though), location, salary range or grade (see the section on federal hiring levels), federal department, job title, and other general information. Keep an eye out for positions that mention multiple vacancies or are listed for longer periods of time—more vacancies mean more chances for you.
- **Duties:** This section describes what the position entails—be sure to use the keywords from this section in your resume and essays (KSAs).
- **Qualifications and Evaluations:** Carefully read this section to be sure you meet the requirements for the job.
- **Benefits and Other Information:** This section includes a general statement about vacation, health insurance, retirement and other benefits, and notes specific to the position.
- **How to Apply:** This section will often lead to you to an online application system external to USAJOBS, which many times will draw the data from your general USAJOBS resume and put it into another database which is used by a particular agency. Some positions still require mailed-in applications. Sometimes a listing will also ask for faxed-in parts of an application, especially if you are claiming veteran's preference or need to show transcripts. You might also need to download and submit certain forms with your application. Be sure to follow all the instructions carefully. In this section, you may also find contact information that you can use to follow up with questions about your application.

NOTE

If you find a position you are interested in, make sure you copy and paste the description, especially the announcement number and any contact information, into an email to yourself, because the description will disappear after the deadline, and you will need it if you have an interview or follow-up questions.

KSAs and Questionnaires

In addition to resumes, many federal jobs also ask for special essays called Knowledge, Skills, and Abilities essays or KSAs. (As of November 2010, federal agencies are supposed to stop requiring KSAs, but they might still be included in some way in the application process. Check www.opm.gov/hiringreform for updates.) Taking the time to write a good essay is very important. The two key points to remember when writing KSAs are to use clear, specific, and measurable accomplishment examples that answer the KSA question and to incorporate keywords from the job description and the KSA question itself as much as possible.

To find good KSA stories, go back to Chapter 1 and look through your Problem-Action-Result stories. This format of introducing the situation you faced, the problem or challenge you had to overcome, the action steps you took, and the quantifiable results you achieved works well for KSAs. You can use examples from work, school, or volunteer experiences. You should write in the first person and write from a half to three quarters of a page per KSA.

You may also encounter questionnaires in the job application process. Typically, they will ask you to measure your abilities according to a five-point rating scale of how well you know how to do certain job functions. Or you may get up to 100 yes-or-no questions. Although you shouldn't lie, I've been told on a few occasions that certain agencies look only at applicants who rated themselves at the top level for each job function. So be generous in your assessment of your own abilities when answering the questionnaires.

On occasion, you may encounter other assessments or questionnaires, such as the Administrative Careers with America (ACWA) assessment for more entry-level positions. This assessment evaluates verbal and quantitative reasoning and other skills.

Federal Hiring Levels (Salary Grades)

Federal job descriptions list "GS levels," which refer to salary levels. For example, GS-5 and GS-7 levels typically require undergraduate education and some experience. GS-9 positions and higher require at least a master's degree or prior years of experience at the GS-7 level. (The USAJOBS website has explanations of the GS levels and how they vary by geographic location.)

I have heard from several hiring managers in the federal government that people should consider applying for positions at lower levels than they are qualified for. For example, you might consider GS-7 positions even if you have a master's degree. This is because if a position is posted at multiple levels, such as GS-7, 9, and 11, the hiring authorities will review each of the applications submitted at each level separately and forward the best candidates who have applied at each level. If you apply at both the GS-7 and the GS-9 level with a master's degree, you might be the best qualified candidate of all the applicants at the GS-7 level, but not at the GS-9 level. You will at least get a chance at an interview at the GS-7 level. If you apply at GS-9 only, you might not get the chance.

Special Hiring Authorities and Excepted Service

Do KSA essays, long federal resumes, and the questionnaires sound daunting to you? Well, you're not alone. Federal agencies are increasingly using other special hiring processes to find candidates. Some of the most popular of these *excepted service* hiring authorities include opportunities for students and recent graduates, such as the Presidential Management Fellowship for recent master's or PhD graduates, the Federal Career Intern Program (FCIP), and the Student Career Experience Program (SCEP). There are other special hiring authorities as well.

> **NOTE** For information on the special hiring process used by the State Department to hire people for the Foreign Service, refer to Chapter 7. If you are interested in working with the United Nations or its affiliates, Chapter 7 also has tips on the UN's specific hiring process. Chapter 8 describes the process the Department of Justice uses to hire FBI special agents.

Presidential Management Fellows Program

One of the most prestigious and competitive fellowships for individuals with graduate degrees, the Presidential Management Fellows Program (PMF) is a two-year, rotational, full-time job in the federal government with additional training and networking opportunities provided. Candidates must apply via a listing on USAJOBS during the fall of their final year of graduate school. Candidates must then be nominated by their school, and if nominated, they complete a multiple-choice test.

A list of finalists is announced, and the finalists can attend a job fair in Washington, DC, typically in March. Every finalist is not guaranteed to receive a job offer, but around 60 percent do, and being a PMF finalist is highly prestigious in its own right. In addition, certain federal agencies (for example, the State Department and USAID) fill a large part of their entry-level civil service hires through the PMF. It can be quite difficult to get into these competitive agencies any other way.

Federal Career Intern Program

The Federal Career Intern Program (FCIP) is perhaps the single biggest hiring authority used by federal agencies to fill entry-level positions (over half of entry-level hires came through FCIP in 2005, according to the U.S. Merit Systems Protection Board). Don't be fooled by the name—FCIP positions are full-time, paid jobs, not part-time or unpaid internships that take place while you are in school.

Although other federal fellowship programs are established and structured, many FCIP positions just pop up on an as-needed basis. Such positions do not have to be publicly listed on USAJOBS, and they may not be advertised except on an agency's website or at a job fair. Networking and doing in-depth research into the federal agency offices you are interested in is a good way to keep abreast of such opportunities. Contact your local Federal Executive Board and search the Blue Pages of your phone book for local federal agencies to reach out to.

What's nice about FCIP positions is that you do not always have to go through the whole federal resume process or write KSAs. Instead, you can apply using your regular resume and cover letter (though it might still help you to have a federal-style resume). Also, FCIP opportunities are open not just to recent graduates, but also to people who graduated a few years ago.

Other Special Hiring Authorities

If you belong to one or more of the following groups, you may qualify as a status candidate for federal jobs:

- **Federal interns:** Many people (even federal hiring managers) don't realize that if you serve a certain number of hours of internships (usually 640) through the Student Career Experience Program (SCEP), you can be converted directly to a full-time position. If you are a student doing an internship in the federal government, be sure to ask your supervisor about this important advantage!
- **Returned Peace Corps volunteers or AmeriCorps participants:** The Peace Corps or AmeriCorps Conversion provides volunteers in these programs one year of *noncompetitive eligibility* after they return, meaning they are considered status candidates. This eligibility means they can search USAJOBS for status positions and apply for them directly, which opens up many more job opportunities.
- **Veterans:** In addition to receiving preference in applications in nearly all other hiring processes in the federal government, veterans also have a few hiring options all their own. (Check the U.S. Office of Personnel Management's veterans employment website at www.fedshirevets.gov for more information.)
- **Individuals with disabilities:** There are some special hiring practices for people with severe physical or mental disabilities, in which individuals with proper documentation of a disability may apply noncompetitively with various agencies. The U.S. Office of Personnel Management outlines this program at www.opm.gov/disability/Peoplewithdisabilities.asp.

Federal Security Clearances

Some federal positions require a current security clearance (a status given to individuals that allows them access to classified information), and others may require you to obtain a clearance as a condition of employment. These clearances are especially important for sensitive government positions, such as those in the intelligence community or Foreign Service, but some level of clearance is required for many other positions.

Some clearances require an in-depth background check on your prior employment, prior residences, education, qualifications, and criminal record. Higher-level clearances may require fingerprinting or a credit check or even a check on relatives, assets, and character references. In some cases, it can take months to receive a clearance.

Federal hiring experts suggest that failing a security clearance may be worse for your federal job prospects than simply not applying for positions that require a clearance—so if you have anything in your background that could prevent you from passing the clearance, you probably should focus on positions that don't require a high level of security clearance. In addition, the potential consequences of misrepresenting anything in your history are far worse than the potential consequences of being honest with an employer and providing an explanation instead.

Federal Legislative Jobs

Many people are highly motivated to work on legislative issues where they can have an impact on the national scene. Working with an elected official, political party, or policy committee is a great way to have an impact. The job search process is quite different from other federal search processes, though.

There are two main types of legislative positions: those working for a specific elected official, in which your job is tied to the re-election of the person you work for, and those in legislative branch agencies that serve all elected officials, such as the Congressional Research Service or Government Accountability Office. Those working for legislative agencies must be able to research policies from any perspective and remain nonpartisan in their work, and the job application process for these positions is similar to other civil service positions.

On the other hand, those working for elected officials really can't be nonpartisan, and they usually find their jobs through networking or campaign work. For example, I know of an individual who is the chief of staff for a U.S. senator and has had a long career working with elected officials—but he has never had a resume. Every position he has had has come from networking. Working on election campaigns, doing numerous internships, volunteering, going to meetings, developing legislative research expertise, or becoming involved with a local chapter of your Republican, Democratic, or other party is a great way to get your foot in the door with political positions.

Many people come to Washington, DC, to work as interns as a method for finding full-time jobs. Not only are many internships not advertised (and found only through networking or referrals), but you can even help set one up yourself by inquiring and offering to intern for a member of Congress. Some internships are paid, particularly in Congress, though many are not.

Although interning and networking are the best way in, there are also some good websites that list Congressional positions; these are listed at the end of the chapter.

Jobs with the President

Positions working directly with the President of the United States are, of course, some of the most prestigious and competitive of all. The President's direct staff includes a chief of staff, deputy chiefs of staff, and senior advisors. There are also positions within the Executive Office of the President, which includes the Council of Economic Advisors, National Security Council, Office of Management and Budget, and Office of Science and Technology Policy. Other entities include supportive functions such as the President's Advance (which prepares locations for a Presidential visit), Office of Communications, and other offices such as the Office of Urban Affairs Policy or Office of Social Innovation. These offices may change with each administration.

Other positions within the administration are listed in the *United States Government Policy and Supporting Positions* book, otherwise known as the *Plum Book,* which lists positions that are appointed by the President. (It seems to have gotten the name because it had a purple-colored cover in its printed form and because the 7,000 positions listed are all "plum" jobs.) An even more exclusive list of Presidential appointments is the *Prune Book* (called this because the positions are for more experienced staff who are likely to be older and wrinklier). Of course, these types of positions are typically filled by the most highly experienced individuals with the most connections.

Applying for a Job in State Government

Like the federal government, many state governments have particular hiring processes. Every state has its own employment website. Researching the hiring process for the state agencies you are interested in well in advance of an active job search is essential because their policies can differ vastly. Some state employment sites link to jobs on the various agency websites directly, but most offer a central clearinghouse of all state government jobs. In general, each state government tends to do hiring in one (or a combination) of three ways: through civil service tests, through specialized applications, or through a resume and cover letter submittal process that is more like private sector hiring.

Civil Service Tests

The rationale behind testing is to ensure that the civil service hires the most qualified candidates without preference based on nepotism or political connections. Based on my research reading the hiring websites of all 50 states, about half of the states require some kind of civil service test for employment, at least for some jobs. Fourteen states (Alabama, California, Connecticut, Delaware, Hawaii, Idaho, Illinois, Louisiana, Massachusetts, New Hampshire, New Jersey, New York, Oklahoma, and Pennsylvania) seem to require a test for the majority of positions. In some states, certain tests are offered on an ongoing basis. In others, certain tests are offered infrequently (for example, in New York State, the fisheries biologist exam has apparently been given on about a five-year interval lately).

In most cases, you have to apply in advance and be found minimally qualified before you will be allowed to take a civil service test. Once you take the exam, if you have a passing score (usually at least 70 percent—this number varies by state), you are then added to a list of individuals ranked by their test scores. When an opportunity becomes available, eligible candidates, usually those who have scored in the top tier—some states, such as Colorado and Idaho, define the top tier as the top 3 or 10 candidates only—are notified (by mail or otherwise) and given an opportunity to consider the position, either by sending in a form stating their interest in the position or by scheduling an interview. Candidates who express interest may then be interviewed for the opportunity.

In some cases, if you do not respond to a certain number of offered opportunities, you will be removed from the list and have to take the test again. Your test scores last only a certain length of time before you must retake the exam.

A variety of civil service tests exist, ranging from a "test" that consists of a point-based evaluation of your application materials and qualifications to a multiple-choice exam relating to job knowledge. Other examples include the following:

- An achievement history questionnaire, which is a self-assessment of job-related accomplishments
- Essay exams administered in a testing center, consisting of questions about hypothetical job-related situations
- An oral examination that is much like a structured job interview (and that may be recorded in some agencies)

Certain positions may also require a physical exam or a test of physical ability. For example, law enforcement officers and park rangers may be required to demonstrate agility, balance, strength, and endurance. Others require an in-basket exercise that simulates the work you would do on the job on a typical day. Occasionally, and especially for law enforcement positions, a psychological test may be required to determine your ability to handle stressful situations.

Some written tests are rather general, including questions about judgment, interpersonal skills, understanding of government procedures, and writing or math ability. Many offer questions that focus on reading comprehension, basic math, or logic problems. An example of a broad-based civil service exam is New York State's Professional Careers Test. Other tests are quite specific to the job and assume in-depth knowledge of the field.

Various resources are available to help people prepare for civil service tests. In New York State, for instance, study guides are available for the broad-based portions of many exams, such as the sections covering reading comprehension, written communication, working with tabular data, supervision, and interacting with the public. However, the technical portions of many tests vary according to the specifics of the job, and may or may not have an available study guide. Some states offer study guides and resources on their websites, and some refer candidates to published civil service test guides. In addition, it is highly recommended to join professional associations in your field and do additional networking (see the Networking section of Chapter 10) to get other tips about how to prepare for exams. Examples of test study guides are listed in the References and Resources section at the end of the chapter.

Civil Service Applications

Instead of requiring tests, some states have a formal application form (either online or mailed in) in addition to supplemental, job-specific questions or questionnaires and may require knowledge, skills, and abilities essays similar to the federal government. Many of the states requiring application forms clearly state that a resume is a purely optional, supporting document and is absolutely not enough to apply with on its own—the application form must be filled in. It is vital to follow all the instructions carefully in order to ensure that your application provides enough detail so that the "grader" reading your application can clearly tell that you meet the requirements for the job (do not expect the person to make any inferences). In addition, some states require you to send in copies of school transcripts or licenses, and some ask for specific personally identifying information on the application form, such as a Social Security number. Some states simplify the process for you by asking only for a resume and cover letter.

Other Requirements and Preferences

Some states, such as Colorado, require state residency to apply for civil service positions. Many others offer in-person tests only in their state. Certain states also have veteran's preference in hiring, and many give preference to individuals who have recently been laid off from state jobs, are current state employees, or are former state employees. In some states, civil service exams are required for classified positions, but not for some higher-level positions. To find out more about state hiring, visit your state's employment or human resources page.

Jobs with State Legislatures and Governors

The process of obtaining positions with state legislatures and governors is similar in many respects to that described in the section on working with Congress and the President. Many states have civil service opportunities working in legislative research. Other positions, such as advisors to a governor or staff for an elected official, are usually found through political and networking connections. You may also consider positions representing various states' interests to the federal government. There are also regional gubernatorial jobs, such as with the Southern Governors Association.

Applying for a Local Government Job

Like the federal government, local government is experiencing a demographic crisis—many experienced city managers are due to retire soon, and fewer young people have considered this career path. If you like being able to see the results of your work in your own local community, local government positions might be for you.

NOTE

Like governors, mayors have their own staff, as do council members of larger cities and counties. Various positions can exist in a mayor's office, ranging from policy analysis to press positions. Again, networking is key to getting a job with a local elected official.

Cities and counties are structured in different ways around the country, and each has its own personality. Like states, some cities and counties require that you pass a civil service test to be considered for employment (see the previous Civil Service Tests section for more details on these tests). Of the largest 20 cities in the United States, 5 seem to hire the majority of their candidates through tests (New York; Los Angeles; Philadelphia; San Francisco; and Columbus, Ohio), and others require tests for certain positions (Chicago, Houston, and Indianapolis). Some require an online application with answers to specific supplemental questions related to a job or require you to send supplemental materials such as transcripts (Dallas, San Jose, and many others). For many cities, the hiring process is closer to that of the private sector, requiring only a resume and cover letter. Similarly, on the county government level, some counties hire solely with tests (such as Los Angeles County and Suffolk County, New York), some require tests only for certain positions (such as Cook County, Illinois; Riverside County, California; and Broward County, Florida), and some accept special application forms or just resumes and cover letters.

As with state civil service tests, you usually must apply to be considered eligible to sit for a city or county civil service test. Tests may be offered rarely, so it's very important to research this avenue to entry for the cities you are interested in. Visit the website of the city or county you are interested in working for, and ask its Personnel

Department to notify you when a test is coming up or ask how the department usually advertises that a test is open.

> **NOTE**
> The International City/County Management Association provides a list of local government management associations, many of which also link to local government hiring websites or have lists of local government jobs, on its website at http://icma.org under Links. ICMA also offers a prestigious Local Government Management Fellowship program for individuals pursuing a Master of Public Administration.

In addition to or instead of a test, many cities require a special city job application form and specifically mention on their websites that submitting a resume is optional and not sufficient to serve as an application. As with state or federal applications, follow the directions and gather the requested information in advance. Examples of requested information could include the following:

- Driver's license information
- Criminal background record information
- Military service information (note that many cities give veterans preference in hiring)
- Previous city employment information
- License or certification information including dates, ID numbers, expiration, and issuing agency
- Work history including employer, address, phone number, supervisor, salary history, job duties, and other job facts
- Other special skills, such as shorthand or typing words per minute
- A list of any relatives who work for the city or county

Some cities, such as Chicago, also require you to be a resident of the city in order to apply for jobs. Others require you to become a resident if you are hired.

Getting Elected Yourself

The decision to commit yourself to public service by seeking elected office is a highly personal one. Some people couldn't be paid enough to accept the many challenges faced by candidates for office, such as criticism by the press and dissatisfied members of the public, the constant worry that you will be defeated in the next election, and the challenges of getting your agenda passed by the rest of the legislature. Others see elected office as the best way to make a real impact and provide a true public service by representing their fellow citizens.

Some individuals who consider seeking elected office start on the local level by attending city or county council meetings or running for city or county council. I met the mayor of a small city who told me that he ended up becoming mayor mainly because he attended city council meetings; the city council members noticed his attendance at meetings and eventually asked him to run for office. Getting involved in local commissions or boards is another way to develop more exposure to the legislative process. In order to be elected on a local level, most candidates need to submit a certain number of nomination petition signatures, conduct a campaign, and hope that they are then elected by popular vote.

To seek elected office on the state or national levels, significant support is needed. Candidates need to be nominated by their political party and then develop support through both a good campaign team and through financial donations. Big campaigns require money for staff, ads, mailings, travel, and more. The cost of running a U.S. Senate race in 2006 was $7.8 million, for example (according to Democracy Matters). Reaching out to one's constituency is also vital. A state senator I met said he had to personally knock on several thousand doors in his district as part of his campaign.

Finding a Nonprofit Job

The job search process for the great majority of nonprofit organizations more closely resembles that described at the beginning of Chapter 10, in that most organizations don't require special tests, unusual resume formats, or long essays. Instead, they usually ask for a regular resume and cover letter.

However, there are important differences between a nonprofit organization and a private or public sector organization. Most nonprofits prefer to see a demonstrated commitment to their mission. That commitment or passion could be shown through volunteer work, internships, studies, or prior work experience, but it usually needs to be there somewhere (there are a few positions, such as accounting positions, where it might not be as important to illustrate your devotion to the cause—but doing so would still be much appreciated by the organization). This passion is necessary but *not* sufficient. Specific skills are needed for nonprofit positions, and you must meet the requirements of the position to be considered.

Because most nonprofits lack the budget to spend money on general job boards or recruiters, you may need to do more in-depth research and networking to find positions. Researching the nonprofits in your field of interest and geographic region, including visiting their websites, is a good place to start. Do not limit yourself to just the largest or best-known nonprofit organizations. Instead, make sure you try to connect with smaller nonprofits as well, where the competition for positions may be slightly less.

Nonprofit organizations tend to have a small, close-knit community in which everyone knows everyone else. There are often local networks of nonprofit organizations, both generally for a geographic area and more broadly for a particular issue area. Get involved with such networks as much as possible so you can be the first to hear about job opportunities and current trends.

Lastly, be careful to learn about the specific culture and jargon used in the field you are interested in. For example, many nonprofits carefully avoid using certain terms for their clients, calling them "customers" or "consumers," and avoid describing populations with words like "handicapped" (instead using the phrase "individuals who have disabilities") or "at-risk." Make sure you use the culturally appropriate terminology in your resume and cover letter.

References and Resources

For more information on the topics presented in this chapter, refer to the following sources.

Identifying Job Opportunities

Federal Business Opportunities, www.fbo.gov

GovLoop, www.govloop.com

Krannich, Ron, and Krannich, Caryl; *The Savvy Networker: Building Your Job Net for Success* (Impact Publications, 2001)

LinkedIn, www.linkedin.com

Understanding the Federal Job Search

Information Solutions Inc., *30 KSA Samples,* www.federaljobsearch.com/insiders/ksa_guide.doc

Partnership for Public Service, Call to Serve program, http://ourpublicservice.org/OPS/programs/calltoserve

Troutman, Kathryn Kraemer, and Troutman, Emily K.; *The Student's Federal Career Guide: 10 Steps to Find and Win Top Government Jobs and Internships* (Resume Place, 2004)

USAJOBS, www.usajobs.opm.gov

USAJOBS, General Schedule Pay Scales, www.usajobs.gov/ei/generalschedulepay.asp

U.S. Merit Systems Protection Board, *Federal Appointment Authorities: Cutting Through the Confusion,* www.mspb.gov

Whiteman, Lily; *How to Land a Top-Paying Federal Job: Your Complete Guide to Opportunities, Internships, Resumes and Cover Letters, Application Essays (KSAs), Interviews, Salaries, Promotions and More!* (AMACOM, 2008)

Special Hiring Authorities and Excepted Service

Congressional Research Service, *Internships, Fellowships, and Other Work Experience Opportunities in the Federal Government,* www.senate.gov/reference/resources/pdf/98-654.pdf

Federal Executive Boards, www.feb.gov

Feds Hire Vets, www.fedshirevets.gov

Idealist.org, Fellowships in Public Service, http://idealist.org/en/career/fellowship.html

National Association of Schools of Public Affairs and Administration, Introduction to the Student Educational Employment Programs (SEEP) and the Federal Career Internship Program (FCIP), www.naspaa.org/presentations/2008FederalOpportunity/FO.asp
Presidential Management Fellows Program, www.pmf.opm.gov
U.S. Office of Personnel Management, Federal Employment of People with Disabilities, www.opm.gov/disability/Peoplewithdisabilities.asp

Legislative Jobs

Congressional Quarterly, Hill Jobs, http://corporate.cq.com/wmspage.cfm?parm1=57
Endicott, William; *An Insider's Guide to Political Jobs in Washington* (Wiley, 2003)
The Hill, http://thehill.com/
HillZoo, www.hillzoo.com
The Original U.S. Congress Handbook, www.uscongresshandbook.com
Roll Call, RC Jobs, www.rcjobs.com/jobs/
United States House of Representatives, Applicant Instructions, www.house.gov/cao-hr
United States Senate, Employment, www.senate.gov/reference/Index/Employment.htm
Washington Post, Washington, DC, Area Jobs and Careers, www.washingtonpost.com/wl/jobs/home
WorkforCongress.com, www.workforcongress.com

Jobs with the President

Executive Office of the President, www.whitehouse.gov/administration/eop
Plum Book, www.gpoaccess.gov/plumbook
PrunesOnline, www.excellenceintransition.org/
White House Fellows (a postgraduate opportunity), www.whitehouse.gov/about/fellows
White House Internships, www.whitehouse.gov/about/Internships

Applying for a Job in State Government

Careers in Government, www.careersingovernment.com
Council of State Governments, www.csg.org
The Internet Job Source, State Government Jobs (list of the 50 states' hiring websites), www.50statejobs.com/gov.html
National Association of State Personnel Executives, www.naspe.net
National Conference of State Legislatures, www.ncsl.org
National Governors Association, www.nga.org
State and Local Government on the Net, www.statelocalgov.net

Civil Service Tests

Kaplan Civil Service Exams (Kaplan Publishing, 2008)
Master the Civil Service Exams (Arco, 2009)
National Learning Corporation, Career Examination Passbooks, www.passbooks.com
New York City Department of Citywide Administrative Services, *Exams for Jobs* guide (has examples of city civil service tests), www.nyc.gov/html/dcas/downloads/pdf/misc/examsforjobs.pdf
Public Service Employees Network, Civil Service Exam and Test, www.pse-net.com/library.htm

Applying for a Local Government Job

GovernmentJobs.com, http://governmentjobs.com
GovtJob.net, www.govtjob.net
Govtjobs.com, www.govtjobs.com

International City/County Management Association, www.icma.org
National Association of Counties, www.naco.org
National League of Cities, www.nlc.org
United States Conference of Mayors, http://usmayors.org

Getting Elected Yourself

Democracy Matters, wwww.democracymatters.org

Finding a Nonprofit Job

Chronicle of Philanthropy, Jobs, http://philanthropy.com/jobs
Commongood Careers, www.cgcareers.org
Community Career Center, http://nonprofitjobs.org
execSearches.com, www.execsearches.com
Idealist.org, Idealist Guides to Nonprofit Careers (free downloads), www.idealist.org/guide
Independent Sector, Member Job Announcements, www.independentsector.org/members/job_postings.htm
National Council for Charitable Statistics, http://nccsdataweb.urban.org/PubApps/990search.php
Nonprofit Career Network, http://nonprofitcareer.com
Nonprofit Jobs Cooperative, www.nonprofitjobscoop.org
Nonprofit Times, NPT Jobs, www.nptimes.com/careers.html
Opportunity Knocks, www.opportunityknocks.org
United Way (provides lists of grant recipients in your local area), www.liveunited.org

CHAPTER 12

Launching Your Public Service Career: Interviewing, Negotiating Offers, and Getting Promoted

"It takes 20 years to make an overnight success."—Eddie Cantor

Congratulations! You have been asked to interview for a public service job. However, it's not quite time to celebrate yet, as many interviews don't turn into job offers. Keep on applying to other positions in the meantime, but harness your excitement into becoming a well-prepared candidate so you can increase your chances of landing an offer. Use the tips in this chapter to help you prepare.

If you do receive an offer, you should take a moment to assess your situation to make sure you make the right decision. This chapter outlines what you should do to negotiate the terms that are right for you.

After you accept a job, the real work begins. You have to learn the ropes and find ways to build on your successes. The advice in this chapter can help you make the most of your new job in public service and turn it into a meaningful career.

Interviewing

An interview can be compared to a theatrical performance, involving special roles, scripts, costumes, and props. Your role in the interview is twofold: to convince the employer to pick you for the position and to gather some information about the employer to determine whether you want the position. Your script—which should not be memorized, because that will sound unnatural and also will be difficult to remember—includes the answers to common interview questions. Your costume should be, typically, business attire. Props include copies of your resume and references, carried in a nice briefcase or portfolio, and possibly samples of your work. The following sections provide further direction for the different acts in the interview performance.

Setting Up the Interview

Be aware that you are being evaluated throughout the application process, including during the time you set up your interview. (The way you follow up on an application—see Chapter 11—is also part of this evaluation.) The person scheduling your interview may or may not be on the hiring committee, so show your gratitude and enthusiasm about being chosen for an interview. Try not to be difficult in your scheduling—having to reschedule is a red flag to most employers, who are trying to determine your trustworthiness and commitment before you walk in the door.

Whenever you receive a call or email message from an employer, return it immediately—waiting even 24 hours can signal to an employer that you are not that interested and cause the employer to move on to the next candidate. Responding promptly to calls and email messages is a sign of professionalism, even if your response is to say that you are no longer available. Likewise, your outgoing voicemail greeting and email address are part of your professional image, so keep them businesslike, especially when you are job searching.

For the interview itself, be sure to arrive about 10 minutes early—too early inconveniences your interviewer and shows desperation; and too late is a huge job search no-no. If—heaven forbid!—you ever do run late for an interview (something you should try to avoid at all costs), call as far in advance as humanly possible, with a message like the following:

> *Jane Employer: Hello, Jane here.*
>
> *Bob Jobseeker: Good morning, Ms. Employer, this is Bob Jobseeker. I know we have our interview scheduled for 11 a.m., and this interview is extremely important to me. I'm so sorry to tell you this, but my car broke down this morning, and I had to take a taxi. I should be able to get to your office at 11:15 a.m. I want you to know that I know your time is very valuable, and if you want to reschedule this interview, I totally understand. This emergency was completely out of my control, and I just want you to know that I would never reschedule in any other circumstance.*

During the interview itself, you should be friendly and polite to each person you meet, including the receptionist and anyone you meet in the elevator. It is not unheard of for two candidates to be equally qualified, and the decision of whom to hire is based on how nice each person was to the receptionist.

Preparing for the Interview: Research

Researching the organization you will be interviewing with is vital. Doing research will help you choose good interview questions to ask and will help you be ready to answer questions, such as "What do you know about our organization?" or "Why do you want to work here?" or even "What challenges do you think our organization faces?" You will also gain information that will help you make a good decision about whether to accept a potential job offer.

Start your research by reading over the organization's website, but don't stop there. Do a Google search, and look though news articles on Google News, LexisNexis, and other news databases. Investigate trends in the field, and find out what other major organizations exist in the field. Contact people in your network to see what they might have to say about the organization, and look up the people who work for the organization on LinkedIn. Make sure you know the basics of the organization, such as who the top executive is, its basic organizational chart, its mission, and ideally the demographics of the clients it serves.

Look into its projects. If it is a nonprofit organization, look up its IRS 990 tax return (on www2.guidestar.org) to see its budget. Find out about the history of the organization and its governance structure. If you are interviewing with an agency that publishes reports, make sure to read over some of its published materials. If you are interviewing with the office of an elected official, look closely at the person's biography and voting history (you can find voting histories from Project Vote Smart at www.votesmart.org).

Dressing for an Interview

Part of the "performance" of the interview is the costume. Making a good first impression is important, and what you wear to the interview counts. What you wear depends on the employer that is interviewing you (and even the city you're interviewing in). Certain regions of the country (for example, many East Coast cities such as New York or Washington, DC) are more formal than others, and certain organizations, such as smaller arts and advocacy nonprofits, are often less formal. Most of the time it is a safe bet to dress formally, but if you are concerned that you might appear as though you don't fit in with the organization's culture if you wear a suit, use your network to find out what would be appropriate to wear (or you might even ask when scheduling the interview). You always can err on the side of caution by wearing a suit and then removing the jacket if a more casual appearance seems best.

The following suggestions are general tips about the "safest" way to dress and apply especially to job fairs and interviews:

- **Suit:** Look for a suit in one of the three most typical colors: navy blue, gray, or black. Make sure the suit fits and is neither too snug nor too loose. Sleeves should end at the wrist and the pants should end just below the ankle. Women's skirts should be cut at or a bit below the knee. The blazer and pants or skirt should match and, like all your clothes, should be clean and pressed.
- **Blouse/Shirt:** For men, a button-down shirt or one with collar stays in white or light blue is appropriate. Ties should also not be too loud (avoid bright colors or bold or distracting patterns). For women, a white or off-white blouse that is either a button-down or a scoop neck (without being revealing) is fine.
- **Shoes:** Men should wear well-polished wing-tip or conservative-style shoes. Women should wear pumps with one- or two-inch heels that match the color of the suit. Do not wear sandals, platform shoes, boots, or stilettos. For men, dark dress socks that match the suit and go up to the calf are best. For women, hose that is either neutral in color or matches the suit color is ideal. Always bring an extra pair in case they snag on the way to the interview.
- **Accessories:** Men should keep jewelry to a minimum. Women should avoid any distracting jewelry such as dangly earrings. Bring a conservative purse or briefcase/portfolio with extra copies of your resumes and references as well as a notepad and pen.
- **Grooming:** For men, make sure your hair is clean and neat, but not slick. Nails should be clean and short. For women, keep your fingernails clean and not too long. Polish is okay if it is clear or conservative. Hair should be neatly styled, clean, and off the face. Makeup should be light and natural, especially eye shadow, liner, and lipstick. Always avoid spicy foods and freshen your breath before each interview. Wear an unscented or lightly scented deodorant, but do not wear strong perfume or cologne—you never know which interviewer will be allergic.
- **Extra:** In addition to extra copies of your resume and references, you may also bring samples of your work (assuming they are not confidential), memos, graphs or charts you have created, letters of reference, or a long work history with names of employers in case they are asked for. You can offer to show such items to the employer, but be sure not to overzealously force them on an employer who might not be open to them.

Gathering References

Most employers ask candidates to provide them with a list of references (usually three, sometimes more or fewer). Therefore, you need to think through who your references will be before starting a new job search. A reference can be any professional who has first-hand knowledge of your experience and qualifications and a positive opinion of you, though it is best to have a supervisor as a reference. Other options include teachers, professors, advisors, or coworkers; leaders or coworkers on volunteer, student organization, or community service projects; and vendors or customers.

When attending an interview, you should have a reference list, formatted like the one in the following figure, on a separate sheet of paper from your resume. This way you have one ready if the employer requests it.

Michael Adams
1 Public Benefit Boulevard Jobsville, TX 99999
(987) 987-6543
madams@xyz.com

REFERENCES

Dr. Robert Smith, PhD, Professor of Public Affairs
Former professor/mentor
University of Texas
201 Educational Boulevard, Box 999, Austin TX 99999
(206) 123-5000
Robert_smith@texas.edu

Ms. Susan Bossie
Former supervisor (20XX–20XX)
Washington State Department of Health
100 3rd Ave. N, Seattle WA 98109
(206) 345-6789
sbossie@washington.gov

Mr. David Lee
Former supervisor (20XX–20XX)
New York City College Library
1 XYZ, Box 100, New York NY 10010
(646) 312-1000
dlee@xyz.gov

Sample reference sheet.

Make sure to speak with your references *before* you give out their names and contact information and send them an updated version of your resume. (If it's been a while since you worked together, you might even remind them of what kind of work you did.) Inform all your references when they might be receiving a call from a prospective employer, and thank your references for their support every time an employer has contacted them, whether or not you get an offer.

If you have had a difficult work situation in the past and cannot use your former supervisor as a reference, ask a coworker or client to be a reference instead. You may, under certain circumstances, have to address the issue (don't bring it up unless the employer asks you or unless you know the employer is planning to call all your former supervisors). Try to make the story neutral, focusing on personality differences or culture clashes between you and your boss or the office you worked in. Depicting your former boss as a sociopath (even if it is true) or describing at length how you were victimized on a prior job is likely to alarm your future employer.

Understanding the Flow of the Interview

Most interviews have a somewhat predictable structure. Typically, you should arrive a few minutes early. You will wait until you are called for your interview, at which point you should stand, extend your right hand for a handshake, smile, make eye contact, and thank the interviewer for his or her time.

You most likely follow the interviewer into an office or conference room, having a few moments of chit-chat on the way (be sure to be pleasant at all times). Then the interviewer or interviewers will likely launch into questions. Depending on the organization, these questions can be read from a prearranged list, or they may be informal and conversational in tone. Most of the interview time is usually spent being asked questions by the interviewer. Near the end, your interviewer will ask if you have any questions, and you will usually have a chance to ask two or three at most.

Of course, every interview is different. Some interviewers don't ask questions and instead just talk, and others will just keep asking if you have any questions, so prepare more questions than you think you will need just in case.

You will end the interview the same way as you started it, by standing, smiling, shaking hands, and thanking the interviewers for their time. Do not forget to ask for a business card from each interviewer if at all possible as well, so you can send thank-you notes.

Dealing with Different Types of Interview Situations

Numerous special types of interviews go beyond a typical one-on-one interview. For example, many employers use a panel of interviewers to assess candidates. The main trick here is to not get overly nervous and make sure you make eye contact with each person interviewing you, so they all feel you are listening to them.

You may also have a phone interview. This type of interview is quite common when you are interviewing across long distances. The challenge with a phone interview is that you do not have the interviewer's facial expression to help you determine whether you have been talking too long. Therefore, you have to time yourself to keep your answers to no more than about two minutes or so to ensure you don't ramble on too much. In phone interviews, like other interviews, it is especially important not to use filler words such as "um," "you know," and "like." These make you sound less professional and are magnified when the employer is only hearing your voice.

Other examples of special interviews include the following:

- In-box exercises involve being given a sample project to work on and having to complete it during a specified time frame.
- In case-study interviews, you have to provide solutions to a case study or problem similar to what you might encounter on the job.
- In group interviews, several job seekers are interviewed as a group by a panel of interviewers (this type of interview is more common in consulting firms).
- Computer technical tests require you to perform a task using computer software that you have said you know how to use and that is a major requirement for the job.

Keep in mind that anything you put on your resume is fair game in an interview. For instance, if you state you are fluent in Mandarin Chinese, and you are interviewing for a position where this skill is relevant, you may well have your interview conducted in Chinese. To be as prepared as possible, try to find out in advance what the interview will entail and practice in advance with a friend, career counselor, or even in the mirror if possible.

Answering Questions

The main focus of interview preparation should be on preparing possible talking points for job interview questions. Job interview questions can be boiled down into three broad categories:

- Can you do the job (skills questions)?
- Do you want the job (motivation questions)?
- Can you get along with other people (personality questions)?

Skills Questions

Employers want to know if you have the skills, training, or ability to do the job or at least learn how to do the job. To determine your level of skill, employers may ask a question such as one of the following:

- "Can you give me an example of a time when you used your research skills?"
- "What are your strengths?"
- "What can you bring to the organization?"
- "Why should we hire you?"

The best way to answer questions about your skills is to go back to your Problem-Action-Result stories from Chapter 1. Before your interview, write out at least one PAR for every requirement in the job description. If you can't think of one for each PAR, try to think of examples that illustrate transferable skills.

Talk over your PARs with a friend to make sure they are compelling—and most importantly, do not forget to highlight your results. The two biggest mistakes people make when trying to explain their accomplishments are being far too vague (for instance, not giving a concrete example at all) or leaving out their results. Sometimes people also do not remember to take credit for their work, especially when it was accomplished as part of a team. It is also important to make sure your examples fit the question and to specifically tie them back to the question.

If you are truly stumped, or simply don't have one of the job requirements, realize that employers usually don't call people in for interviews who aren't qualified for the job. It is acceptable to admit that you do not have a specific skill they are asking for, but instead to emphasize either a related skill or to give an example that illustrates your ability to learn quickly. Most importantly, if an employer asks a factual question you do not know the answer to, *don't* make up your answer. Admit you don't know, and make your best guess based on what you do know.

Another example of a question that could fit the skills category is a hypothetical question; for example, "What would you do if a client came to you with xyz problem?" Here, your research on the organization's culture, your networking and knowledge of the field in general, as well as your judgment and prior experience will help you talk through how you would solve the problem. Ideally, you can tie the answer back in to a real-life example of something related that you did. If not, give a hypothetical answer.

Motivation Questions

The following questions boil down to seeing if you are motivated enough to work hard and do a good job:

- "Where do you see yourself in five years?"
- "Why did you choose your course of study?"
- "What do you know about our organization?"
- "What would your ideal job be?"

It is important to speak with enthusiasm throughout your interview, but especially when answering these questions. Tell your career story as if your entire career leads you to work in this field.

In public service, motivation to work towards the mission of the organization you are interviewing for is paramount. Much of the time, the people who are interviewing you have made a lifetime commitment to solving a societal problem by working for a particular kind of organization, and they expect nothing less from you. Therefore, you can be a bit more passionate and personal when talking about why you care about an issue.

You can frame your career story by starting with an experience you had which originally sparked your interest in the field, and follow by outlining relevant work or volunteer experience that demonstrates that you are committed to this career. For example, a student of mine chose a career path in refugee aid because of her experience volunteering with refugee teenagers when she was a high school student. She met a refugee who had escaped from a war-torn country and had witnessed his father being killed in front of the family by soldiers. His story was so compelling that she became determined to devote her life to helping people like him.

Enthusiasm for the job and the mission of the organization goes a long way towards getting hired in public service. If you are speaking to others who are passionate about the field as well, your passion will make you stand out further.

Personality Questions

You could have aced the first two kinds of questions, and think you are the best qualified person for the job, but if you can't prove that you can get along with others, you won't land the job. When employers see numerous candidates who are qualified at the same level and who seem equally motivated, the question becomes Who is more likeable? Who has better interpersonal skills or better judgment? Who is more friendly and polite? Who shares the employer's sense of humor? Who could the employer imagine working long hours with, socializing after work with, and sitting next to on a long plane ride? Some of these qualities are assessed through the employer taking note of how you handle interview etiquette, such as nonverbal communication, grooming, and attire, rather than by asking you questions.

Interviewers are likely to assess your common sense and good judgment by asking some of the more negative interview questions, such as "What is your worst weakness?" or "Tell me about a time when you had a conflict in a team. How did you overcome it?" The key to answering these questions is to focus on how you overcame a challenge, how you learned from a mistake, and/or how the weakness is a strength in disguise. Don't use it as an opportunity to complain, no matter how much a question might lead you in that direction, and pick a weakness that is not directly related to the job.

The following example would work for a job where being outgoing is *not* a major requirement. Notice that it uses the PAR format:

> *I used to be a little bit shy (problem). I chose to attend a college where I didn't know anyone, and I made an effort to get to know my classmates and roommates. I also decided to join a student organization on campus, Students for Better Tomorrows, that organized volunteer opportunities in the community (action). By becoming a member of the organization, I got involved with many volunteer activities on and off campus, and over time, I made many new friends. By constantly putting myself in situations where I met new people, I was able to become less shy. I now have many friends and have far less trouble connecting with new people (result).*

When answering questions about weaknesses, avoid the highly overused "My weakness is that I work too hard...." It's been said too many times before.

Other interview questions are unpredictable or off-the-wall, such as "If you were in a circus, what role would you play and why?" These may be attempts to understand your personality or see if you can think on your feet. Consider what the employer might be looking for, but don't be afraid to be yourself.

The Classic Interview Question

The typical first interview question is "Tell me about yourself." This question is stunningly challenging if you haven't heard it before. Where should you start? Grade school?

A good answer to this question should be 90 seconds to 2 minutes long and should give a brief overview of your career story. You can start with a brief statement about your motivation, perhaps about how you started in the field and why you are excited about the career, followed by a few points about your early career experiences, leading up to your current position or situation. Finish off your statement with why you are excited to be in the interview, as in the following example:

> *First of all, I am delighted to be here today because I admire the work of the Roosevelt County Parks Department. I have been passionate about working with kids in outdoor settings, starting with one of my first jobs as a camp counselor. Because of this interest, I chose geology as my undergraduate major and went on to get my master's in education. I have been a public high school earth science teacher for many years, and during that time I developed many educational programs that included outdoor education. I've also been a volunteer interpreter in Roosevelt County Parks for the last year and have enjoyed the experience of teaching kids and adults about nature in an outdoor setting. I am now looking for an opportunity to use my education background to build new public programs for the Parks Department, and the recreation coordinator opportunity would be a perfect fit for my background.*

Illegal Questions

Certain questions are not legal to ask prospective employees in the United States. These include questions about marital status, age (unless verifying eligibility to work), citizenship (unless this is a prerequisite, as in a federal job—though other employers are allowed to ask whether you are legally able to work in the U.S. for any employer without visa sponsorship), religion, race or ethnicity, number of children you have, and so on. Typically questions like this arise because employers are ignorant of labor law and/or because they start thinking an interview is a friendly chat and they get too personal. It happens more often with small or new employers than larger, more established ones.

You are within your rights to simply say, "That is an illegal question." Doing this is likely to end your interview early and lead to bad feelings. Instead, you might try determining why the employer is asking you the question, but respond in a manner that does not answer the question directly. For example, if asked about whether you have children, you might answer with "If you are concerned that my having children would cause scheduling conflicts, I can assure you that I have numerous years of experience, and it has not been an issue in the past." If you want a slightly pushier, but not interview-ending, response, you can always say, "Can you tell me how that is related to the requirements for this job?" That usually brings the conversation back to what is important—whether you qualify for the job.

Understanding Nonverbal Communication in the Interview

Not all the information we gather when communicating with other people comes from the words they say. A large percentage comes from posture, tone of voice, facial expression, and other nonverbal communication.

Pay some attention to the nonverbal part of your communication when interviewing, but try not to worry about it so much that you become distracted from what you are saying. The most important idea is to project confidence and professionalism. If you find yourself becoming very nervous about interviewing, realize that this is normal. Practice interviewing in front of a mirror, on video, or with a friend or career coach until you feel a bit more comfortable.

NOTE

Nonverbal communication is quite culturally defined. If you are interviewing across cultures, be sure to know what is expected of you.

The following tips apply to interviews in most parts of the United States:

- **Handshake:** A firm handshake is considered a sign of confidence. Take the other person's hand in your right hand (don't use both hands), so that the space between your thumb and first finger touches theirs. Give a firm, but not crushing, squeeze, and shake the person's hand up and down slightly, once. If you have sweaty hands, be sure to dry them before your interview.
- **Posture and physical distance:** When sitting in a chair, sit up straight or lean forward slightly (don't slouch). If you will be crossing your legs, do it so that one knee is stacked on top of the other or cross your ankles. (Do not cross your legs so that one foot is on top of your other knee.) Alternatively, keep both feet on the floor. Do not stretch your legs out in front of you or sit with your legs spread far apart—it looks too casual. When standing near someone, about three feet of distance is standard in most parts of the United States. Standing closer than this can be quite uncomfortable for others.
- **Arms and hands:** You can "talk with your hands" to some extent, but do not do so to the extent of distracting your interviewer. Sitting with your arms crossed in front of you can look defensive. Instead, try to have a more open posture. Don't fidget, play with your hair or a pen, or bite your nails!
- **Eye contact:** Look in the eyes of the person interviewing you. Looking down or away frequently gives a message of not being confident or being confused. Rolling your eyes up is considered a sign of disrespect. Don't stare intensely at the interviewer; just look him or her in the eye as much as possible.

- **Facial expression:** Smiling is an important way of showing that you are a friendly individual and that you are enthusiastic about the position. Smile at the beginning and the end of the interview at a minimum. This can't be emphasized enough—I know several people for whom lack of smiling was a major barrier to employment!
- **Voice:** If you tend to have a quiet voice, be sure to speak clearly and try to project your voice so that the other person understands you. If you tend to have a loud voice, be sure not to overwhelm the interviewer by shouting. Use your vocal tone and pitch to show enthusiasm (a monotone will not work). If you have a name that might be hard for your interviewer to pronounce, say it slowly and clearly when introducing yourself.
- **Mirroring:** You can also take note of the posture and expressions of your interviewer, and adopt some of his or her tone. Be careful, though—even if an interviewer is quite friendly and casual, that does not mean you should be too casual. It is still a professional job interview.

Asking Questions

After you have been asked a number of questions, the employer will give you a chance to ask your own questions as well. Be sure to have a number prepared. Some general favorites of mine are the following:

- **"What are you seeking in the ideal candidate for this position?"** This question allows you to counter by adding any particular skills or qualities you have left out in the interview, but which the employer thinks are important.
- **"How would you describe your management style?"** When you are being interviewed by a hiring manager to whom you would report, this is a great question for gathering insights into whether you might get along.
- **"Can you give me some examples of the types of projects I may be working on?"** If the job description was a bit vague on the types of assignments you would be doing or if you are otherwise unclear on this, this question is essential to ask.
- **"What do you like best about working for this organization?"** This question not only gives great insight into the culture of the organization, it also makes the person answering the question feel good. In addition, if the person answering can't come up with something good to say, this is a red flag about the place you might be working!
- **"How did this position become available?"** This question is a bit pushy, but it is quite important if you do not know how the position opened. Is

the organization expanding? Or did the last person leave, and can you subtly find out why?

- **"What would you like to see happen 6 to 12 months after you hire a new person for this position?"** This question is akin to "How will I be evaluated?" or "How do you measure success in this role?" It can also clue you in on whether the expectations for the job are realistic.
- **"What resources are available for this position?"** This question addresses the technology, staff, or budget resources you will have and gives many insights into whether the organization is being realistic about what you can accomplish given the resources available.
- **"Is there anything you are still wondering about my candidacy that might keep you from offering me the position? Is there anything further I could clarify?"** This question shows you are open to feedback or critique and also tells the employer you want every opportunity to reassure him or her that you would be a great candidate.
- **"What is the next step in the process? May I have your business card?"** This final question can help relieve your anxiety after the interview because you at least have some clue about how long it will be before the employer gets back to you. Ask for business cards from each person interviewing you so you can send thank-you notes.

Questions *not* to ask include questions about salary, negative questions (such as any questions about a scandal the organization has experienced or questions about office politics), or personal questions about the interviewer.

Following Up After an Interview

Show your appreciation for the opportunity to interview, and thank each and every person who interviews you at the beginning and the end of your interview. At the very end of your interview, try to get a business card from each person interviewing you. Barring that, at least ask for the spelling of each person's name and write it down.

Within 24 hours of the interview, send a thank-you email message, followed by a written thank-you note. Why both? My opinion is that email is quicker, but the written note is much classier (and less common). People who are of a generation that did not grow up with email expect a written thank-you. I'm a fan of a thank-you letter, in a business letter format (because the interview is a business meeting), on letter-quality paper stock. Send one to each person who interviewed you, and ideally, thank the receptionist who scheduled the interview as well. After you send out thank-you letters, you have to wait to hear back from the employer.

Dear Ms. Jackson,

Thank you for taking the time to interview me today for the Program Manager position. I left even more excited to contribute to the mission of XYZ Human Services.

As I mentioned in the interview, I believe my strong background as a Program Assistant at ABC Organization, combined with my education and training in social work, would make me an excellent fit for the Program Manager role. I also believe that my understanding of the issues faced by the many working mothers you work with, both on a personal and policy level, will make me best able to meet the needs of this population.

I hope to speak to you again soon about this opportunity. If you have any questions or concerns, please do not hesitate to contact me at 212-987-6543 or staceygriffin@hotmail.com.

Sincerely,

Stacey Griffin

Thank-you note example.

Asking for a Response

On occasion, you may go on an interview and then not hear back from the employer about whether you have been accepted, even after the date he or she told you to expect a decision. Employers often find out that they need more time to make a decision than they previously thought, so give the employer a grace period of a few days before following up on your interview. Then consider calling to follow up or sending an email message like the one in the following figure. Once you have been interviewed, employers should give you at least some sort of response, even if it is to say they are still determining their next steps.

Dear Mr. Jones:

I enjoyed meeting you several weeks ago during my interview for the analyst position. I would like to thank you again for the interview. I left feeling very excited about the opportunity to work at ABC Environmental Associates.

As I had mentioned in the interview, I feel I can bring my combination of strong academic training, as well as my skills in financial analysis, to your company.

I am still very interested in the position, and was wondering if you might know when decisions will be made. If there is anything I can do to forward my candidacy, or if you have any additional questions about my background, please don't hesitate to contact me at (917) 123-4567 or email me at tburnett@yahoo.com. Thank you again.

Sincerely,

Taneisha Burnett

Follow-up email example.

Handling Rejection

No matter how smart or qualified you are, you are going to be rejected at some point during the job search process (everyone is). If this happens, never show your anger or frustration to employers, because this will jeopardize your future chances with them. However, if you handle rejection with grace, you might be considered favorably for future opportunities when they arise. I know of a few instances of people who were second-choice candidates for a position—and who handled their rejection by thanking the employer, stating their continued interest, and asking for any feedback for improvement—and were later offered the position when the first-choice candidate did not work out. When you receive a rejection, try writing an email message or making a phone call that conveys a message similar to the one in the following figure.

Dear Ms. Jackson:

Thank you again for interviewing me. Although I understand that I was not selected for the Program Manager position, I still appreciate the chance you gave me to meet with you and learn more about XYZ Human Services. I also hope that you will keep me in mind for future opportunities.

In addition, I am always seeking to improve my interviewing skills. I would greatly appreciate it if you have any suggestions that could help me improve in future interviews. If you could take a moment to either email me or call me with any advice or tips on how I could improve my candidacy for future opportunities, I would be very grateful. My email is staceygriffin@hotmail.com, and my phone number is 212-987-6543. If you do not have time, of course I understand.

Thank you so much again for your time.

Sincerely,

Stacey Griffin

Rejection response example.

Evaluating and Negotiating Job Offers

Negotiation with an employer starts well before you receive an offer, during any pre-offer salary discussion. If an employer does not insist on seeing your prior salary, and you can avoid telling it, it is better not to disclose it. If you disclose salary and it is too low, the employer has an incentive not to provide you a much higher salary than you already earn. If your current salary is too high, the employer may quickly decide you will be dissatisfied with his or her offer and not pursue you further (even if you would be glad to take a pay cut for a better position). In some cases, your prior salary doesn't reflect your current market value—for example, if you have recently completed a graduate or certification program, and this new education should increase your earning potential. On the other hand, if you are switching careers or moving to a less expensive city, your old salary might be higher than you can now expect. If you are in an interview and are asked for your salary requirements, say something along the lines of "I'm sure you offer a fair salary, and I would be glad to discuss that with you in the future when we know we are interested in working together."

> **NOTE**
> Sometimes hiding your previous salary is impossible. For example, the USAJOBS resume format requires you to list the salaries of all your prior positions (though this does not affect the salary you are offered). Also, if you work for the government or for a nonprofit that lists salaries in its 990 tax return, your salary might already be public information.

There are sometimes moments along the way in the hiring process where an employer might say something that sounds a lot like an offer, but isn't, such as, "When can you start?" This question isn't a real offer. A real offer should always include a job title, a starting salary, a start date, and an outline of benefits.

Suppose you've followed all the steps in this book and have landed a job offer. Naturally, you are excited, but before you accept the offer, it's important to assess your situation to make sure you make the right decision. Be sure you clearly understand what the offer entails and take a moment to analyze your job offer.

Taking Time to Consider the Offer

Once you get a genuine offer, show your interest and appreciation, and then ask for some time to think about the offer. Most organizations will give you time to decide. Although there are some times when you might just decide to accept the offer as-is, it is worth asking for time to decide for three reasons.

First, the window of time between the offer and your acceptance is the main time in the job search process where you have the power. The employer likely does not want to reopen the search and has chosen you as the top candidate. This situation gives you some of the best leverage you can get to ask for what you want. Many employers actually make a "low-ball" offer as their first offer, with the *expectation* that the candidate will counter-offer—so you are often expected to negotiate. Even in an organization in which it seems impossible to negotiate, it might still be worth asking about it. For example, although federal government positions have a posted GS level, there are steps within each level. Some people have been successful at negotiating up a step, even when they can't get a higher grade level.

Second, you should take the time to think about the whole offer. Go back and look at the values you identified in Chapter 1, and compare this job with your current job and/or ideal job. Talk to your family or significant other about the implications of the new job. Discuss with a mentor or advisor to see if this job will take you in the right direction. If you are leaving a current job, consider the costs and benefits of leaving your job. If you do not have a job now, ask yourself if this job is good enough for you to stop looking for new jobs or whether you want to wait for something better. Don't hesitate to ask the employer for more details if you are missing information. You have every right to know the details of the job you are considering.

Third, having time to decide can help if you have had multiple job interviews but only one offer so far. While you are considering the job offer, you can contact the other organizations that have interviewed you to say the following:

> *I appreciate your interviewing me for the position of X last week. I want to update you on my job search process and let you know that I have recently received an offer from another organization, and have until Tuesday at 3 p.m. to decide on the offer. I want you to know that I would much prefer to work for your organization, and I wanted to see if there was anything that could be done to speed the decision making about my candidacy at your organization. If I can help answer anything else for you, please let me know; and if you could give me any update about the status of my candidacy, I would greatly appreciate it.*

Hopefully, by speeding up one offer and slowing the other one down, you have a chance to choose between two offers, which is a rare and wonderful thing.

Once you've "thought about it" enough, it is time to make a counter-offer. A good counter-offer is based on actual research on salaries as well as knowledge of your own market value.

Evaluating Salary and Benefits

Salary data in both the public and nonprofit sectors is often easier to come by than you may find in private corporations. First of all, most jobs in government list a salary range in the job description itself. In addition, the federal government posts its salary ranges online. States and local governments often also have posted salary ranges available online. Technically, government salaries are publicly accessible information much of the time, due to the Freedom of Information Act, as well as state and local government open records laws, though it can take time to obtain this information.

Most nonprofit organizations, except religious ones, are required to file 990s (IRS tax returns) that can be easily searched at GuideStar and the National Center for Charitable Statistics. These tax returns list the entire operating budget of the organization, as well as the salaries of the top staff, which can be very enlightening.

Professional organizations may also be able to provide tips on salary information, and it is safe to ask your networking contacts what a typical starting salary may be for their field (so long as you don't go so far as to ask someone what his or her personal salary is). Also, be aware of the difference in the costs of living between where you currently live and where the new offer is located.

Salary, while important, is only one aspect of an offer. Other benefits can make a huge difference in your life, such as a flexible work schedule, telecommuting option, vacation time, or health insurance. You might identify nonsalary items you want to negotiate for, such as help with relocation expenses or a delayed start date so you can take a vacation. Consider all factors, and choose just those few that are the most important to you. Don't assume you'll get everything you ask for and realize that you should not ask for so much that it offends the employer.

NOTE

If accepting the new job means you will have to relocate, do some research about the new location before you make a decision. Consider commuting issues, recreation opportunities, your spouse or partner's job opportunities, the quality of education, weather/climate, and the cost of real estate. Also, take into account whether your new employer provides any relocation-related benefits, such as reimbursement for moving expenses.

Negotiating a Job Offer

Once you have done your research—something you should have done before you embarked on your career transition—you will have some ammunition when counter-offering to the employer. You will need to be careful in how you approach the employer, especially if you don't have a current job or another competing offer to fall back on. You can hedge your bets by saying,

> *I am very interested in the offer you have made, and I truly appreciate it. Before I go further, I want to make sure I wouldn't jeopardize the offer by asking some questions about salary. Can you reassure me that it would be OK to ask some additional questions about the offer?*

Most employers would not hesitate to agree that you should at least be able to ask some questions.

Then—and this is the scariest part for most people, but the most crucial—state what you are hoping for and why, and then hold your breath. Of course, you shouldn't ask for double the salary, because that will likely offend the employer. But if your research shows that the market value for such a position is higher than what the employer has offered, say so. Especially if your current position or a competing position pays more than what the employer has offered, let the employer know.

Don't focus only on what the market research shows about the job offer, though. Instead, explain how you will bring such a significantly greater value to the organization than any other candidate that it will be worth the extra money. Talk about the areas in which you feel you can go above and beyond what is requested in the job description. If the description asks for program management, emphasize your strengths in that area and talk about how you can also help with grant writing or how you can conduct a survey to evaluate the results of the program, which will then help the organization lobby for more funds. If the job asks for a language translator, emphasize how you not only speak a language, but also can act as a cultural bridge between the agency and people from another culture to greatly increase the organization's standing within that community. Think carefully about what you know about the toughest problems the organization faces and speak convincingly about how you can truly go above and beyond what is asked for in a way that justifies giving you the compensation you feel is fair. Make sure to emphasize issues of importance to the *employer;* issues that are only relevant to your own needs (such as having to send your kids through college or pay off debts) should never be brought up at this stage as a reason why an employer should pay you more.

Even while asking for more money, continue to reassure the employer that you are truly interested in the job, and that your concern is only about the salary or benefits. If you start to sound like you are not interested in the job, the employer's faith in you will quickly waver, and the relationship you have built during the interview process might crumble.

Do not play hardball and say you will walk away if the employer doesn't offer a higher salary unless you are truly prepared to turn down the offer. Instead, consider the negotiation a relationship-building exercise in which both parties win: You will win an offer you can be satisfied with, and the employer will win a sought-after employee.

There are two main scenarios you will encounter: Either the employer can meet your request (or at least come close enough to satisfy you), or the employer cannot meet your request. If an employer truly cannot increase an offer because he or she has offered you all the organization can afford, then it is your decision whether you can still accept the offer, considering all the other factors about the job. On occasion, employers might meet you halfway, and say that they have to start you at a certain salary, but that they will consider giving you a raise at some future point (in six months, for instance). When you hear such a promise, make sure to get it in writing.

If all else fails, and you can't get a higher salary than you are offered initially, at least ask about the promotion potential for the position, including what it takes to get promoted and what the typical promotion time frame and trajectory entail. Then, focus your energy on doing what you need to do to impress your new employer, do a great job, and, eventually, take your next career step.

Accepting the Offer

Now you can finally celebrate! If you have decided to accept an offer, make sure to discuss it verbally with the employer to ensure you are in agreement on the terms and conditions of employment. Ask for the offer in writing. Consider also sending a formal letter of acceptance.

After you accept an offer, thank all the people in your network who helped you along the way: your references, your supporters, and especially anyone in your network who helped you with informational interviews. If someone went above and beyond—for example, helping you get an internal referral or recommending you personally—that person deserves at least a thank-you card, if not a box of chocolates, a bouquet of flowers, or some other small but professional gift.

Making a Good First Impression

Congratulations! You are now in a wonderful new public service job. Before you worry about promotion, it's best to work on making a good impression and doing a great job.

People observe each other in the workplace, so it's important to know that nothing you say or do is really "off the record." Therefore, be reliable, show up to work on time, dress professionally, be positive and enthusiastic about all of your work assignments, avoid gossip, don't bring personal issues to work, and do not use work resources (such as your work phone or computer) for personal communications or projects. (Note that email messages you send as a public sector employee are a matter of public record.) Make an effort to get to know your coworkers and attend work-related social events.

In the first few weeks of your job, try to get a thorough understanding of the culture and power structure of the organization. Take a good look around you. Do people wear gray flannel suits or tie-dyed T-shirts? Do people seem to work long hours, or are they relaxed? Are communications formal or informal? Try to fit the culture. Ask for an organizational chart, operating plan, mission statement, annual report, and budget if at all possible, but keep in mind that an organizational chart doesn't always reveal the real power structure. Ask around, casually but carefully, until you get a sense of how things really work.

If you don't understand something, ask—you are new and can get away with this for a while. Try not to ask the same question twice, though. Check with your supervisor to make sure you are following the correct procedures. All jobs have a learning curve—some jobs take more than a year to adjust to. Give yourself time and focus on doing your best.

Aiming for Promotion

Once you have proven yourself for a while and gotten your bearings, you can consider whether you want to aim for a promotion. It is important to carefully consider whether you actually *want* a promotion. More money or a fancier title is tempting, but make sure to revisit your values (from Chapter 1) to be sure they fit with a new, higher-level job. Promotion usually entails taking on more managerial responsibilities, learning how to supervise others, being held accountable at a higher level, and having to make harder decisions. It can also mean longer hours and more stress.

If you decide you want to try for promotion, first research the opportunities and procedures for promotion. Procedures for promotion vary by organization, and some are more structured than others.

Federal Government Promotion Procedures

In the federal government, many positions that you may apply for will already have a "promotion potential" listed right in the job description. For example, a position may be listed as GS-7/9/11 (see Chapter 11 for more on GS levels). This means that if you accept the position as a GS-7, for example, you have the ability to be promoted up to a GS-11 level. In order to be promoted up a grade, you will need to meet two requirements: one year of specialized experience performed at the current grade level (for example, one year of work conducted at GS-7 level), plus one year of "time in grade." It is common to be promoted up a grade if you are doing your work well.

In addition to being promoted up a grade, you can also be promoted up a step within the grade. For example, perhaps you have been promoted up to GS-11, and that is the top grade level for your job. After one year of time working at GS-11, you will get a step increase each year. There are 10 steps within a grade, but some take longer than others to reach. (For example, steps 1, 2, and 3 require one year of service each, but steps 5, 6, and 7 require two years of service.) Occasionally, people are considered for "quality step increases," which are earlier within-grade increases based upon better performance. In addition to step increases, there are often "general pay increases" set by the President, which are usually 0 to 5 percent raises to reflect cost of living increases.

Noncompetitive promotion may also take place based upon "accretion of duties." This term refers to a situation in which someone's job roles may have changed, for example, if an administrative assistant begins taking on accounting and bookkeeping roles. Such employees may be able to receive a promotion based on their position having new responsibilities not listed in the original job description.

Typically, if you have reached the promotion potential for your job, you may need to consider switching jobs and competing for higher-level positions or even moving across functions or agencies, in order to move up to a higher GS level. Some people also consider taking a step down in order to move to a different position to build new skills.

Once people have reached some of the highest GS levels, they may be interested in pursuing the Senior Executive Service, the "leaders of the federal civilian workforce" according to the Office of Personnel Management. Top leaders are groomed for these positions through cross-agency learning opportunities, endorsements from higher-level supervisors, and leadership programs.

Many, if not most, federal employees are unionized. Although this may or may not affect the mechanics of how a promotion is handled, it might make a difference in who may get promoted. For example, a bargaining agreement might stipulate that promotions must go to current staff rather than being opened to candidates from other agencies.

State and Local Government Promotion Procedures

Promotion systems within state and local governments vary tremendously by area, and often, between different agencies in the same state or location. Of the states and localities that have civil service systems (see Chapter 11), promotion is usually handled in a formal manner, prescribed by the system. For example, when a promotional opportunity arises, internal candidates may take a promotional test to determine their eligibility for the promotion. Factors such as job seniority may also be taken into account in areas where the workplace is unionized.

Different job classifications have different promotional pathways, some more structured than others. For example, some positions are in a promotional series, and uniformed services have their own promotional processes. Some promotional positions are only for internal candidates, and others are for the general public. It is often up to the employee to either ask for a reclassification or to apply for promotional positions.

In states with a less structured civil service system, promotion varies by position. For example, within the Washington State Department of Transportation, staff in technical positions (such as electronic technicians or transportation system technicians) have to take an exam to be promoted. They cannot take the promotional test until they have spent 12 to 36 months of "time in grade" and must also have satisfactory performance reviews. Others, such as maintenance technicians, must only go through "time in grade" and have satisfactory performance to be promoted.

For professional staff, the promotional process might not require exams. Instead, staff members may have individual staff development programs with a matrix that shows their current skills and experience, with advice on what steps must be taken to progress to the next level. Within the Washington Department of Transportation, for example, staff members receive a performance appraisal once or twice a year, covering their technical, communication, and other skills. These evaluations can be checked when an internal promotion position is posted or as part of reference checks within the agency. Candidates have to apply competitively for higher-level positions and typically compete against both external and internal candidates for the positions.

Government agencies often offer classes to help staff improve their technical and managerial skills, such as courses in conflict management, diversity in the workplace, public speaking, technical writing, emergency preparedness, and computer software. Taking advantage of such opportunities can help you reach a new performance level so that you can be promoted. Some agencies also offer executive leadership training programs to help promote middle managers, including extra training, conferences, and skill building for executive management positions.

Promotion Strategies

When you are ready, start asking for more challenging assignments. Go out of your way to get training, continually learn new skills, and stay abreast of developments affecting your field. Take the time to find out what your boss needs, what problems the organization has, and how you can come up with new ideas to solve the organization's problems. Gather expertise and knowledge that sets you apart and try to become an expert in a subject area at your job, but be willing to share your knowledge. Cooperation with others should lead to reciprocity and better team results. Network, get to know people in your organization, and find opportunities to be on committees so people will find out who you are.

Make sure you continue to focus on performing well at your current job. If you make mistakes (who doesn't?), don't cover them up. Apologize quickly and professionally and try to redress grievances rather than escalating problems. Be especially careful with email. For instance, work emails at government agencies are a matter of public record. Make sure you read carefully and double-check the "to" and "cc" addresses you are sending to.

Track your accomplishments (use the Problem-Action-Result method from Chapter 1 to document them). Make sure to keep records and copies of examples of your best work. Ask for feedback on your performance, and use the feedback to improve on your weaknesses and stay on track. In this way, you may build up some good performance reviews in your file.

As part of your research about the promotional process, you can also ask for job descriptions of typical positions that you might get promoted into. Scrutinize the descriptions you receive, and think carefully about how you can build the skills or experiences required for the next level position. Consider setting a measureable set of goals about what you want to achieve and by when, and ask for feedback and evaluations from your supervisors, mentors, and peers periodically. Ask people who were successfully promoted in the past about how they achieved that goal.

NOTE

In smaller organizations in particular, opportunities for promotion may be limited. Although some people use the strategy of waiting for a spot to open when someone above them retires, this proposition is risky. There is no guarantee that you will be promoted up to the spot you want. An organization may prefer to find an external candidate. In such situations, you may need to quietly keep an eye out for opportunities at other organizations.

If needed, consider obtaining further training or education so you can reach the next level in your career. Some employers have tuition reimbursement programs, and some of the larger ones have their own training institutes you can attend.

Before a promotional opportunity arises, be sure you rewrite your resume to reflect your new accomplishments. If you've been keeping track of your accomplishments, you can incorporate them in such a way that they match the description of the promotional opportunity. Once you feel that you have made your mark, gather evidence of your accomplishments, find the right time to ask for a promotion, and go for it!

In Conclusion

The world needs people with the real skills, determination, and passion needed to handle the challenges we face. Whether you decide to work for the public, nonprofit, or private sector, your career in public service can make a difference. I wish you all the best as you take the next steps in your journey to find a fulfilling job that matters.

References and Resources

For more information on the topics presented in this chapter, refer to the following sources.

Evaluating Salary and Benefits

Glassdoor.com, www.glassdoor.com
GuideStar, www.guidestar.org
National Center for Charitable Statistics, http://nccs.urban.org/
PayScale, www.payscale.com
Salary.com, www.salary.com
U.S. Office of Personnel Management, 2010 Salary Tables and Related Information, http://opm.gov/oca/10tables

Negotiating

Chapman, Jack; *Negotiating Your Salary: How to Earn $1,000 a Minute* (Jack Chapman, 2008)

Aiming for Promotion

Liff, Stewart; *Managing Your Government Career: Success Strategies That Work* (AMACOM, 2009)
Senior Executive Service, www.opm.gov/ses/

Index

G

M

N

V

W–Z